T0251112

Volume 1

COGNITIVE RETRAINING USING MICROCOMPUTERS

COGNITIVE RETRAINING USING MICROCOMPUTERS

VERONICA A. BRADLEY, JOHN L. WELCH AND
CLIVE E. SKILBECK

Routledge
Taylor & Francis Group

LONDON AND NEW YORK

First published in 1993 by Lawrence Erlbaum Associates Ltd.

This edition first published in 2019
by Routledge
2 Park Square, Milton Park, Abingdon, Oxon OX14 4RN

and by Routledge
711 Third Avenue, New York, NY 10017

Routledge is an imprint of the Taylor & Francis Group, an informa business

© 1993 by Lawrence Erlbaum Associates Ltd.

British Library Cataloguing in Publication Data
A catalogue record for this book is available from the British Library

ISBN: 978-1-138-48894-6 (Set)
ISBN: 978-0-429-45935-1 (Set) (ebk)
ISBN: 978-1-138-59115-8 (Volume 1) (hbk)
ISBN: 978-0-429-49056-9 (Volume 1) (ebk)

Publisher's Note
The publisher has gone to great lengths to ensure the quality of this reprint but points out that some imperfections in the original copies may be apparent.

Disclaimer
The publisher has made every effort to trace copyright holders and would welcome correspondence from those they have been unable to trace.

COGNITIVE RETRAINING USING MICROCOMPUTERS

Veronica A. Bradley

Hurstwood Park Neurological Centre, Haywards Heath, West Sussex, UK

John L. Welch

Newcastle General Hospital, Newcastle upon Tyne, UK

Clive E. Skilbeck

Royal Victoria Infirmary, Newcastle upon Tyne, UK

LEA LAWRENCE ERLBAUM ASSOCIATES, PUBLISHERS LEA
Hove (UK)   Hillsdale (USA)

Lawrence Erlbaum Associates Ltd., Publishers
27 Palmeira Mansions
Church Road
Hove
East Sussex, BN3 2FA
U.K.

British Library Cataloguing in Publication Data
Bradley, Veronica A.
   Cognitive Retraining Using
   Microcomputers. – (Brain Damage,
   Behaviour & Cognition Series,
   ISSN 0967-9944)
   I. Title   II. Series
   153.40285

   ISBN 0–86377–202–1

Typeset by DP Photosetting, Aylesbury, Bucks
Printed and bound by BPCC Wheatons, Exeter

Contents

Series Preface

From being an area primarily on the periphery of mainstream behavioural and cognitive science, neuropsychology has developed in recent years into an area of central concern for a range of disciplines. We are witnessing not only a revolution in the way in which brain–behaviour–cognition relationships are viewed, but a widening of interest concerning developments in neuropsychology on the part of a range of workers in a variety of fields. Major advances in brain-imaging techniques and the cognitive modelling of the impairments following brain damage promise a wider understanding of the nature of the representation of cognition and behaviour in the damaged and undamaged brain.

Neuropsychology is now centrally important for those working with brain-damaged people, but the very rate of expansion in the area makes it difficult to keep up with findings from current research. The aim of the *Brain Damage, Behaviour and Cognition* series is to publish a wide range of books which present comprehensive and up-to-date overviews of current developments in specific areas of interest.

These books will be of particular interest to those working with the brain-damaged. It is the editors' intention that undergraduates, postgraduates, clinicians and researchers in psychology, speech pathology and medicine will find this series a useful source of information on important current developments. The authors and editors of the books in this series are experts in their respective fields, working at the forefront of contemporary research. They have produced texts which are accessible and scholarly. We thank them for their contribution and their hard work in fulfilling the aims of the series.

CC and DJM
Sydney, Australia and Ipswich, UK
Series editors

Preface

The fields of clinical neuropsychology and the rehabilitation of cognitive deficits continue to develop at a very rapid rate. The authors are all involved in the demanding area of providing neurological rehabilitation services, and as such are under heavy pressure from clinical colleagues to devise cognitive retraining packages for our patients.

For some years we have employed microcomputers both in the assessment of neurologically-impaired patients, and in assisting our cognitive rehabilitation efforts. The provision by the Northern Regional Health Authority of a research grant allowed us to undertake the project described in this book. Our aims in writing the book are to provide a balanced review of the use of microcomputers in cognitive retraining to date, and to describe a major research project designed to evaluate their role in this field.

Acknowledgements

We would like to thank the patients and their families who agreed to participate in our study, and the Neuroscience Consultants who referred them to the project.

We are indebted to Joan Fittes, John Welch's secretary, who typed the manuscript and its drafts with great speed, accuracy and good humour.

Thanks are also due to Jerry Cooper, who developed some of the software, and to Alistair Macdonald and Philip Lowe who provided support from the Regional Medical Physics Department. We also appreciate the help of our Research Assistants Trudi Boorman, Linda Wilkinson, and Marguerite Holliday.

1

Patterns of Recovery in Neurologically Impaired Individuals

1.1 INTRODUCTORY REMARKS

In general terms neuropsychologists working in the field of rehabilitation are interested in conditions in which, to some degree, recovery is predicted. It is, of course, quite feasible to use cognitive retraining techniques with patients who suffer from degenerative conditions such as Alzheimer's disease or multifocal/degenerative states such as multiple sclerosis or multiinfarct dementia. Reality Orientation (Holden & Woods, 1982) is one such example of a cognitive retraining technique which has largely been used with groups of patients suffering from degenerative conditions. However, when dealing with degenerative conditions it is usually necessary to employ a broad psychological approach to treatment and it may turn out that facilitation of adjustment processes for the patient and the carers is the most important role for the clinical neuropsychologist. In addition, in degenerative conditions evaluation is often extremely difficult due to the severity of impairment and alterations of mood state.

It is therefore proposed that the main emphasis of this chapter will be upon conditions such as head injury, stroke and encephalitic illnesses in which continuing deterioration of higher mental functioning is not predicted. The patient population investigated in the Newcastle Cognitive Retraining study was composed of patients suffering severe head injury, stroke or herpes simplex encephalitis, and many of the ideas, particularly the models of rehabilitation which are described fully in later chapters, have been generated with reference to the aforementioned groups of neurologically impaired individuals. Thus, cognitive retraining with groups of patients or individuals suffering from degenerative neurological conditions or less common non-degenerative neuro-logical conditions (e.g. anoxic states, endocrine disorders, or nutritional deficiencies) needs to be the subject of further investigation and is beyond the scope of this volume.

1.2 RECOVERY FROM HEAD INJURY

The degree of spontaneous recovery in head injury varies depending upon the severity of the head injury. Some patients may merely be concussed for a few minutes but others may be in coma for several weeks before signs of a recovery process can be seen. The difference in rate of recovery is associated with severity of the injury. A mild concussive injury leads to temporary disruption of coordinated brain activity but a severe head injury produces coma, structural damage, and a significant degree of brain swelling (cerebral oedema).

There is considerable debate about the mechanism of recovery in head injury. Is it due to a relearning process, whereby the system makes use of preserved neuronal capacity and alternative pathways? Or is it due to restoration and recovery of damaged structures? It is well recognised that elderly patients have reduced neuronal capacity and also recover less well from severe head injury. However, unless some restoration or recovery of the damaged structures occurs, elderly people would presumably show little sign of recovery from a head injury. This would tend to imply that relearning and the establishment of alternative pathways takes place in conjunction with restoration and recovery of damaged structures.

The shape of the recovery curve in severe head injury is determined by a slow, progressive restoration of cerebral function which may or may not lead to the patient functioning at a level equivalent to that enjoyed in their premorbid state. The recovery process has been noted to continue for 10 years after trauma occurs (Thomsen, 1981). However, the majority of recovery tends to occur within the first 6 months after the onset of a severe head injury (Bond & Brooks, 1976). They showed that it was possible to produce recovery curves for specific functions such as verbal or non-verbal intelligence. They used the Mill Hill vocabulary scale and the Raven's Progressive Matrices to demonstrate this. The recovery curve measured by the scores on the Raven's Matrices shows a sharp rise during the first 6 months, followed by a period of relative plateau with another sharp rise at the 2-year stage (Fig. 1.1). The scores on the Mill Hill vocabulary test changed less over time and gave rise to a less steep recovery curve but they started at a higher point initially. These curves reflect the differential effect upon verbal and non-verbal functioning of a severe closed head injury. However, some care needs to be exercised in interpreting this figure as it is from a longitudinal study with different numbers of patients at each time interval.

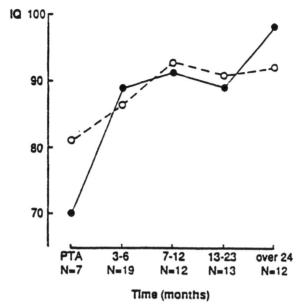

FIG. 1.1. Examples of recovery curves in head injury. Changes in verbal and non-verbal intelligence in severely brain-damaged men up to 2 years after injury.
—•— Raven's progressive Matrices   —o— Mill Hill Vocabulary Scale
(Reproduced from Bond & Brooks, 1976 with permission).

Stages of Recovery

Rosenthal and Bond (1990) suggested that recovery has three stages: (1) neurological recovery; (2) a more general adaptive process; (3) a social process involving the interaction of the injured with those closest to them and any resulting changes of social status.

Changes which occur in the steepness of the recovery curve appeared to be linked to the different stages of the recovery process and from that predictions can be made about final outcome.

Assessing the Changes in Functions

The assessment of changes which occur in the patient's capacity to function following a closed head injury can be investigated in various ways. One of the best indications of recovery in the early stages is the motor response and early evaluation of the patient status can be ascertained by using the Glasgow Coma Scale (Teasdale & Jennett, 1974). The scale consists of three elements: eye opening, limb movement, and verbal response (see Table 1.1).

TABLE 1.1
Glasgow Coma Scale

	Examiner's test	Patient's response	Assigned score
Eye opening	Spontaneous	Opens eyes on own	4
	Speech	Opens eyes when asked to in a loud voice	3
	Pain	Opens eyes when pinched	2
	Pain	Does not open eyes	1
Best motor response	Commands	Follows simple commands	6
	Pain	Pulls examiner's hand away when pinched	5
	Pain	Pulls a part of body away when examiner pinches patient	4
	Pain	Flexes body inappropriately to pain (decorticate posturing)	3
	Pain	Body becomes rigid in an extended position when examiner pinches patient (decerebrate posturing)	2
	Pain	Has no motor response to pinch	1
Verbal response (talking)	Speech	Carries on a conversation correctly and tells examiner where he is, who he is, and the month and year	5
	Speech	Seems confused or disoriented	4
	Speech	Talks so examiner can understand patient but makes no sense	3
	Speech	Makes sounds that examiner can't understand	2
	Speech	Makes no noise	1

Once a patient has passed through the early stages of coma, semiconsciousness, partial confusion, and poor orientation, it is then possible to use a standard neuropsychological assessment in order to measure more subtle changes in behaviour and cognitive functions. In order to investigate the recovery curve, an appropriately sensitive measure of cognitive functioning needs to be used. General intellect, as measured by traditional IQ tests, is not always affected greatly by severe head injury (Newcombe & Fortuny, 1979). However, memory and information processing speed are frequently shown to be impaired, and in order to establish the pattern of natural recovery they should be assessed in some detail.

Memory.   It has been pointed out that difficulties arise in serial assessment as it is sometimes not possible to separate out practice effects from actual recovery of functioning. However, Brooks (1987) suggested use of a retested control group design, or a fully cross-sectional design with no control group, or use of a measure not susceptible to practice, or use of alternate forms of test materials and titration of the change against the severity of injury in order to control for practice effects. Conkey (1938), using a multibaseline test–retest design noted that behaviours involving memory seemed to lag behind other behaviours in both rate of recovery and final outcome. In Conkey's studies, most patients were first assessed when they were still in post-traumatic amnesia but by the second assessment, which was generally about 40 days after the injury, it was possible to note considerable improvement. Recovery of memory functioning has also been reported in studies by Brooks and Aughton (1979) and Bond and Brooks (1976). Patients were assessed at 1, 3, 6 and 12 months after the injury. At the 12-months stage the head injured were still significantly worse than controls on word learning. Brooks (1984) suggested using measures of short-term memory or immediate memory span (e.g. digit span) in order to measure recovery. His results suggested marked recovery within 3 years or less of the injury, often up to the normal level. This contrasts with studies of new verbal learning which have shown slow recovery and marked deficits at least one year after the injury and often a failure to reach the premorbid level of functioning.

Language.   Disturbances of speech are relatively uncommon after closed head injury, and on balance they appear to recover quite well (Thomsen, 1975). Heilman, Safran, and Geschwind (1971) noted that of the 750 head-injured patients admitted to a Boston Hospital during one year, only 2% were judged to have a residual aphasia. However, others such as Groher (1983) have pointed out that communication is a more complex process involving cognitive processes other than speech, and head injuries do result in impairments of perception, reasoning, judgement, and memory, all of which could affect language processes. Thus in its broadest terms, communication problems might arise in as many as 25% of the severe head injured population (Bond, 1986). It would appear that recovery from aphasia will usually take place within the first six to nine months (Newcombe & Fortuny, 1979). Najenson (1978) demonstrated that visual and auditory comprehension skills tend to return first, followed by expressive abilities and writing. However, whilst the abilities that are normally measured by an aphasia battery (e.g. repetition, word recognition, writing) seemed to recover in a number of months, those language functions which required memory for auditory or written information, abstract reasoning ability or the switching from one topic of conversation to another, still appear to be impaired some two years after the injury (Kertesz & McCabe, 1977).

Perception.   A number of studies have reported changes in perceptual functioning following head injury using tests such as Elithorns Mazes, Raven's Matrices, and Block Design (Roberts, 1979; Smith, 1974). On the whole, it is difficult to find evidence of a distinctive pattern of recovery associated with perceptual functioning. One exception to this might be auditory discrimination functions which consistently appear to show subtle deficits for at least one year following head injury (Bergman, Hirsch, & Nagenson, 1977).

Attention.   Studies of attention have presented evidence to suggest that head-injured patients do not suffer from a selective attention deficit and are just as capable of filtering out a distractor as control subjects (Denker & Lofving, 1958; Gronwall & Sampson, 1974). Van Zomeren, Brouwer, and Deelman (1984) did report that head-injured patients have more difficulties than matched controls in dealing with distractions on a number of tasks such as card sorting or mirror drawing. The head-injured subjects were clearly slower in dealing with interference from irrelevant stimulation. Van Zomeren concluded that the difference between head-injured and non-head-injured subjects is in their mental slowness when processing such information, although alertness when attending to a stimulus is also a significant factor but its role has not been researched fully.

Although very little has been written about the recovery of attentional impairments, van Zomeren, Brouwer, & Deelman (1984), in particular, would seem to suggest that distractions can occur which result in subtle dysfunction of cognitive processes, involving decision-making time and response discrimination, which can last up to, and beyond, two years following the head injury.

Recovery of Personality.   It is well reported that behavioural disturbance and psychiatric illness can create more disruption to family life and working life than physical problems (Bond, 1975; Oddy, Humphrey, & Uttley 1978).

Levin, Grossman, Rose, and Teasdale (1979) summarised the types of personality problem resulting from head injury as follows:

1. Thinking disturbance with conceptual disorganisation and unusual thought content.
2. Hostility, suspiciousness and uncooperativeness.
3. Withdrawal/retardation. Emotional withdrawal and motor retardation with blunted affect.
4. Anxiety with depression, anxiety with guilt feelings and depression.

Lezak (1978) characterised personality changes in head-injured patients according to five categories of emotional change, impaired social perceptiveness, impaired self-control, increased dependency, and behavioural rigidity. Longitudinal studies relating to behaviour changes following head injury have come from work at Glasgow University from, amongst others, Brooks and McKinlay (e.g. Brooks et al., 1987). They suggested that the most frequently reported changes are slowness, tiredness, irritability, and poor memory. Emotional changes such as poor temper control, irritability, and loss of mood stability are also reported relatively frequently. The Glasgow group found that some personality characteristics such as irritability actually increased in prominence over the first year and by the fifth year 64% of the relatives continued to report irritability as a problem. This research suggested that not only is behavioural disturbance liable to worsen in many cases within the first 12 months after a head injury, but thereafter it may become a permanent disability.

The pattern of recovery in closed head injury is by no means consistent and well defined. It depends upon factors such as age, severity, and site of injury as well as the underlying cognitive function which is being measured. The Coma Scale (Teasdale & Jennett, 1974) or the Outcome Scale (Bond, 1975), which are used regularly in neurosurgical and neurological practice, do not give information of sufficient detail to reflect the subtle cognitive deficits and changes in personality which still seem to be present some two or more years after the insult. If it is possible at all to generalise from the available evidence it could be said that the majority of spontaneous recovery of function in severe head injury occurs with respect to:

1. Confusion in 2 to 3 months.
2. Aphasia in 6 to 9 months.
3. Auditory perceptual discrimination in 12 months.
4. Selective attention, distraction, information processing speed, new verbal learning, verbal and non-verbal recall, abstract reasoning, and conceptual shifting in approximately 2 years.
5. Personality dimensions, such as irritability and lack of drive/initiative, in as many as 5 to 7 years.

1.3 RECOVERY FROM STROKE

In the discussion of rehabilitation from stroke Wade, Langton-Hewer, Skilbeck, and David (1985a) and Wade et al. (1985b) make the useful distinction between *adaptive recovery* and *intrinsic recovery*. *Adaptive recovery* refers to a process of learning to use unaffected areas of functioning in new ways and *intrinsic recovery* means a return of direct neurological control over the affected function. Cognitive retraining, as will be seen in later chapters, probably influences adaptive more than intrinsic recovery but the changes which are first seen in recovery from stroke are largely the result of intrinsic recovery. Wade et al. (1985a) list the possible processes involved in intrinsic recovery in Table 1.2.

The recovery of function is recognised as being most rapid during the first few weeks after a stroke occurs and then as progressively slowing down. Several studies have indicated that statistically significant spontaneous recovery of functioning is limited to the first 6 months, e.g. Skilbeck, Wade, Langton-Hewer, and Wood (1983) studying ADL (Activities of Daily Living) function, communication, walking, and arm function. Meerwaldt (1983) reported results on spatial disorientation. Very few patients show any signs of recovery beyond

TABLE 1.2
Intrinsic Recovery: Some Possible Processes

Pathophysiological
Resolution of oedema (reduction of brain swelling)
Diaschisis and restitution of function (spontaneous recovery of "depressed" neurones allowing recovery of function)

Systems
Redundancy and multiple control (the theory that the brain has excess capacity and remaining tissue allows function to continue)
Functional substitution (undamaged areas of brain can take over function)
Global reorganisation (the whole brain shares out the remaining load after brain injury)

Anatomical
Axonal regeneration and sprouting (reconnection of damaged nerves and takeover of pathway by undamaged nerves)
Synaptic changes and denervation supersensitivity (synapses increase their effectiveness to compensate for damage)

Reproduced from Wade et al. (1985a) with permission.

the 6-month period, although Hier, Mondlock, and Caplan (1983) found that recovery on some tests of right parietal function did continue for one year after a stroke. It would therefore seem that whatever function is being examined, whether it be a higher mental function such as language or a motor function such as arm movement, the crucial period in which spontaneous recovery occurs is relatively short. The spontaneous recovery curve associated with impaired higher mental functions after stroke might therefore look something like the example shown in Fig. 1.2.

Disturbances of general intellectual ability appear to be of greater use in studies of stroke than they are in head injury, as can be shown by the fact that gross level of cognitive preservation soon after stroke is an important prognostic factor (Matthews & Oxbury, 1975). Several studies (reviewed in an excellent article by Heaton and Pendleton, 1981) have predicted functional outcome using measures of general intellect such as the Wechsler Adult Intelligence Scale (Wechsler, 1981), and David and Skilbeck (1984) were able to demonstrate that patients who died within the first 6 months post-stroke had significantly lower IQs than those who survived (although no mechanism is suggested to explain such a finding).

Language

Studies of spontaneous recovery in language give very detailed information as to when measurable recovery appears to have ceased. The range appears to be from 1 month (Culton, 1969) to 6 months (Hagen, 1983). The majority of studies seem

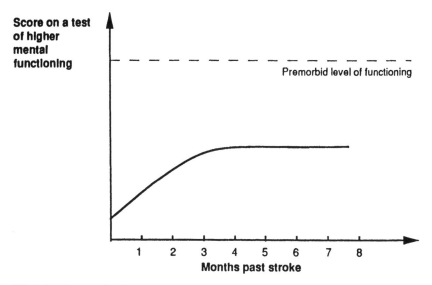

FIG. 1.2.   An example of a recovery curve following stroke.

to agree that most spontaneous recovery has occurred during the first 3 months following a stroke. All further recovery would be seen in terms of adaptive processes. There have been some debates within speech therapy as to whether comprehension improves more in the early stages than expression (Prins, Snow, & Wagenaar, 1978). However, within the overall context of cognitive retraining, which is largely concerned with the development of adaptive recovery processes, such debates are largely irrelevant as treatment is unlikely to start within the first 3 months. In such circumstances when cognitive retraining is commenced spontaneous recovery would almost certainly be complete.

Perception

Meerwaldt (1983) studied posterior right hemisphere stroke patients at 2 weeks, 6 weeks, 3 months, 6 months and 12 months after their strokes. Only 1 out of 16 of the patients was still impaired at 6 months post stroke. By contrast, some studies have indicated that up to one third of stroke patients who suffer from unilateral visual neglect as a result of their stroke continue to do so at 6-month follow up (Denes, Semenza, Stoppa, & Lis, 1982). Visual disorders such as cortical blindness are extremely rare and if recovery from cortical blindness is going to occur it will do so very quickly (Willanger, Danielsen, & Ankerhus, 1981). Hier, Mondlock, & Caplan (1983) noted in their studies of stroke patients that recovery of prosopagnosia (impairment of facial recognition) occurred at a median level of 9 weeks and they observed that this was quicker than the recovery for hemianopia, hemiparesis, motor impersistence, and constructional apraxia.

Memory

Memory impairment after stroke is common (Wade, Parker, & Langton-Hewer, 1986; Wade, Skilbeck, & Langton Hewer, 1989). In the earlier study Wade reported that at 3 months post-stroke 14% of non-aphasic survivors remembered nothing of a story after 30 minutes and 35% remembered nothing of a drawing. Wade points out that recovery of memory in the early stages is as yet poorly researched, but in the studies from Wade et al. recovery does seem to occur between 3 and 6 months.

Emotional Problems

Wade et al., (1985a) reported that stroke patients are frequently depressed. Some studies, including Robinson and Price (1982) have provided evidence to suggest that the prevalence of depression after stroke is about 25–35%. The severity of depression is reported by Robinson and Price to be greatest between 6 months and 2 years post stroke but it should be noted that the groups in the studies were very small. Similar figures of prevalence are reported by Wade et al. (1985a;b).

Wade et al. (1985a; b) reported mood changes still in evidence at 6 months post-stroke and their studies suggested that loss of confidence and increased irritability were the most common changes (Table 1.3).

It is also interesting to note that a greater number of patients report being more relaxed following stroke than before the stroke (although the mechanism for this is by no means clear). Wade et al. (1985a) identified items which were inter-related (in a mood change questionnaire) and by factor analysis they

TABLE 1.3
Mood Changes at 6 Months Post-stroke

Mood change	Much less	Less	Same	More	Much more
Low or run down	6	17	114	36	12
Happy	11	17	136	17	4
Depressed	3	12	130	23	17
Irritable	2	11	115	45	12
Confident	20	38	112	12	3
Anxious	6	25	99	40	15
Relaxed	11	26	109	34	5
Calm	11	29	130	13	2

n = 185
Taken from Wade et al. (1985a) with permission.

established three major factors: loss of confidence, anxiety and depression, and irritability.

Not surprisingly, social functioning is affected greatly after stoke (Feibel & Springer, 1982; Susset, Vorbecky, & Black, 1979). The loss of social life is clearly associated with factors such as the extent of the physical disability, loss of occupation, financial constraints, loss of independence in travel, and imposed feelings of depression and anxiety. As a result, the recovery in terms of social functioning can be quite varied, depending on the individual circumstances and sense of loss. A study by Gresham et al. (1979) gives an indication of the reduction in social activities following stroke (Table 1.4).

Christie (1982) looked at 85 survivors living independently 6 months after stroke. This group represented about 39% of 6-month survivors. Holbrook (1982) followed up 92 patients in Bristol and found that only 5 (of the 30 who were in work prior to the stroke) were actively working two years after the stroke. It would therefore seem that even in those patients who have made a good recovery from the physical effects and cognitive effects of stroke there still remain significant problems associated with social functioning up to two years post-stroke.

The studies of recovery of function in stroke patients have tended to concentrate upon the first 6 months of the patient's rehabilitation. In the realms of cognitive functioning most spontaneous recovery appears to occur between 3 and 6 months post-stroke. Language function, particularly those areas tradition-ally assessed by asphasia screening tests such as the Boston aphasia screening test or the Frenchay aphasia screening test, appears to be recovering during the first

TABLE 1.4
Reduction in Social Activity after Stroke

	Percentage showing reduction in each group			
Activities reduced	Group 1	Group 1(a)	Group 2	Group 2(a)
Vocational function	63	38	36	29*
Socialization outside home	59	32	28	19
Household tasks	56	28	20	19
Interests and hobbies	47	27	20	12
Socialization at home	43	23	28	20*
Ability to use transport	44	21	13	4

*Not significant difference for group 1(a) against group 2(a).
Group 1:   stroke survivors (n = 148): overall reduction.
Group 1(a): stroke survivors, excluding reductions due to other disease.
Group 2:   stroke-free matched controls (n = 148): overall reduction.
Group 2(a): controls, excluding reductions due to the same other diseases.

Taken from Gresham et al. (1979) with permission.

3 months post-stroke, and recovery occurs within the first 6 months in terms of functions such as more complex verbal reasoning and verbal memory. Social and emotional changes tend to be reported up to 2 years post-stroke and, rather as in the case of head injury, some aspects are seen to be worse later in the recovery process than they were earlier in the recovery process (e.g. in relation to depression).

1.4 RECOVERY FROM HERPES SIMPLEX VIRUS ENCEPHALITIS

Herpes simplex virus encephalitis is a common and a severe form of sporadic encephalitis. The clinical features of the illness are associated with symmetrical frontal and temporal lobe inflammatory processes. The clinical course is extremely variable with rapid changes over a period of a few days involving symptoms such as headache, hallucination, bizarre behaviour, and seizures, often of the temporal lobe variety. The progression is either to death or resolution with variable degrees of intellectual, especially memory deficit (Baringer, 1978).

Brierley (1977) noted the striking amnesic sequelae resulting from encephalitis. Rose and Symonds (1960) reported patchy retrograde amnesia of up to 30 years during the initial febrile episode, but this later shrank considerably with the major defect of memory being for recent events. A period of retention of 30 seconds was quoted in one case. Studies by Cermak (1976) and Cermak and O'Connor (1983) reported in one case that a marked anterograde amnesia noted at the first assessment of a survivor of encephalitis was still easily demonstrated some 14 years later. Lack of recovery in terms of anterograde amnesia and in some cases of retrograde amnesia (Butters & Miliotis, 1985; Damasio et al., 1985) have made such patients the focus of many studies in cognitive neuropsychology (e.g. Wood et al., 1982), as well as very suitable cases for those investigating the effectiveness of cognitive retraining programmes, e.g. Gianutsos and Grynbaum (1983), and Wilson (1987).

In summary, the natural history of encephalitic illnesses arising from the herpes simplex virus appears in general to be associated with a short initial period of a few weeks in which gross neurological disturbance occurs with features of bizarre behaviour, memory loss, and dysphasia, which is then followed by a life-long impairment of retrograde amnesia ranging from a few weeks and up to 20 years in some cases and persistent anterograde amnesia in all reported cases.

1.5 SUMMARY

It can be seen from the above review that the pattern of recovery in head injury, stroke, and herpes simplex virus encephalitis can be quite different, reflecting the differences in the nature of the cerebral insult, the site of involvement, the age of the sufferers, and the physiological mechanisms involved in the recovery process. When carrying out cognitive rehabilitation such differences must be recognised and appropriate designs for therapy must be applied in order to take account of differing rates of spontaneous recovery.

Stroke patients appear to be ideal candidates for the study of cognitive retraining as virtually all cognitive recovery that is likely to occur will have taken place prior to the start of retraining. However, secondary psychological factors such as depression may continue to have an influence throughout treatment. Cases of herpes simplex virus encephalitis also appear at present with a relatively stable picture in terms of spontaneous recovery of cognitive functioning once the initial acute stage of the illness which, in many cases, lasts no more than a few weeks, is over. Severe head injury, on the other hand, presents a pattern of recovery in which different cognitive functions appear to recover at different rates. Subtle cognitive deficits and secondary personality changes are still very much in evidence two years post head injury; cognitive retraining will almost certainly commence against a background of improving higher mental functions with a further possible complication of deteriorating secondary psychological factors. Under such circumstances the design of the intervention is of critical importance.

2

Treatment Issues

2.1 AIMS OF INTERVENTION

Achieving Functional Improvement: The Issue of Generalisation

Many writers in the field of rehabilitation who have considered the aims of intervention have emphasised both the importance of improving the quality of everyday life and the doubtful validity of achieving gains which can only be demonstrated on experimental or psychometric measures. For example, in an evaluation of aphasia therapy, Schuell and her colleagues (Jenkins, Jimenez-Pabon, Shaw, & Sefer, 1975) found that a group of globally aphasic patients improved their scores on the Minnesota Test during treatment but that none of them achieved functional language skills in any area of spoken, written, or gestural communication. In order to avoid representing improvement only on test measures and not in everyday life, researchers in recent times have looked in some detail at the way in which treatment outcome is evaluated and the effect that the results might have upon the continuation of therapy.

In a thoughtful analysis of the way in which speech therapists apportion treatment time, Marshall (1987) discusses reasons why therapists may continue sessions with global aphasics who are not achieving functional gains. These patients are well-motivated, hard-working and grateful for the therapist's attention and such qualities often motivate the therapist to continue treatment. In addition more is known about the preserved abilities in global aphasia than in mild aphasia and well-established treatment procedures are available for use in the treatment of the global aphasics. Despite such obvious reinforcers for the therapist, Schuell (1965) and Marshall (1987) conclude that it may be appropriate to terminate therapy in cases where it is clear that functional gains are not being made.

A more positive finding is discussed by Diller and Gordon (1981). They describe a programme in which a group of brain-damaged patients were trained on the Block Design Subtest of the Wechsler Adult Intelligence Scale (Wechsler, 1955). Patients improved their scores on this particular subtest, but more importantly gains were also observed in ADLs (activities of daily living) which depend upon the effective functioning of visuospatial and visuomotor skills in the real world. Analysis of videotapes of eating behaviour revealed improvement in the organisational aspects of eating for the experimental group when compared with a control group. On the issue of continuation of treatment, Diller and Gordon (p. 728) conclude:

> If within task gains continue to occur with carryover to external tasks (in this case ADLs), it is clear that training should continue. If only within task activities improve, but not external tasks, continuation of training should be judged by the clinical context in which the trade-off of continued efforts, available resources for training, and consequences of stopping training must be weighed.

Gordon (1987, p. 125) has summarised three different levels at which generalisation may occur.

> Level I generalisation is the persistence of gains on task performance from one session to the next and from one form of the task to parallel forms.
> Level II generalisation is the carryover of gains to psychometric tests. These tests may have task demands which are similar or different to the demands of the training task.
> Level III generalisation is described as "The highest order of generalisation which involves the transfer of what has been learned from training to functioning as it occurs in day-to-day living."

One obstacle to generalisation is suggested by Wood (1987) in that he contends that cognitive skills (for example the ability to attend to appropriate events or the ability to judge spatial orientation) do not generalise as easily as other types of behaviour which depend largely on motor learning or social learning. He points out that particular attention must be paid to the issue of generalisation when computer-based training is used. He argues that for many patients, computer interaction does not have a direct functional significance and in support cites a study by Wood and Fussey (1987). In this study Wood and Fussey found that patients trained on a computer showed improved performance on the computerised training task. However, they did not show any generalisation to other measures of the same ability which shared many of the performance characteristics of the computer task.

It therefore seems that the problem of generalisation is a complex one. It appears to be dependent on the type of behaviour being trained, the cognitive system involved, and the method of training used.

In spite of the developing recognition of the importance of measuring outcome of therapy in terms of its effect on ADL, this type of learning has as yet to receive sufficient attention from neuropsychologists. This may be related to the difficulty of measuring change in everyday performance. Tallis (1987, pp. 1 and 3) when considering this issue of measurement of change following rehabilitative intervention stated:

> It is often said that rehabilitation can never become a science because the things that really matter to the patient cannot be measured . . . everyday life cannot be reduced to a finite number of parameters to which values can be assigned.

However, he concludes that although limitations must be recognised, measurement of the effect of intervention is possible and rehabilitation, like the other branches of medicine, can be scientific. What this would mean in practical terms is that additional rather than alternative pre- and post-intervention assessment is recommended. Therapists may still continue to glean important clinical data from the use of standard psychometric tests but useful additional information regarding the effects on everyday life can be obtained with the aid of skills assessment or the use of appropriate questionnaires to measure changes in activity patterns, frequency of cognitive failures and emotional adjustment. There is a wide variety of published scales and questionnaires and these are reviewed in 3.4 in Chapter 3.

One final question which is raised by the discussion of functional improvement concerns the rationale for retraining cognitive functions rather than teaching ADL skills directly. The justification for cognitive retraining is that it remediates deficits which may underlie a whole range of functional problems. In other words successful cognitive retraining might allow a generalised improvement in many, if not all, daily activities. Piasetsky et al. (1982, p. 205) describe research into the cognitive component of rehabilitation as "seeking methods by which to remediate primary cognitive domains so as to promote the broadest basis for independent functioning." Clearly, if an hour spent in cognitive retraining can improve performance in a range of ADLs then that hour is well spent and considerably more productive than spending that same hour teaching one particular ADL. It may be that, in the ideal rehabilitation programme, cognitive retraining sessions should run in parallel with training in specific skills in order to maximise transfer of cognitive gains to "real life" settings.

Improving Rate or Level of Recovery

Intervention may be aimed at speeding up the natural recovery process or may be undertaken with a view to enhancing development beyond the point of spontaneous recovery. These two aims are not, of course, in conflict and it may be that an intervention will achieve both. The implication of adopting the goal of speeding the recovery process is that the intervention must be timed to take place within the period during which spontaneous recovery is occurring. The therapist must therefore be aware of the neurological history which has resulted in the cognitive impairment and the shape of the recovery curve normally associated with different neurological conditions. These have been described in some detail in the previous chapter and reference to such normal recovery curves is advisable before embarking on any treatment programme. The relative merits of early and late intervention are discussed in the following section.

2.2 PRACTICAL AND THEORETICAL ASPECTS OF INTERVENTION

Timing of Intervention

Miller (1984) has noted that it is a common assumption that the earlier intervention is instituted following brain injury the more effective it is likely to be. There is some empirical evidence to support such an assumption. For example, Cope and Hall (1982) found that head-injured patients entering a rehabilitation programme less than 35 days after the injury reached a level where they were considered fit for discharge in half the time taken by patients who were entered into the rehabilitation programme more than 35 days after the injury. In this particular study the long-term outcome was similar for both groups. There is also a small amount of evidence from animal studies which suggests that early intervention can lead to greater improvement in the overall level of recovery (Black, Markowitz, & Cianci, 1975; Goldman, 1976).

On the other hand in support of late intervention, Ben-Yishay, Piasetsky, and Rattok (1987) demonstrated the efficacy of a programme for improving the attentional capacity of head-injured patients whose impairments were uniformly chronic (at least 1 year and typically 2–4 years post-injury). There is clear evidence that improvements in cognitive functioning can follow late interventions and certainly, from our own work, we would maintain that rehabilitative intervention should not be withheld simply because brain injury is not recent.

Clearly, there are some problems connected with mobility and primary sensory loss which may make interaction with a computer immediately post-injury quite impractical. Entry to a rehabilitation programme should not have some universally applied criteria associated with it but should take into account the severity of injury, confusional state, motor impairments, and emotional stability of the patient concerned. This will remain the case until a definitive answer to the question of whether or not early intervention is preferable is reached on the basis of evidence from methodologically sound studies with human subjects suffering from a range of neurological impairments.

Generalisation Across Subjects

Many rehabilitation specialists stress the importance of rigorous assessment and detailed specification of deficits prior to the development of a "tailor-made" retraining programme for a brain-damaged individual (e.g. Crosson & Buenning, 1984). The case for individualised retraining is a strong one and investigation of the effectiveness of case-specific techniques often form the basis for experimental studies (e.g.Gianutsos & Gianutsos, 1979; Scott, 1987). The arguments in its favour follow:

1. The case-specific approach is in line with the approach most frequently adopted by cognitive neuropsychologists currently working within the experimental field (Shallice, 1979; Marshall & Newcombe, 1984). The identification of functionally-distinct subsystems is a primary concern of cognitive neuropsychology and it is argued that the evidence of dissociation of function observed in individual cases constitutes proof of dissociability. Specific dissociations would be less likely to be recorded in group studies since subsystems which are functionally related may also be anatomically close and, in the majority of cases, a number of subsystems are impaired following cerebral damage. A parallel argument may be advanced in relation to retraining interventions. Evidence from a single-case study, which records improvement following intervention directed at a single cognitive system or subsystem, constitutes an existence proof of the retrainability of that subsystem and is of theoretical as well as practical interest.

2. In the consideration of group versus single-case studies it has been argued that it is unrealistic to expect generalisation across subjects to occur as, for example, there is great difficulty in selecting groups that are truly homogenous in respect of aetiology, lesion, site, and extent of neurological impairment (Gordon 1987). In fact traditional group experiments may not be feasible because a sufficiently large pool of patients with similar patterns of impairment is not available.

3. On the same theme Wilson (1987) explains that, even when research has established that one particular strategy is significantly superior to another, it does not follow that every individual will benefit from that superior strategy. She goes on to say (p. 5) that "most treatment research studies are carried out with people who have one particular deficit ... [but] many patients undergoing rehabilitation have several cognitive deficits or behavioural problems making it less likely that they will respond to treatment in a similar way to patients in single case research studies." Certainly, if a patient has an unusual complex of

impairments the development of an individualised retraining programme may prove to be the only way forward and has the advantage of enabling the therapist to consider the interactions between different impairments.

4. There have been advances in the development of statistical techniques which can be used in single-case designs to render them methodologically sound (Barlow & Hersen, 1984; Hersen & Barlow, 1976). In particular, multiple baseline across behaviours designs enable the researcher to compare performance on tasks subserved by a system that has been targeted by a retraining programme with performance on tasks subserved by systems that have not been targeted by the programme. Gray and Robertson (1989, p. 164) offer a helpful description of this type of design:

> Here a number of behaviours within the same individual are identified and measured over time to provide baselines against which change can be evaluated. A treatment variable is applied sequentially to each of the target variables, and is effective when the level of that behaviour changes while untreated behaviours remain unchanged. Both treated and untreated behaviours must be potentially capable of change and both must generally improve with spontaneous recovery.

Time series analysis, in which level of performance on a given task is repeatedly sampled before, during and after intervention is particularly helpful in separating out the effects of retraining from the effects of spontaneous recovery (McLeary & Hay 1980).

Whereas we would not question the desirability of individually designed treatment plans the practical and theoretical advantages of the group approach should not be ignored. We see the advantages as follows:

1. When it is demonstrated that an intervention has been effective with one person few conclusions can be drawn regarding future applications. Group studies open the way for analysis of the characteristics of the patient who is most likely to benefit from the intervention. For example, the age of the patient, time elapsed since the occurrence of the injury and the location of damage (e.g. in the right or the left hemisphere or bilaterally) may all have implications for response to treatment.

2. Although the effectiveness of a treatment programme with a single individual may yield valuable information in respect of theoretical models of cognitive function and retrainability of function, it provides limited evidence relating to the efficacy of the particular treatment programme as compared with other programmes. Certainly claims for a programme's effectiveness are stronger if they are based on evidence from a number of patients with a range of impairments.

3. Studies requiring the use of control groups which are as closely matched as possible with the experimental group in respect of age, sex, chronicity, and site

and severity of lesion may, as already noted, be difficult to set up. If adequate control groups are available, however, the traditional design provides a valid alternative to time-series and multiple baseline analyses in separating the effects of spontaneous recovery from the effects of intervention. There may be practical problems involved in requiring patients' repeated attendance at the rehabilitation centre before the start of the intervention.

4. In the clinical setting where the therapist's time and resources are limited the design and preparation of materials for individual retraining programmes may not be feasible. In particular, when computerised retraining packages are in use the time involved in writing a programme for the use of a single patient is extremely hard to justify. There are, of course, degrees of individualisation and the retraining package may be composed of a number of existing programmes selected from existing packages. The selection of programmes on a "mix and match" basis is clearly less time-consuming than writing a series of programmes from scratch but may nevertheless absorb a significant proportion of the therapist's time especially as alternative selections related to the speed at which the patient progresses on a given task may need to be included in the treatment plan.

5. Although the occurrence of discrete deficits in isolation is reported in published accounts, the majority of cases seen in hospital neuropsychology departments, as Wilson (1987) has pointed out above, present with multiple deficits. Although the neurological correlates of the deficits may vary widely, similar practical problems are reported by a surprisingly large number of patients. For example, difficulty in responding rapidly to environmental demands is a problem which is reported almost universally following stroke, head injury, and many other neurological conditions. Diverse memory deficits can lead to the common experience of difficulty in keeping track of a conversation.

It would seem therefore that if a retraining programme is developed from the standpoint of reported practical problems and is broadly-based enough to cover several domains of higher mental functioning (e.g. attention, memory, processing speed, visual perception, and language) then it is likely to prove appropriate for use in a wide variety of cases. One of the advantages of computerised tasks is that they can be flexible enough to be performed by patients with impairments of varying severity. Even when there is no significant impairment in an area of cognitive functioning, performance of a task designed to retrain in that area may still be helpful both in building upon existing strengths and in increasing self-confidence by enabling the patient to experience success which may be much more difficult to achieve in areas of deficit.

In fact there is some evidence that a standard retraining programme can be used to good effect with a group of patients. Ben-Yishay et al. (1987) developed a set of five tasks aimed at remediating attention/concentration deficits following severe head injury. The tasks were administered in standard format to a group of 40 patients. These patients had all sustained severe head injury but were not matched for the extent of neurological impairment, age, or chronicity (time since insult varied from 1 to 4 years). The patients progressed from initially impaired performance to performance within the normal range.

There will, of course, be some patients with isolated deficits or unusual combinations of symptoms who have specific retraining needs, but a therapist who develops a retraining programme should expect to be able to use the programme with a number of patients. In the long term, time may be most economically spent in the careful development of a programme which has the necessary flexibility to be appropriate in remediating a range of deficits of differing severity levels than in developing simpler tasks aimed at remediating a specific pattern of deficit which is unlikely to occur in more than a few patients.

Adjustment to Cognitive Impairment

Once a patient's spontaneous recovery appears to have plateaued, it is important that he or she adjusts to changes in cognitive abilities (see 4.2 and 4.3 in Chapter 4 for fuller discussion of issues relating to adjustment). This point is stressed by Prigatano (1986, p. 56) who argues that cognitive retraining should "enhance the patient's awareness of his or her residual strengths as well as deficits." He describes two cases of head injury in which problems arose as the result of an initial failure to attain such a view. In the first case, the patient's misjudgement of his own abilities led him to hold unrealistic occupational goals; in the second, failure to accept that memory problems were present led to a refusal to use compensatory approaches such as the use of lists and diaries to help him remember important information. Following cognitive retraining, improvement in adjustment was observed in that, in both cases described, the patients were helped towards a realistic view of their own levels of cognitive functioning.

An area of concern is the case in which a realistic acceptance of the nature and extent of deficits has been reached prior to the offer of cognitive retraining. The majority of participants in retraining programmes are not self-referrals. A professional may refer the patient for retraining on the basis of a knowledge of the existence of deficits even when the patient is not dissatisfied with his or her lot. The promise of retraining could lead to unrealistic hopes of dramatic improvement—a return to premorbid lifestyle—which could in turn lead to the need for a further readjustment period following training if the patient's high expectations are not fulfilled. This is particularly likely in the case of a computerised retraining programme because there is a certain mystique attached to this "high-tech" approach to retraining which is not attached to programmes which rely on the use of pencil and paper exercises. For this reason it is extremely important that the programme is described in such a way as to discourage the prospective participant from developing unrealistically high expectations of it.

2.3 PATIENT SELECTION FOR INTERVENTION

Prognosis for Spontaneous Recovery

It is not possible to establish hard and fast rules which would enable the therapist to predict with absolute accuracy a given patient's eventual level of recovery. However, there are a number of characteristics of the individual which have been recognised in the literature and have been assumed to influence recovery. There is also some experimental evidence relating to these assumptions.

Age.   Kennard (1936; 1942), on the basis of evidence from animal studies and after reviewing literature on recovery following brain injury in humans, concluded that recovery of motor function is better in younger subjects. This principle, often referred to as the Kennard principle, has been assumed to operate in many areas including recovery of cognitive function. Other animal studies which tend to support this principle are Benjamin and Thompson (1959) and Goldman (1974). Studies carried out with human subjects have also presented evidence in support of the Kennard principle. For example, Carlsson, Van Essen, and Lofgren (1968) followed a large group (496 cases) of head-injured subjects for a period of 10 years and found that a return to autonomous functioning in the community was observed in almost all individuals under the age of 20 at the time of injury regardless of duration of coma. It was also observed in the majority of the 21- to 50-year-olds for whom duration of coma was less than 24 hours. For the over 50 age group, coma durations of more than a few days were more strongly associated with an inability to return to autonomous functioning than in the younger age groups. More recently Timming, Orrison, and Mikula (1982) and Kotila et al. (1984) have reported better outcomes for younger subjects in terms of functional independence for a head-injured group and a stroke group respectively.

However, the principle is now challenged by findings from both animal and human studies. Miller (1984) reviewed the literature, particularly the detailed evidence produced by animal studies, and concluded that the relationship between age and recovery is a complex one and is influenced by numerous factors including locus and extent of lesion, performance measures used, and time since the lesion occurred.

In the human literature also there is evidence which contradicts the Kennard principle. For example, Sarno (1980) found no effect of age on recovery from aphasia and Hier, Mondlock, and Caplan (1983) found no effect of age on recovery of the ability to do the Block Design and Rey Figure tasks in a psychometric battery. In the same study, Hier et al. (1983) found a trend for subjects in their older age group to recover faster from hemiparesis of the upper limb following stroke.

In summary it would seem that there is evidence from human as well as animal studies that younger subjects will spontaneously recover better than older subjects but this is a trend rather than an absolute certainty.

Premorbid Abilities.   The general clinical impression is that the higher the IQ and educational level before brain injury is sustained the better the prognosis. There is some evidence to support this impression. Dresser et al. (1973) and Teuber (1975) studied two groups of war veterans who had sustained head injury. They measured level of recovery in terms of employment at 15 years post-trauma. They found that long-term outcome was closely related to premorbid IQ. A large proportion of their experimental group were working in professional jobs at follow-up and the proportion in this type of job was comparable to that in a control group who had not sustained brain injury. However, an investigation carried out by Basso and colleagues (Basso, 1987) investigated the relationship between outcome of therapy as measured by performance on comprehension tests and IQ at outset of training. They found that there was no evidence of a negative influence of a low IQ level on recovery.

Once again, the evidence is contradictory. Overall, higher educational levels and IQ tend to be associated with a more favourable prognosis but other factors appear to interact with the level of intellect in influencing the final outcome.

Ribot's Law and Pitres' Law.   Ribot's law and Pitres' law relate to the use of a psychological function or system prior to impairment due to neurological damage. Ribot's law states that the skills that have been learned first recover first following cerebral insult, whilst the skills that are acquired shortly before the insult will be most subject to disruption. By contrast, Pitres' law states that skills that are most frequently used will recover more rapidly and more fully than skills that are not in constant use. The implication of Pitres' law is that over-learning may "protect" a skill following cerebral insult.

These laws were developed in the context of effects of trauma on language processes. The evidence relating to these laws is mainly from bilingual aphasia and is discussed in detail by Albert and Obler (1978). The issue is considered in terms of bilingualism in the following example: A native speaker of Italian is brought up in an Italian-speaking home and is educated in Italian but becomes fluent in French. He then emigrates to France while his parents remain in Italy. He completes his studies in French at the Sorbonne and marries a French fellow student. He obtains a job in France and speaks French at work and at home. He rarely uses Italian except when visiting friends and family in Italy. At the age of 35 he sustains a CVA and the language areas are involved. Which language is likely to be most severely affected? It is clear from this example that Ribot's and Pitres' law make contradictory predictions although in many cases the first-learned language would also be the most used language. There is evidence to support both laws. In general terms evidence was consistent with Pitres' law in approximately twice as many cases as the evidence contradicted it. Ribot's law was contradicted slightly more often than it was confirmed. It would therefore seem that overlearning and primacy of learning are important factors in the recovery of cognitive functioning following brain injury. The amount of influence each will have in cases where over-learned skills are not the first-learned skills cannot be predicted with any certainty but generally the over-learned skills will be the most resistant to cerebral insult.

Severity of Insult.   It is not always possible to measure severity of cerebral insult independently except in terms of functional loss. EEG recordings, CT scans, and measures of cerebral blood flow can all provide data relating to the number of lesioned areas and their size but are not available in all cases. In head injury a measure in terms of length of post-traumatic amnesia (PTA) is available (see Brooks, 1984, for description). Brooks and his colleagues investigated the relationship between the level of impairment as measured by a test of reasoning ability (Raven's Progressive Matrices; Raven, 1960) and length of PTA. They found a consistent reduction in ability with increasing PTA.

Assessing severity of focal lesions is more problematic. Hier et al. (1983) considered the effect of size of lesion in a group of right-hemisphere stroke patients. They found that recovery of both physical and mental function was often better for smaller than for larger lesions. However, site of lesion is a confounding factor in relation to measurement of severity. For example, quite massive frontal ablations can fail to produce any changes in IQ scores (Hebb, 1945). Cases such as this, however, are the exception rather than the rule and as a general rule of thumb, recovery after large, diffuse lesions will be slower and less complete than recovery after smaller, focal lesions (Darley, 1975; Meerwaldt, 1983; Milner, 1966).

Time Since Onset.   The recovery curves associated with different neurological conditions are discussed in Chapter 1. A summary is provided here. When cerebral damage is of abrupt onset, as in the case of stroke or head injury, the major part of spontaneous improvement takes place in the first 3 to 6 months. Following this period recovery continues but at a slower rate for up to 2 years following the injury (Bond, 1979; Brooks et al., 1984; Kotila et al., 1984). Differential rates of recovery have been noted for different functions (Meier, Strauman, & Thompson, 1987), higher-level functions—such as organisational and planning abilities—tending to recover more slowly than focal functions such as unilateral visual neglect. A caveat in relation to time since onset is that recovery curves obtained from group studies tend to mask individual differences in rate of recovery. Brooks et al. (1984) note that the difference between a mean recovery curve and recovery curves of some individual patients "may be very striking indeed" and the therapist should be aware of the possibility of spontaneous recovery taking place outside the limits that are generally observed.

Sex.   Investigations of lateral specialisation of function have suggested sex differences reflected in superior verbal processing in females and superior visuospatial integration in males although the extent to which such differences are attributable to interaction with environmental factors is unclear (McGlone, 1980). Additionally, as Meier et al. (1987) point out there is considerable overlap in the distributions of these functions. Thus, no firm predictions can be made about the lateralisation of, or level of ability in, these areas and hence about the nature of the recovery process in any one individual. There is some evidence of sex differences in recovery from aphasia but reported results are inconsistent when different studies are compared. Basso, Capitani, and Moraschini (1982a) and Basso, Capitani, and Zanobio (1982b) found no significant differences between males and females in recovery of auditory comprehension but observed a higher level of recovery of oral expression in females than in males. The period of time which elapsed between first and second examinations was 6 months. By contrast, Pizzamiglio Mammucari, and Razzano (1985) compared scores in naming and comprehension tasks in a group of stroke patients tested within the first 3 months after their stroke and retested 3 months later. They found no significant differences between males and females on the naming task. Better recovery was observed in a female than in a male group of global aphasics on 3 out of 4 comprehension tasks; there was no significant difference between the groups on a fourth comprehension task. This type of inconsistency in the research evidence has led researchers to question the existence of sex differences in recovery from aphasia, and Lendrem, McGuirk, and Lincoln (1988) state that "it is generally agreed that sex of the patient has no relationship to language recovery." Results from studies investigating this variable are particularly difficult to interpret because of the effect of environmental factors on aptitude, motivation, and choice of strategy.

Meier et al. (1987) conclude that "longitudinal studies of recovery have not revealed striking sex differences" and "the influence of gender on recovery is not well understood if the factor plays a role at all."

Motor deficits.   Although psychological factors are recognised to have the strongest influence on eventual outcome after brain injury (Bruckner & Randle, 1972; Brooks et al., 1987) a number of studies have suggested that the presence of motor disability is a negative prognostic sign (Kotila et al., 1984; Oddy, Humphrey, & Uttley, 1978). These studies have measured psychological outcome in terms of factors such as return to work, independence in self-care and social adjustment. A related outcome study (Dye, Milby, & Saxon, 1989) is of particular interest in that it suggests that motor disabilities recorded immediately post-injury are associated with poorer cognitive performance in the long term.

Decision to Intervene

As can be seen from the above discussion a number of variables such as severity of insult, age, premorbid ability, and stage and development at which a skill has been acquired are likely to affect the course of spontaneous recovery. If all such factors are taken into account, a prognosis may be made with some degree of confidence. However, the therapist is still left to consider whether an intervention is best directed at those for whom the prognosis is going to be good in terms of spontaneous recovery or those for whom the prognosis is likely to be poor and who, without therapeutic intervention, may experience minimal recovery of function. Such decisions are not easy to resolve but the therapist may be helped in making a decision by taking into account the extent to which the patient is motivated as regards the intervention and by the identification of factors which may affect the individual's ability to benefit from various types of intervention.

Motivation.   Motivation is a factor which many therapists report as being of primary importance in selection for therapy. It is generally accepted that a patient who is poorly motivated will not respond well to intervention. Lashley (1938) recounts an amusing incident concerning a man who failed to learn the alphabet after 900 repetitions. Lashley made a bet with this man that he could not learn the alphabet within a week. The stake was 100 cigarettes (this incident having taken place before recognition of the effects of smoking on health!). Lashley lost his bet, the cigarettes clearly providing the extra motivation that had not been in evidence in the previous 900 trials.

Motivation is a complex factor and can be very hard to assess. The area is discussed in some detail in 4.2 and 4.3 in Chapter 4. It is sufficient to note here that one of the ways in which well-motivated patients can differ from poorly-motivated patients is the extent to which their view of the nature and outcome of their therapy is realistic. A well-motivated patient sets readily attainable goals to be achieved within realistic time periods whilst the poorly-motivated patient may well show no signs of adjustment to his or her disability and demand a return to the premorbid state without being prepared to put in the necessary work.

Prigatano, Fordyce, and Zinen (1986) reported arranging 6–8 one-hour sessions with patients prior to making the decision to admit or not to admit them to a retraining programme. Realism was noted as an important factor in preliminary assessment. The patient's own expression of interest and the fact that help was sought were also taken into account. The much-quoted anecdote of Lashley raises the issue of whether it is possible for the therapist to improve a patient's motivation. It may be that the way in which a retraining programme is presented to the patient and his family is important in determining initial level of motivation.

Prigatano argued that aspects of the retraining programme can help to sustain that level of motivation. Clear feedback from the therapist is also of value. It has been suggested that computers are in themselves highly motivating and they have the advantage of being able to be programmed to present clear feedback while therapists are sometimes tempted to "wrap up" negative feedback for fear of damaging the patient's self-esteem (Brookshire, Nicholas, Redmond, & Krueger, 1979; Kinsey 1987).

Denial of Deficits. A patient may deny that he or she has cognitive deficits. Denial of mental or physical sequelae of brain injury is known as anosognosia and occurs quite frequently following damage to the right side of the brain (Frederiks, 1969). Denial of deficits may also occur as a psychological response to trauma. Until a patient has accepted that they have difficulties in certain areas of mental functioning, they are unlikely to see the value of attending a course designed to remediate the difficulties.

Impaired Executive Function. The term "executive function" has been used (for example, by Lezak, 1987) to cover the range of functions impairment of which is usually associated with damage to the frontal areas of the cerebral hemispheres. Such impairment can lead to difficulty in planning and organising activities, poor self-control and lack of insight into the relevance and implications of certain actions or activities. These problems inevitably affect the patient's capacity to benefit from treatment. As Lezak (1987, p. 43) points out, they may show up in "erratic attendance; confusion of relevant and irrelevant events or expectations; and difficulty in appreciating that dull, repetitive, or what seem to the patient to be silly or degrading training exercises are means to an end." Thus, at the most practical level these impairments may lead to irregular attendance, lack of application during training sessions, and failure to utilise newly-acquired skills in settings outside the department where retraining is carried out. In such cases the therapist may need to organise behavioural intervention aimed at improving the patient's organisational skills before embarking on a cognitive retraining programme. In practice, good attendance can usually be achieved with the help of a relative who can remind the patient of appointments and encourage them to leave the house, whether accompanied or unaccompanied, at an appropriate time. The therapist can help by mentioning the time of the next appointment at the end of each session. It seems that computerised tasks are frequently experienced as interesting and highly motivating (Finlayson, Alfano, & Sullivan, 1987; Long & Wagner, 1986), and thus particularly appropriate in the retraining of patients with these types of problem; we have never found patients unwilling to complete computerised tasks, and the literature suggests that other researchers have had similar experiences (Carr, Ghosh, & Ancill, 1983; Lucas 1977; Slack & Slack, 1977). The highly structured nature of computerised retraining tasks also appears to be helpful in retraining patients who have difficulty with the organisation of activities. However, since work with computers may seem an activity far-distant from other activities in everyday life particular effort may need to be directed towards specific teaching of generalisation of retrained skills into everyday life.

Attentional and Memory Deficits.   Impaired memory and learning may affect the ability to benefit from retraining programmes aimed at alleviating other areas of deficit. Similarly, a short attention span will cause problems in concentration throughout the retraining session regardless of the type of retraining material being used. Many head-injured patients do present with deficits of this type which affect their ability to benefit from the retraining programme. With regard to attentional deficits the point made in previous sections about the motivating quality of computerised retraining techniques is relevant. Detailed and frequent feedback and the interactive nature of the tasks all help the patient to maintain concentration during the retraining session. With regard to memory difficulties it is frequently the case that, while there is difficulty in retaining new information for explicit recall, procedural knowledge is much easier to acquire. Thus, whereas a patient may be unable to describe the use of a particular strategy, they may use it spontaneously when aiming to attain a high level of performance on a retraining task.

Finally, both attentional and memory deficits can be targeted for retraining. In cases where such deficits are severe the therapist may regard the retraining of the deficits which have most effect on the ability to benefit from the programme (most frequently these will be impaired memory, learning, and concentration) as the first stage in the programme, with other problems being targeted at a later stage even if they are apparently causing the patient more distress. Alternatively, retraining of any subsystem in which there is a deficit could be run concurrently in the programme. The presence of such deficits should not lead to exclusion from a retraining programme but must be taken into account in planning the programme.

2.4 SUMMARY

This chapter has considered the issue of generalisation of improvements achieved as a result of rehabilitative intervention. In the context of intervention, it is noted that there is now a recognised need to demonstrate functional improvement as well as or in preference to gains in performance on clinical or experimental tests and the assessment of functional change is discussed.

A second issue considered in this context is that of whether intervention is planned in order to speed up the rate of recovery or with a view to achieving a higher level of recovery. It would seem from the available evidence that the two aims need not be mutually exclusive and that decisions relating to these aims require knowledge of the recovery curves associated with different neurological conditions. In the discussion relating to timing of intervention it is noted that the evidence is as yet equivocal. Data from a study of human subjects support the view that early intervention can improve rate of recovery whereas the animal literature suggests that early intervention can lead to improvement in the eventual level of recovery. Nevertheless, there is also clear evidence of gains in higher mental function when late intervention is adopted with human subjects.

In the consideration of generalisation, the important question of whether a single retraining programme can be used effectively with a number of subjects or whether it is preferable to design individualised programmes has been addressed. Arguments for and against these approaches are discussed and it is concluded that, although the development of individualised programmes is preferable, there is both practical and theoretical justification for continuing with the use of group retraining methods.

However, no matter which type of retraining programme is contemplated (i.e. individual or group) a number of individual characteristics can be identified which could influence recovery. In particular, the majority of evidence suggests that: younger patients will recover more quickly then older patients; patients with high premorbid IQs do better than those with low premorbid IQs; over-learned skills and well established skills recover first; smaller focal lesions produce quicker recovery than larger diffuse lesions; the absence of motor deficit is a good prognostic indicator; a realistic view of deficits and good motivation result in better outcomes; and patients with central executive function deficit, attention deficit, or severe amnesia will have more difficulty with the demands of a retraining programme itself than those who have other kinds of cognitive dysfunction.

3

Cognitive Systems: Assessment for Rehabilitation

3.1 AIMS OF ASSESSMENT FOR COGNITIVE RETRAINING

The assessment which is carried out prior to remediation provides a profile of the brain-injured individual upon which rehabilitation plans are based. The most obvious of the aims which the assessment serves is to provide a description of the patient's areas of deficit. The nature of the retraining programme to be used determines the breadth of the assessment and the degree to which the deficits are investigated.

If a "tailor-made" retraining programme is to be developed for a single brain-damaged individual then standard clinical tests may be only the first step in the assessment procedure and should be followed by the use of specially designed instruments which will aim to specify precisely the nature of the deficit. Such specific tests will probably be developed in the context of an information-processing model of cognitive functioning derived from experimental psychology. However, the development and application of this type of test is time-consuming and clinicians may not always be able to justify the allocation of such a high proportion of their time to a single patient.

In clinical practice, a less detailed description of the deficit is often considered sufficient and existing standard clinical tests should prove adequate. These are available for the assessment of a wide range of cognitive functions and enable the therapist to identify impaired areas of functioning. However, they do not usually provide the information required for an in-depth analysis of the deficit. An advantage of using standard clinical tests is that, in the majority of cases, norms are available and the patient's abilities can be interpreted in the context of the abilities of the general population.

A second aim of assessment is to obtain information about preserved skills. Strengths are as important as deficits in planning the total rehabilitation programme. Consider, for example, two patients who have visual memory deficits. The remedial techniques developed for use with these patients may be very different if one has well-preserved verbal memory while the other has severe impairments of verbal as well as visual memory. In the first case the therapist might encourage the patient to describe to-be-remembered scenes or routes using verbal mnemonics to facilitate learning. In the second example tactile learning or motor coding might be used as alternative strategies to remediate the visual/ verbal memory impairment. The use of verbal mnemonics would be redundant in this case.

A third aim of the assessment is to identify factors which may affect the individual's ability to benefit from various types of intervention. The possible effects of impaired executive functioning and deficits in attentional capacity, memory, and learning have been described in 2.3 in Chapter 2. It is important that such deficits are identified as early as possible since information about their presence or absence is required for rehabilitation planning.

Another extremely important aim of assessment is to provide a baseline measure of the level of functioning of the impaired cognitive systems which can be compared with the results of a similar assessment carried out following intervention. The repeat assessment is important in describing areas of impairment after intervention which will provide information about residual deficits. This information is crucial in respect of the advice which is given to the patient about the extent to which he or she can hope to resume premorbid/ pretraumatic activities. In addition, such information is required in order to evaluate the effectiveness of different types of intervention. It may also be advisable to repeat testing on a number of occasions prior to training with a view to establishing whether or not spontaneous recovery is taking place.

3.2 NEUROPSYCHOLOGICAL TEST BATTERIES

Advantages and Disadvantages of Test Batteries

Neuropsychological test batteries such as the Halstead Reitan battery (Reitan & Davison, 1974) or the Luria Neuropsychological Investigation (Christensen, 1975) are attempts to measure mental functioning across different modalities and then to use the information obtained to make a good diagnostic discrimination about the presence or absence of organicity. However, ready-made test batteries do not allow flexibility in their administration and thus it is not possible to add or subtract sub-tests depending on the needs of the patient being examined. In addition, composite test batteries are often extremely lengthy which will tire the patient and may destroy good will. Substantial amounts of information irrelevant to the patient's pathology are often obtained and the intact areas of functioning can more easily be ascertained by clinical bedside testing or short clinico-experimental tests. An exception is the Adult Memory and Information Processing Battery developed by Coughlan and Hollows (1985). This useful collection of tests comprises two tests of speed of information processing, verbal memory tests (list learning and story recall) and visual memory tests (design learning and figure recall). Norms are provided for each individual test and tests can be selected from the battery as required. Two forms of the test are provided.

One of the advantages of a large battery approach could be said to lie in the fact that the administration could be completed by a technician as no flexibility is required in test administration. However, qualitative aspects of functioning are likely to be missed in this case, and even if the patient were to endure the entire assessment procedure the chances of him or her cooperating in a further rehabilitation programme might be reduced by the experience. In other words, decisions about the patient's ability to cope with the assessment procedure need to be made by experienced clinicians, not technicians. Interpretation of results obtained can be facilitated by the use of microcomputer-based interpretation programs. These are available for the Revised WAIS (Wechsler, 1981) and the Revised WISC (Wechsler, 1976); both are published by the Psychological Corporation.

In practice most neuropsychologists tend to assemble their own test batteries for assessment of neuropsychological dysfunction. These batteries—e.g. Smith (1975), Lezak (1983, pp. 107, 108), Bradley and Welch (1987; see Chapter 6 of this volume)—try to sample different modalities and the functioning of different psychological systems but allow variation in their usage to accommodate the handicaps and limitations of response by individual patients. Practitioners constructing such batteries will be very much aware of time constraints upon testing, the need for portability of test materials, and the possible lack of expensive equipment in many departments. The contents of a battery can be continually updated in order to make use of the best tests currently available.

The Features of a Good Test

Brevity.   If a test is to be administered as part of a comprehensive assessment schedule its administration should not be too lengthy a process. The use of a test which is slow to administer can only be justified if it provides a large amount of information or information which cannot be obtained by a shorter test. In the clinical setting the therapist's time is a valuable commodity and account must also be taken of fatigue which patients will experience in a prolonged assessment session.

Repeatability.   Repeated administrations of tests are necessary in the assessment of brain-injured patients in connection with retraining programmes. The use of parallel forms of tests will help to ensure that improvements in performance are not simply the results of practice effects due to familiarity of the test material. Two parallel forms may be sufficient if assessments are limited to one pre- and one post-training session. If, however, repeated assessments are used to establish a baseline before commencing retraining, a number of parallel forms will be required.

Sensitivity.   Tests used in the rehabilitation setting must be sensitive enough to pick up small gains in performance. A simple impaired/unimpaired scoring system is inappropriate for this purpose. The range of scores must be great enough to ensure that results are not invalidated by floor or ceiling effects.

Applicability to Real-world Situations.   In the discussion of generalisation in Chapter 2, we note the importance of recording whether or not gains observed in psychometric test performance carry over to improved functioning in everyday life. The converse is important in relation to the use of psychometric tests. We are concerned with measuring deficits which affect the quality of everyday life for the brain-injured individual. We therefore need tests which will reflect such deficits in the assessment. The majority of clinical tests do, of course, perform this function albeit at a gross level and the majority of patients who present to a neuropsychology service with complaints of memory dysfunction, for example, will show poor performance on clinical memory tests.

A number of studies have investigated the value of neuropsychological tests in predicting level of ability in everyday functioning. Of relevance here is Heaton, Chelune, and Lehman's (1978) finding that certain psychological tests (specifically the Halstead–Reitan battery [Halstead, 1947; Reitan & Davison, 1974] and some subtests of the WAIS) are of value in predicting employment status. Heaton and Pendleton (1981), in discussion of this issue, concluded that there is evidence to suggest that neuropsychological test scores are statistically associated with ultimate level of self-care following stroke. Chelune and Moehle (1986, p. 514) argue that "many of the tests which have been shown to be useful for neurodiagnostic purposes are also helpful in addressing questions about patients' probable success in everyday tasks and activities." However, they also emphasised that new research paradigms and strategies are necessary in this area of research, a point which was also made by Williams (1988) who argued that, in addition to further investigation of the relationship between existing tests and everyday abilities, test developers should "modify tests to include everyday tasks whenever possible." Recently, tests have been developed with the explicit intention of simulating everyday activities in the clinical setting. The first commercially-available tests of this type are the Rivermead Behavioural Memory Test (Wilson, Cockburn, & Baddeley, 1985) and the Behavioural

Inattention Test (Wilson, Cockburn, & Halligan, 1987). A similar approach was reported by Crook and Larrabee (1988) who measured memory functioning using telephone dialling, name–face association, facial recognition, and object location tasks. Kewman, Yanus, and Kirsch (1988) simulated the act of engaging in conversation in a noisy room by presenting subjects with a spoken passage, on which they had to answer comprehension questions, against a background of competing vocal stimuli. Unfortunately, adequate normative data is not yet available for all of these newly developed tests but in many cases the screening of a wider population than initially reported is planned or underway. Norms for the adult population (age range 16–65) are now available for the Rivermead Behavioural Memory Test (Wilson, Cockburn, Baddeley, & Hiorns, 1989) and supplementary norms for the elderly have been included in the test pack since 1989 (Cockburn & Smith, 1989). The Behavioural Inattention Test manual (Wilson et al., 1987) gives results obtained from a group of 50 control subjects in order to establish cut-off points in test performance, scores below which are indicative of impairment.

Computerised or Non-computerised Assessment

There are advantages and disadvantages attached to the use of computerised assessment prior to computer-based cognitive retraining. The use of computerised assessment procedures enables the therapist to observe the way in which the patient interacts with a computer and helps the patient to form realistic expectations about the type of task which would be involved in the retraining programme. However, when looking at the extent to which gains in computer-trained skills have generalised to performance of tasks other than the retraining tasks themselves the therapist may wish to include non-computerised tests presented in different modalities since computerised tests and tasks will generally have identical presentation and response modes (i.e. stimuli are presented visually and a motor response is required). Nevertheless, the task demands made by assessment and training tasks can vary even when both are computerised.

In discussing the features of a good test we mentioned brevity, repeatability, sensitivity, and applicability to real-world situations. With regard to the first of these features, computerised tests can decrease the demands on therapist time (Elwood, 1972, a, b), although currently available batteries require the therapist to be present to print out results and to move the patient from one test to the next.

The provision of a number of parallel forms of the test is, in theory, facilitated by computerisation, especially when alternative forms can be produced by means of random generation of the stimuli. In practice, the authors of existing computerised batteries have not capitalised on this facility and there is a pressing need for parallel forms of computerised tests to be devised. We are not aware of any batteries in which these are already provided.

The sensitivity of the test should, in theory, be facilitated by computerisation; automatic transfer to an appropriate short-form could be made on the basis of initial responses. More often than not the sensitivity of computerised tests tends to match that of non-computerised tests since the authors of tests have followed the original form as closely as possible when computerising existing tests (e.g. Warburg, 1988).

With regard to applicability to real-world situations it is sometimes assumed that a computerised task is one step further removed from reality than is a test administered by the psychologist in a clinical setting. This need not be the case if attention is paid to task demands in designing the computerised test. It is relevant to note that the simulated everyday memory tasks discussed in the previous section (Crook & Larrabee, 1988) were computerised.

The relative advantages and disadvantages of computerised assessment have been enumerated elsewhere (e.g. Norris, Skilbeck, Hayward, & Torpy, 1985; Romanczyk, 1986; Space, 1981) and the overall advantages and disadvantages of the clinical use of microcomputers are discussed in Chapter 5 of this volume. Time saving, ease of administration, ease of data analysis and production of accurately timed responses stand out as primary advantages. However, perhaps the most important advantage of computer administration is that of flexibility. Microcomputers are capable of analysing the patient's responses and changing the level of difficulty as appropriate whilst the programme is running. Even the most sensitive and responsive clinician cannot achieve such a degree of flexibility, as ongoing scoring and analysis is not always a reality in face to face clinical contact. One other advantage of microcomputer administration to be noted is the improvements in controlled testing condition which can be reproduced at every testing session. Computer administration has sometimes been criticised for depersonalising the patient, although this is unlikely to occur unless there is a total absence of human interaction in the assessment process. Furthermore, there is evidence that many patients prefer computer interactions to personal interactions (e.g. Angle, Hay, Hay, & Ellinwood, 1975; Cliffe, 1985) as embarrassment and test anxiety is reduced by the non-evaluated nature of the feedback from the computer.

The use of computerised assessment is limited by the small number of batteries currently available for microcomputers. A recent review of currently available software has been written by Skilbeck (in press). The most widely used battery is the BMAPS (Bexley–Maudsley Automated Psychological Screen; Acker & Acker, 1982) which includes visual memory, verbal memory, symbol digit, visuoperceptual and right–left orientation tasks. It runs on the Commodore (C64 and PET models) and Apple II computers. In the United States the California Neuropsychological System has been developed (Fridlund & Delis, 1983). The original version is currently being expanded. The tests can be administered and scored either manually or by means of the IBM PC and Apple microcomputers. The system is not a fixed battery but is designed for flexible use so that tests are selected according to the needs of the individual patient. An advantage of the computerised scoring system is that it is capable of evaluating qualitative data on test performance. An example described by Incagnoli (1986) is the scoring of the Rey–Osterreith Complex Figure task (Rey, 1941). The subject draws the figure on the monitor using a light pen. The computer will regenerate the patient's drawing on request and asks for information about the way in which it was drawn (e.g. Was the large rectangle drawn as a unit?). The computer then tabulates and summarises this data. Other tests included in this system are a verbal learning test similar to the Rey Auditory Learning Test (Rey, 1964), a test requiring definition of proverbs and a finger tapping test which is sensitive to motor impersistence.

Swiercinsky (1978) described a computerised system (SAINT) for the analysis of data obtained from manual administration of the Halstead–Reitan Neuropsychological Battery. A computerised administration and scoring system (SAINT-II) was described by Swiercinsky (1984). SAINT-II consists of 10 neuropsychological tests, many of which are computerised analogues of the Halstead–Reitan tasks. Abilities tested are spatial orientation, motor persistence, verbal and visual memory, visual information processing speed (symbol-digit task), vocabulary, sequencing, rhythm discrimination, numerical ability, and ability to shift attention. These tests are not commercially available, however, and are not currently in use by the author. Other available software is described below, categorised according to the cognitive system under assessment. If appropriate software for frequently-used tests is not commercially available, clinicians may consider writing programs which will enable them to administer these tests by means of a microcomputer. Apart from the programming time involved, a major problem with this procedure is that, since it involves altering the standard form of presentation, existing norms may not apply to results obtained from computerised administration. Although the clinician would need to collect normative data for the computerised test if reliable comparison with the general population were required, there is some evidence to suggest that automated presentations may not, in fact, have significant effects upon scores. For example Elwood (1969; 1972 a, b) compared results on standard and automated versions of the WAIS and found that test–retest reliabilities were high for both forms of presentation and that there were high correlations between the two forms of the test. Brierley (1971) reported similar findings when investigating automated and standard forms of Anstey's Dominoes Test (Vernon & Parry, 1949), a test which parallels Raven's Matrices (Raven 1960; 1965). It should be noted that these tests were automated rather than computerised. The equipment for administration was developed before low-cost microcomputers were available, and appears cumbersome and dated by comparison with these machines. In a later study in which the Peabody Picture Vocabulary Test (Dunn, 1965) was computerised, Elwood and Clark (1978) similarly found high correlations between standard and computerised versions. High test–retest correlations and high correlations between standard and computerised forms of a test designed to measure cognitive style on the reflection–impulsivity dimension (The Matching Figures Test: Kagan et al., 1964) were reported by Van Merrienboer and Jelsma (1988). However, the results of a large scale, multi-centre study organised in the Psychology Department at the University of Leicester in which eight psychological tests were administered to 367 subjects led the authors to urge caution when automating existing tests because on some tests (e.g. Raven's Standard Progressive Matrices) significant differences were found between the means of scores obtained using standard and computerised versions (Beaumont & French, 1987; French & Beaumont, 1990). However, alternative/standard form test–retest reliabilities compared favourably in many cases with those obtained in the original reliability studies. Computerised assessment proved to be entirely acceptable to the sample who participated in this study (French & Beaumont, 1987).

We conclude that the most appropriate assessment for cognitive retraining will include computerised and non-computerised tests. The overall aim of the assessment is to obtain as broad a data-base as possible which provides information about strengths as well weaknesses for each individual. Yet the amount of therapist time required for assessment should not be prohibitively great. The inclusion of computerised tests helps to minimise the amount of time which the therapist spends on the assessment and provides additional information about the ability to work independently and the ability to interact with a computer. At present there is a much wider range of non-computerised than computerised tests available and inclusion of non-computerised tests is necessary to ensure that the assessment covers all appropriate areas of cognitive functioning.

An ideal battery used for assessment for retraining will include newly-developed tests aimed at providing data about everyday abilities alongside traditional tests which have well-established norms.

3.3 TEST PROCEDURES FOR THE INVESTIGATION OF SPECIFIC COGNITIVE SYSTEMS

A range of regularly used clinical test procedures and some newly-developed adaptations and methods for the assessment of different psychological systems is discussed.

Attention

Attention was described in general terms by William James in 1890 (p. 404) thus: "focalisation, concentration of consciousness are of its essence. It implies withdrawal from some things in order to deal better with others." More recently, attention has been characterised by the concepts of selectivity or alertness/vigilance. Attentional defects therefore appear as distractibility or impaired ability for focused behaviour in the brain-damaged patient and unimpaired attention is a necessary precondition of both concentration and mental tracking activities. In the brain-damaged patient the difficulty in focusing attention leads to difficulties in solving problems or following a sequence of ideas. The attentional deficit is not always a global problem but can be specific to visual or verbal modalities and thereby associated with a lesion in the right or left hemisphere respectively (Diller & Weinberg, 1972).

A simple way of examining the ability to sustain attention is by the use of vigilance tests such as cancellation tasks. These normally involve the sequential presentation of stimuli such as strings of letters or numbers over an extended period of time with instructions to the patient to indicate in some way when a target letter or number is perceived. The level of difficulty of such tests can be varied by asking the subject to respond to two or more target items or respond only when the target item is preceded by a specified item. Cancellation tasks can involve many different stimuli. Diller et al. (1974) constructed 9 different cancellation tasks, 2 using digits, 2 using letters, 2 using easy three-letter words, 2 using geometric figures and 1 using simple pictures. Talland and Schwab (1964) constructed a letter cancellation test which is typically used with neuropsychologically impaired patients, and Diller et al. (1974) devised a letter cancellation task which is used in the assessment of neurologically impaired patients for rehabilitation. The task consists of six 52-character rows in which the target character (or characters) is (or are) randomly interspersed approximately 18 times in each row. Results from studies involving this task (e.g. Diller & Weinberg, 1977) indicate that stroke patients with right hemisphere lesions were not much slower than control subjects but made many more errors, normally of omission. The failure on this cancellation task was thought to be associated with spatial neglect in patients who had right hemisphere lesions, and with difficulties in temporal processing of information in left hemisphere patients. Mirsky (1989) describes a "Continuous Performance Test", which is a visual vigilance task. The subject is required to press a response key when a specified target letter appears and to withhold responses for a 10-minute period, and is thus particularly sensitive to impairments in the ability to sustain attention.

Another form of attention which is frequently tested is mental tracking. Digit recall or digit span is one of the simplest forms of mental tracking but performance on complex conceptual tracking tasks such as digits backwards (Weinberg, Diller, Gerstman, & Schulman, 1972) or spelling a long word or name in reverse (Bender, 1979), particularly if the task is complicated by requiring the subject to track two or more stimuli or ideas simultaneously, indicates basic difficulties in selective attention.

In psychiatric and neurological clinics, subtracting serial sevens is a task which is often used to estimate how well a patient can sustain mental activity. The subject is instructed to take 7 from 100 and to continue subtracting until they cannot go any further. However, there are no norms for this test and a significant number of errors can be found in a substantial number of the normal population (e.g. Smith, 1967).

The Paced Auditory Serial Addition Test (PASAT) (Gronwall & Sampson, 1974) is a sensitive test which has been used to examine mental tracking, particularly in patients who have sustained head injury. The test requires the patient to add 60 pairs of randomised digits so that each is added to the digit immediately preceding it. The digits are presented at varying rates ranging from one every 1.2 seconds to one every 2.4 seconds. The PASAT is very sensitive to deficits in information processing ability and has been used to determine when a patient can return to normal social and work activities. A disadvantage of the test, however, is that it requires calculation skill. Weber (1988) has described an alternative (The Attentional Capacity Test) which makes similar demands on information processing capacity but does not require the subject to add digits. In the Attentional Capacity Test subjects listen to taped numerical stimuli and count the number of targets presented in a series. Targets become increasingly complex so that they may first count the number of times 8 appears and later move to counting the number of times when 5 occurs preceded by an 8. The response is in each case a single number representing the total number of stimuli counted.

A number of tests exist which combine visual search and visual scanning. Such tasks demand focused concentration and directed visual shifting. An example of such a task is the Wechsler Digit Symbol Subtest (Wechsler 1955; 1981). In 90 seconds the subject is required to fill in blank spaces below randomly assigned numbers from 1 to 9 by making reference to a printed key which pairs each number with a different symbol. A poor performance on the Wechsler Digit Symbol Subtest is taken to indicate difficulty in one or more of the following abilities: (1) sustained attention; (2) visual scanning; (3) shifting visual set; (4) speed of mental processing; (5) motor speed (Kaufman, 1968).

Another test which involves attention is the "Trail Making" Test (Reitan, 1958). It is an easily administered test of visual conceptual and visuomotor tracking. It has two parts, A and B, and the patient is required to draw lines between consecutive numbered circles. In the second part of the test the patient has to alternate between numbers and letters. Performance is measured in terms of time taken to complete the array and errors made.

Computerised Assessment of Attention. One computerised test which is sensitive to the presence of attentional deficits is the symbol digit test from the BMAPS (Acker & Acker, 1982) from which standardised scores of speed and accuracy can be obtained. BMAPS runs on the Commodore PET and C64 as well as the Apple II computer and is available commercially from NFER–Nelson. Moerland, Alderkamp, and De Alpherts (1986) developed a battery for the Apple II–e which includes vigilance and visual search tasks that depend heavily upon attentional processes. This battery lacks normative data but relevant data is currently being accumulated and there are plans for research on reliability, validity, and standardisation.

Visuoperceptual and Visuoconstructional Abilities

When assessing visuoperceptual and visuoconstructional abilities it is important to recognise that there appears to be a dissociation between spatial and non-spatial visual tasks which broadly correlates with the site of lesion. Newcombe and Russell (1969) illustrated a dissociation between closure (Mooney, 1957) and spatial ability (Benton, Hamsher, Varney, & Spreen, 1963) tasks in patients who had right hemisphere injury. Such dissociations led Benton (1979) to draw up a provisional classification of clinically differentiated forms of visuoperceptual, visuospatial, and visuoconstructive disorders (see Table 3.1).

Visual Object Agnosia.   This is an impairment of object recognition that is not secondary to visual sensory deficit, language deficit, or a general intellectual deficit, though these can co-occur. Usually, appropriate responses will occur when the patient is allowed to handle an object rather than merely to observe the object. Visual object agnosia can be tested for by asking the patient to examine common objects and to name them or by asking the patient to name pictures of

TABLE 3.1
Classification of Visuoperceptual, Visuospatial and Visuoconstructive Disorders

I   *Visuoperceptual*

      A. Visual object agnosia
      B. Defective visual analysis and synthesis
      C. Impairment of facial recognition
          1. Facial agnosia (prosopagnosia)
          2. Defective discrimination of unfamiliar faces
      D. Impairment in colour recognition

II   *Visuospatial*

      A. Defective localisation of points in space
      B. Defective judgement of direction and distance
      C. Defective topographical orientation
      D. Unilateral visual neglect

III   *Visuoconstructive*

      A. Defective assembling performance
      B. Defective graphomotor performance

Taken from Benton (1979) by permission of Oxford University Press.

objects—for example using the Graded Naming Test (McKenna & Warrington, 1983). Alternatively, recognition of pictured objects from unfamiliar angles can be used to investigate the perceptual processes involved in recognition of objects. For example Warrington and Taylor (1973) were able to demonstrate that patients with right brain damage did poorly on a task in which objects were presented in unconventional views. Riddoch and Humphreys (1986) investigated agnostic responses to unconventional views in detail. They established that patients can be differentially sensitive to different ways of transforming a picture of an object. Some patients were most affected by foreshortening, some by "feature reduction" (a term used to describe a view of an object taken so that the saliency of its primary distinctive feature was reduced) alone, and some by "feature reduction" plus size disparity.

Visual Analysis and Synthesis.   There is a vast array of tests which are used to investigate visual analysis and synthesis. The subject is required to make sense out of ambiguous, incomplete, fragmented, or distorted visual stimuli. Tests such as the picture completion subtest from the Wechsler Adult Intelligence Scale (Wechsler, 1955; 1981), Mooney's Closure Test (Mooney, 1957), Gollin figures (Gollin, 1960), Street Completion Test (Street, 1931) and the Minnesota Paper Form Board Test (Likert & Quasha, 1970) all investigate this type of visual organisation. Other tests such as the Hidden Figures Test (Talland 1965), the visual closure subtest from the Illinois Test of Psycholinguistic Abilities (ITPA) (Kirk, McCarthy & Kirk, 1968) or the Overlapping Figures Test (Poppelreuter, 1917) investigate visual perceptual abilities involved in analysing figure–ground relationships in order to distinguish the figure from the interfering element.

Visual discrimination and recognition can also be investigated by looking at the perception of angular relationships (e.g. Judgement of Line Orientation; Benton et al., 1983). This test consists of 30 items which show a different pair of angled lines to be matched to display cards which have 11 numbered radii forming a semicircle. The angle of each of the lines presented in the stimulus perfectly matches the angle of one of these radii in the response set. However, the length of the stimulus line is shorter than that of lines in the response set and may match proximal, middle, or distal segments of them. The patient is asked to respond by giving the numbers of the lines in the response set which are at the same angle as the stimulus lines. A pointing response is acceptable if the patient has difficulty with number recognition.

A specific form of visual analysis and synthesis is involved in facial recognition. Impairments have been divided into prosopagnosia, an inability to identify familiar people, or facial agnosia which implies defective discrimination of unfamiliar faces. Benton and Van Allen (1968) devised a test of facial recognition. This test enabled the recognition of faces without reliance upon memory. The patient has to match identical front views, front with side views and front views photographed under different lighting conditions. In order to investigate cases where prosopagnosia is suspected the clinician could use photographs of the patient's friends and relatives. Care should be taken to select photographs showing faces only, since prosopagnosic patients are frequently able to identify people by their clothing (de Haan, Young, & Newcombe, 1987). Alternatively photographs of well-known people may be used. These can be collected from newspapers (Marslen-Wilson and Teuber, 1975). A standardised Recognition of Famous Faces Test has been prepared by Lancaster University in collaboration with the Radcliffe Infirmary, Oxford. It is not commercially available but is described in some detail, with normative data provided, by Hanley, Young, and Pearson, (1989). The latter also note that prosopagnosia should be distinguished from a more general impairment of person identification. The latter impairment seems to be related to deficits in semantic memory rather than to a failure of visual perception and may be identified when the patient fails to recognise familiar people even when cued with their voices or their names. A "Famous Voices Test", which is helpful in distinguishing prosopagnosia from the more generalised impairment described above, has been developed by Meudell, Northern, Snowden, and Neary (1980).

Tests have also been designed to examine facial expression of emotion (e.g. De Kosky, Heilman, Bowers, & Valenstein, 1980). Patients with right hemisphere damage tend to make emotional discriminations less well than control subjects or those with left lateralised lesions.

Colour Recognition. Ishihara Plates (Ishihara, 1954; 1985) can be used to discriminate colour blindness. The Farnsworth–Munsel 100-Hue and Dichotomous Test for Colour Vision (Farnsworth, 1943), which requires the subject to arrange coloured paper chips according to hue, can be used to identify colour agnosia. Other tests which require patients to choose the correctly coloured crayon to colour in simple line drawings of familiar objects (e.g. Damasio, 1979) have been used to distinguish colour agnosia from an anomic disorder involving the use of colour words.

Visuospatial Abilities. Test performance of patients with visuospatial problems is indicative of failure to appreciate spatial aspects of visual experience. Such dysfunction can result in defective judgement of direction and distance. Pointing to a light source on a projection screen is often used as a way of measuring localisation of points in space. The multiple choice version of the Benton Visual Retention Test (Benton, 1950) appears to be sensitive to subtle changes in perception of spatial relations (Walsh, 1978). The Benton Line Orientation task mentioned earlier can be used for identification of problems with directional orientation. Defective topographical orientation can be established by asking a patient to describe a trip from one point to another point in their home or other familiar surroundings. A more formal assessment of the ability to describe topographical relations is Money's Standardised Road-Map

Test of Direction Sense (Money, 1976). In this test the patient requires the ability to use visual imagery in order to describe the right and left turns necessary to follow a specified route through the map. Ratcliff and Newcombe (1973) noted that a distinction should be made between visuospatial tasks in which the subject explores spatial relations without any major change in body position and those which measure the subject's topographical orientation ability in a dynamic situation. The latter type of test may well be preferable for inclusion in an assessment for retraining since the tasks involved are likely to share more of the demands of real-life tasks. A test developed many years ago which can prove useful in assessment for rehabilitation is that developed by Semmes, Weinstein, Ghent, and Teuber, (1955). The test consists of a number of diagrams showing paths linking dots. The 9 dots on the diagrams represent 9 circles on the floor of a room. The subject is required to hold the diagram in a constant orientation and to follow the designated path round the room. The test does, of course, require access to a reasonably large and uncluttered room. Tactile versions of the diagrams were developed in addition to the visually-presented diagrams.

Defective ability to conceptualise spatial transformations such as rotations, inversions and, three-dimensional forms of two-dimensional stimuli have long been of interest to neuropsychology (e.g. Luria, 1966). Ratcliff (1979) devised a mental reorientation task, known as the Little Men Test. The little men are presented on cards or a computer screen, in 1 of 4 orientations shown in Fig. 3.1. The subjects are asked to indicate in which hand there is a black circle. Ratcliff found that patients with right posterior lesions made more errors than any other group.

Unilateral Visual Neglect.   Patients suffering from unilateral visual neglect have an absence of awareness of visual stimuli in either the left or right field of vision, in the absence of visual field defects. It is most frequently the left field of vision which is neglected as the condition is more commonly associated with right hemisphere lesions (e.g. Hecaen, 1962). One of the most frequently used methods of testing unilateral visual neglect is a line-bisection task (e.g. Schenkenberg, Bradford, & Ajax, 1980). The subject is asked to mark the middle

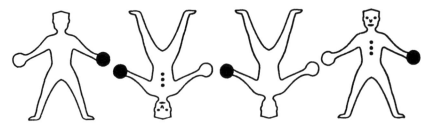

FIG. 3.1.   Orientations of the "Little Men" figure.

of each of a set of 20 lines of different sizes, arranged so that 6 are centred to the left of the midline, 6 to the right of the midline and 6 in the centre. The percentage deviation is calculated for each of the 3 sets of differently centred lines. This is a useful test because it provides information from many trials by a relatively brief assessment which increases the likelihood of demonstrating inattention, particularly in cases of mild neglect. Reading tasks and complex drawing tasks such as drawing a bicycle or a clock face also reveal evidence of unilateral visual neglect (Battersby, Bender, Pollack, & Kahn, 1956; Taylor, 1959). The Rivermead Perceptual Assessment Battery (Whiting, Lincoln, Bhavnani, & Cockburn, 1985) is a standardised assessment originally developed for use by occupational therapists. It consists of 16 subtests which include a picture-matching and a cancellation task and a range of copying tasks which are sensitive to visual inattention. Normative data is available for adult subjects. Normal subjects take about an hour to complete the test. Lincoln and Edmans (1989) investigated whether the test could be shortened in order to reduce administration time. They used three shortened versions, each of which proved acceptable for clinical use although a decrease in sensitivity was noted in each case. The clinician must weigh up the advantage of a 40% reduction in administration time against a 19% reduction in sensitivity (that is, this version failed to identify 19% of patients identified as having perceptual deficits by the full battery) in the case of version A and even larger reductions in sensitivity in the case of the other versions. It should be noted that the use of the non-dominant hand in timed cancellation and copying tasks can slow performance significantly. Cramond, Clark, and Smith (1989) found that some members of a cerebrally-intact group appeared to have a right-sided inattention when asked to use their non-preferred hands. This factor must be taken into account when using the battery with hemiplegic or hemiparetic neurological patients who are forced to use their non-preferred hands.

Visuoconstructive Disability.   Constructional praxis is the skilled behaviour, coordinated in time and space, required to put parts together in order to form a single entity or object. Implicit in constructional praxis is the organisational activity in which spatial relations among the component parts are accurately perceived.

Copying and free drawing have, for many years, been used to investigate constructional impairment. The Bender–Gestalt Test (Bender, 1938) has been used regularly. It is a very quick and easily administered test of 9 designs, originally used to demonstrate the tendency of the perceptual system to organise visual stimuli into configurational wholes. The complex figure test (CFT) devised by Rey (1941) to investigate both perceptual organisation and visual memory is another drawing test which is able to detect constructional impairment in its copy administration. It has the advantage of normative data for children from the ages of 4 to 15 and adults from 16 to 60. The "Copy" administration of the Benton Visual Retention test (Benton, 1974), and the two simple block construction tasks from the Stanford-Binet scale (Terman & Merrill, 1960) are also suitable for the examination of constructional impairment.

Building and assembling have been used for many years to investigate constructional disability and are useful in helping the examiner discriminate between spatial and visual aspects of a problem. The Block Design and Object Assembly subtests of the Wechsler Intelligence Scales are typical examples of two dimensional constructions. Goodglass and Kaplan (1983) provide a useful description of subtests within their Spatial-Quantitative Battery which are sensitive to constructional difficulties. These subtests, for which a scoring system is provided, require the patient to draw items to command, to construct designs with matchsticks, and to copy three dimensional block designs.

Benton et al. (1983) present a test of three-dimensional block construction in which the subject is required to reproduce a copy of a construction from a photographic representation. The number of omissions, additions, substitutions, and displacements are counted and in line with other block construction tasks, the time taken to complete the constructions is measured.

Computerised Tests of Visuospatial and Visuoperceptual Ability. Computerised tasks can, potentially, play a particularly important role in the assessment of visuoperceptual deficits through the provision of dynamic displays and precise temporal and spatial control of stimuli. Rosamund Gianutsos has developed a number of tests which run on the Apple II computer and the IBM–PC (Gianutsos, Cochran, & Blouin, 1984; Gianutsos & Klitzner, 1981; Gianutsos & Matheson, 1983). Examples are SDSST (Single and Double Simultaneous Stimulation), in which the patient must identify stimuli flashed on one or both sides of the screen, and BISECT, in which the patient must mark the centre of a line displayed on the monitor (Gianutsos et al; 1983). Both tasks are sensitive to the presence of a visual neglect. Skilbeck (1984) has also produced a computerised line bisection task which varies line length and calculates results in terms of percentage error. This test runs on the Commodore PET and the Commodore C64. Halligan and Marshall (1989) developed a version of the task which runs on the BBC Master. Line lengths range from 18 mm to 180 mm. The cursor arrow is moved from an AMX "mouse" pointer. An interesting variation of the task, which is useful in experimental investigations, is described by Halligan and Marshall. In the "perceptuo–motor compatibility" condition, the mouse and the cursor arrow move in the same direction. In the "perceptuo–motor incompatibility" condition this relationship is inverted and the cursor arrow moves in the opposite direction to that in which the "mouse" is moved. Moerland et al.'s (1986) battery also contains a test for visual neglect (the Visual Half Field Test) and Robertson and Smart (1988) working at the Astley Ainslie Hospital in Edinburgh have produced a package for the retraining of visual neglect which also contains an assessment programme. This is commercially available through Lochee Publications. Normative data is not available for these tests. The BMAPS battery (Acker and Acker, 1982) includes a test of visuoperceptual discrimination which yields a standardised score. This test involves spotting the "odd man out" in three complex designs. The computerised version of the Rey–Osterreith Complex Figure Task, which is part of the California Neuropsychological System (Fridlund and Delis, 1983), has been described in the discussion of computerised test batteries. A relatively simple computerised visual matching-to-sample test was originally developed for use with a dementing elderly population by Carr, Woods, & Moore (1986). It runs on a Commodore C64 computer with colour-monitor and touch-sensitive screen. Details of availability can be supplied by the second author, on request.

Memory

Memory has been described as the means by which an organism registers some previous exposure to an event or experience (Lezak, 1982) but what is generally called memory is not a unitary function and includes a variety of functions which are often conceptualised in stage models (e.g. Squire, 1975). Registration of *sensory memory* holds information very briefly for 1 to 2 seconds (Loftus & Loftus, 1976). *Immediate memory* is described as the first stage of short-term memory storage and serves as a limited capacity store from which information may be transferred to a more permanent store. *Long-term memory*, sometimes called "secondary memory", refers to the individual's ability to store information permanently; this system may come into operation as soon as information has entered the short-term storage system. The efficiency of the memory system is judged by its ability to recall information or to recognise information which has been previously learned. Some patients have deficits which are material specific, e.g. verbal or non-verbal (Butters, Lewis, Cermak, & Goodglass, 1973) and other distinctions such as episodic as opposed to semantic or procedural memory (Baddeley, 1982) are useful and may have implications for the clinical interpretation of results.

An important variable applicable to memory across all modalities is the amount of processing which to-be-remembered material receives. In real-life situations the level to which material is processed depends upon a variety of factors including importance and relevance to the individual, the time available for processing the material and so on. The case for different levels of processing was first argued by Craik and Lockhart in 1972. Central to their argument is the theme that longer retention is associated with the "depth" to which the material is processed, a deeper level of processing (i.e. elaborated processing in which material is linked with other material already stored in memory) leading to longer retention. Some of the tasks included in memory assessment clearly require only superficial processing. For example, if a patient is asked to memorise a list of numbers for immediate recall he or she is unlikely to form meaningful associations with other material in memory. Presentation of a passage of prose may elicit a deeper level of processing. According to Lezak (1987) the memory examination should therefore cover span of immediate retention, the extent of recent memory as tested by tasks requiring immediate recall, learning capacity (that is whether the subject is able to benefit from repeated presentation of to-be-remembered material), how well newly-learned material is retained over time, and efficiency of retrieval of both recently-learned and long-stored information.

In clinical practice the Wechsler Memory Scale (Wechsler & Stone, 1945) has gained widespread acceptance, primarily because it covers a number of different aspects of memory functioning in a relatively short and easily administered test. The subtests cover the areas of personal and current information, orientation, mental control, logical memory, digit span, visual reproduction, and paired associate learning. The Wechsler Memory Scale has a number of weaknesses. All but one of the subtests involve verbal memory of some kind. Also, the Memory Quotient obtained correlates very highly with IQ, suggesting that it is reflecting general intelligence as well as memory capability. In addition the normative information is based on a relatively small number of people and its original normative data did not go beyond the age of 60. However, it does have a consistent factor structure comprising 3 component factors: (1) immediate learning and recall; (2) attention and concentration; (3) orientation and long-term information recall (Skilbeck & Woods, 1980). The Wechsler Memory Scale has recently been revised (WMS–R; Wechsler, 1988) such that it now has useful additions such as delayed administrations of both memory passages and visual reproductions. The extended WMS, however, has become far less user-friendly to patients and clinician alike, and often takes over 45 minutes to administer.

Recently, clinicians have become more aware that clinical memory tests, such as the Wechsler Memory Scale, do not involve stimulus materials which are found in everyday life. Wilson et al. (1985) developed the Rivermead Behavioural Memory Test (RBMT) in order to improve face validity of memory assessment. The RBMT involves the following items: orientation, remembering a name, remembering a hidden belonging, remembering an appointment, picture recognition, immediate prose recall, face recognition, remembering a route, and delivering a message—which have been found by Wilson and her colleagues to reflect the kinds of memory failure which regularly affect the brain-injured in everyday life.

The following memory tests are also regularly used in clinical practice, often to supplement the information obtained from a memory battery such as the RBMT or the WMS. The Rey Auditory Verbal Learning test (Rey, 1964) gives a measure of immediate memory span and yields a learning curve. It enables the clinician to measure the effect of retroactive interference, confusion, and confabulation and also indicates the types of strategy used in learning. The Rey test consists of 5 presentations with recall of 15 words. There is also a forced choice recognition task at the end of the test. The Warrington recognition memory test (Warrington, 1984) allows comparison between recognition of words and recognition of faces and as such is useful in distinguishing between right and left hemisphere damage. The Rey complex figure test described above has a recall administration given between 30 minutes (Brooks, 1972) and 45 minutes (Taylor, 1979) after the original administration. The Benton visual retention test (BVRT) (Benton, 1974) is another widely-used visual recall test which gives a 10-second exposure to each of 10 cards with geometric designs followed by an immediate recall in each case.

One area of memory which has received little attention from clinicians over the years is visual learning. Comparatively recently, a visual learning test was devised as part of an information processing and memory battery (AMIPB; Coughlan & Hollows, 1985). The test follows the pattern of the AVLT in that it gives the subject five brief exposures to the stimulus items. In the case of the Coughlan test, a line drawing on a grid made from dots is shown. After each exposure the subject is required to draw as much of the drawing as he or she can remember. After the fifth trial a new drawing is shown and, finally, a recall of the original drawing is required without further exposure. From the number of lines drawn it is possible to calculate the rate of new non-verbal learning which can then be checked against the authors' normative data for different age groups.

Computerised Assessment of Memory.   Some computerised memory tests are available. Both the BMAPS and Moerland et al.'s (1986) battery contain visual and verbal memory tasks. The BMAPS tasks involve recognition memory while Moerland et al.'s tasks require free recall. Visual memory span can also be measured using BLOX, a test developed by Lindsay Wilson at the University of Stirling (described by Wilson, Wiedmann, Hadley, & Brooks, 1990) for the BBC-B, B+ or Master and adapted to run on the Apple by Logie (1986).

Normative data is being accumulated in relation to visual span. The California Neuropsychological System, discussed earlier, contains computerised analogues of the Rey Auditory Verbal Learning Task and SAINT-II, also discussed in the section on computerised batteries, contains computerised versions of the Halstead–Reitan verbal and visual memory tasks.

Mental Speed

A few tests may be regarded as predominantly measuring mental speed although there is clearly overlap with other tests measuring attention or orientation (e.g. the Digit Symbol Substitution Test from the WAIS and the Trail-making Test from the Halstead–Reitan battery). Two other tests of mental speed which should be mentioned are the AMIPB Information Processing Tasks, A and B

(Coughlan & Hollows, 1985). In Task A the subject has to select the second highest number from a row containing five two-digit numbers. The number of correct responses given in a 4-minute period gives a measure of the patient's information processing speed. In task B the subject has to examine two rows of numbers. The second row of numbers contains all the numbers contained in the first row randomly arranged, plus one additional number. The subject has to find and cross out additional numbers in the second row completing as many items as possible in 4 minutes.

Computerised Assessment of Mental Speed.   Another procedure which investigates mental speed is Sternberg's paradigm (Sternberg, 1969) by which a small number of items are memorised (e.g. digits 2, 5, 6) which are called a positive set. The remaining digits (0, 1, 3, 4, 7, 8 and 9) comprise the negative set. A number of digits are then presented randomly on a computer screen, if the target belongs to the positive set (e.g. 5) then the subject presses a button as quickly as possible. If the target is in the negative set, then the subject presses another button, again as fast as possible. In normal subjects a linear relationship exists between reaction time and positive set size. The normal reaction time for a positive set of only one item is approximately 400 milliseconds and as the positive set increases the reaction time increases by about 40 milliseconds per item in memory. The effect of increasing memory load of brain-injured subjects can be easily investigated using this simple paradigm. The procedure is extremely sensitive to the presence of brain damage and results can be displayed readily in a simple graphical form. Skilbeck (1984) adapted the Sternberg paradigm for use on the Commodore PET microcomputer. This version has the advantages of the original Sternberg administration but with the added facility of computer administration.

As with visuoperceptual abilities, computerised tests have the advantage of precise timing which enables reliable presentation of stimuli and more accurate recording of responses. A number of simple or choice reaction-time tasks have been written. Some are available commercially (e.g. Bracy, 1982; Gianutsos & Klitzner, 1981), others may be available from the authors (e.g. Robertson & Smart, 1987; Warburg, 1988).

Frontal Lobe Function

Often associated with diffuse cerebral damage is conceptual inflexibility or mental inflexibility, which implies difficulties in forming and applying abstract concepts. Almost invariably, this occurs when there is frontal lobe involvement (Zangwill, 1966). A number of tests have been devised to investigate the concrete thinking that is associated with this type of impairment. In clinical bedside testing proverb interpretation or object usage items (e.g. How many uses can you think of for a lid from a tin of boot polish?) are frequently used. Standardised tests often have drawbacks of being extremely time-consuming and requiring specialised equipment (e.g. The Category Test; Halstead, 1947).

The Wisconsin Card Sorting Task (Berg, 1948) is a more manageable test, which looks at abstract behaviour and shift of set. The subject has to sort patterned cards according to some principle, e.g. the number of stimulus items on the card or the colour of the stimulus items. Having made 10 successful sorts the examiner then shifts the principle by telling the subject that they are wrong. This process is repeated six times. The degree to which the subjects respond to the shift of category can be measured and the number of preservative errors which occur can be noted. The Wisconsin Card Sorting Task can be a very demoralising test for patients with frontal lobe disorder as their tendency to perseverate responses often means that they get one item after another wrong and in many cases they do not make the required conceptual shift at all. It is also a procedure that is quite difficult to score as the number of perseverative and other types of errors need to be noted as well as the number of categories that have been achieved.

Another test, which is regularly used in clinical practice, and which examines high-level abstract thought processes, is Raven's Progressive Matrices (Raven, 1960). This test is very easy to administer. It has 60 items in which a pattern has one part removed and the subject has to pick one of the six alternatives given, only one of which will correctly complete the pattern. A wide range of age norms are available and the progressive matrices also have the advantage that the raw scores can be converted into percentiles using tables developed by Peck, 1970.

A further area of ability which is included under the heading of frontal lobe function is word fluency which is normally measured by the number of words produced within a given time limit. The controlled oral word association test (Benton & Hamsher, 1976) uses two sets of letters—C, F, L and P, R, W—for which norms have been produced. The early version of the test used the letters, F, A, S and the test was often known as "the FAS test". However, use of the lettersets C, F, L and P, R, W is preferable, because the two sets are matched for letter frequency. The importance of availability of alternative forms of any test which is to be used in assessment for rehabilitation has already been stressed. The norms have an adjustment formula which takes into account the numbers of years spent in education and gives an age percentile score, which is useful when comparing the performance of brain-injured subjects. Benton (1968) found that patients with left frontal lesions produced almost one third fewer words on a controlled word fluency test than patients with right frontal lesions and patients with bilateral frontal lesions produced even fewer words on this test.

Adamovich, Henderson, & Auerbach (1985) suggest a number of tasks designed to investigate cognitive abilities in such a way as to facilitate treatment planning. Those which may be classified as tests of frontal lobe ability are those presented by the authors under the headings "Organisation" and "Higher Level

Thought Processes". The tasks described under these headings are particularly useful as supplements to existing tests, although norms are not provided. The "Organisation" section includes category sorting tasks, suitable for a greater range of abilities than the Wisconsin Card Sorting Task. For example, the subject may simply be asked to sort 12 items (3 colours, 3 vegetables, 3 vehicles, and 3 animals) into groups. This test may be useful for patients with very severe impairments who are unable to attempt the Wisconsin Test. There are a number of tests which look at sequencing ability ranging from a very simple task in which the patient is required to place 6 triangles in order of size to more complex tasks in which the patient must place sentences in order to form a meaningful paragraph or order steps involved in complex procedures such as booking and setting off on holiday. Tests of "High Level Thought Processes" include tests of convergent and divergent thinking, deductive and inductive reasoning, and "multiprocess" reasoning when assessing for rehabilitation. A particularly useful item in the latter group is that which measures "task-specific insight". Patients are asked to consider everyday activities (e.g. going on a shopping trip) and to answer questions in the light of their knowledge of their own limitations due to disability.

Computerised Tests of Frontal Lobe Function.   The Wisconsin Card Sorting Task has been mentioned and the complexity of its administration noted. A computerised version (The Bexley Maudsley Card Sort Task) has been developed by Acker and Acker (1982) and is on the same disc as the BMAPS package. This test is simple to administer and provides detailed information about responses including the number of perseverative errors recorded. Beaumont (1975) administered the Halstead–Reitan Category Test by means of a LINC–8 computer in conjunction with the standard slide projection equipment. The computer initiated slide change and recorded responses. No problems were encountered with computer-aided administration but Beaumont questioned the validity of the test in that it did not discriminate adequately between a brain-damaged group and a group of psychiatric patients without organic brain damage.

Language

The majority of classification systems based on models of language developed from the perspective of cognitive psychology (e.g. Ellis, 1982; Patterson & Shewell, 1987) treat language as a complex system which can be broken down into a number of subsystems. Patterson and Shewell's model subdivides receptive abilities into acoustic analysis, matching of the auditory stimulus with a stored representation of the word and access to semantics. Similarly, with the expressive system the semantic representation is matched with a phonologically-coded representation before being articulated. Similarly, in Ellis' complex information processing model of language processes, which includes "spelling, writing, reading and speaking" the following stages of speech comprehension are identified: acoustic analysis, acoustic-phonemic conversion (in certain circumstances), matching of the representation obtained by means of these preliminary analyses with a stored whole-word representation, and accessing the "cognitive system" where semantic information is stored. As regards expressive speech the semantic representation is matched with a whole-word "speech output" representation, which is fed into a phonemic buffer before neuromuscular execution of the speech sounds takes place. Classifications developed in clinical settings—for example that which provides the rationale for the widely-used Boston Diagnostic Aphasia Examination (Goodglass & Kaplan, 1939)—differ substantially from this type of model but, nevertheless, cover many different aspects of language. The BDAE classification assesses fluency of speech, naming, and repetition independently. Comprehension and production of written language is also assessed. Models of written language processing drawn from cognitive neuropsychology subdivide this type of language processing into subsystems, and different types of acquired dyslexia and dysgraphia can be identified on the basis of the pattern of preserved abilities (e.g. Coltheart, 1987). Inclusion of subtests that assess written as well as spoken language in clinical tests emphasises the fact that the communication system can be divided into different modalities. Five such modalities are listed by Shewan and Bandur (1986). These are: auditory processing, visual processing, gestural and combined gestural–verbal communication, oral expression, and graphic expression. It is important that all modalities are assessed prior to the development of a treatment plan.

Large test batteries like the BDAE, the Western Aphasia Battery (Kertesz, 1982), and the Minnesota Test for the Differential Diagnosis of Aphasia (Schuell, 1965) are valuable in assessing mild to moderate impairments of language. Where there is evidence of a severe aphasia, a briefer test focusing on the ability to perform low-level linguistic activities may be more appropriate. Examples of such materials are the Aphasia Screening Test developed by Whurr (1974) and the Halstead–Wepman Aphasia Screening Test which forms part of the Halstead–Reitan Neuropsychological Assessment Battery (Halstead & Wepman, 1959). These tests look at the ability to match, copy, comprehend, and produce simple stimuli in different modalities. The patient is not presented with complex information nor with a high volume of information. In cases where there is profound impairment of language functioning residual abilities may be assessed by building up a functional communication profile (e.g. Functional Communication Profile; Sarno, 1969; Edinburgh Functional Communication Profile; Skinner, Wirz, Thompson, & Davidson, 1984). This is achieved by rating the patient's ability to make themselves understood in a range of situations. The clarity of the communication is the prime concern and the way in which communication is made is of less importance—for example, a patient may rely entirely on gesture to carry out a transaction in a shop. An example of an instrument that formalises the ratings is Communication Abilities in Daily Living (Holland, 1980).

The larger assessment batteries, although valuable for revealing approximate level of functioning, are now recognised as lacking the sensitivity to measure changes in performance following treatment directed at a specific area of language functioning. Additional tests, which may need to be developed specifically for the individual patient, will be required to measure such change.

Kertesz (1989) notes that, in order to be comprehensive, the clinician may need to assess abilities beyond language function since "the overlap between intelligence, memory and language is considerable." The breadth of testing which is required for the full assessment of aphasia may render the process confusing. Kertesz (1989, pp. 250–256) argues that there is a consensus among aphasiologists regarding the most important items to be included in the assessment. This consensus is reflected by the most commonly used subtests which examine the following areas: (1) spontaneous speech; (2) information content of spontaneous speech; (3) comprehension; (4) repetition; (5) naming; (6) reading and writing. Calculation skills, gesture, pantomime, and symbolic movement may also be included as supplementary tests.

Computerised Tests of Language.   Some of the subtests of both the large batteries and the screening instruments lend themselves to computerisation but computerised versions of standardised tests are not widely used and norms are not available. If computerisation of a full battery is to be possible a hardware system which includes speech synthesis and speech analysis facilities is a prerequisite. Examples of computerised analysis of specific areas of speech and language can be found. For example The Newcastle Speech Assessment (Beresford, 1988) of which a computerised version is available, rates a range of speech characteristics and presents a profile for each individual assessed. It is suitable for use with adults or children. Qualitative and quantitative data are included in the profile. The Lingquest packages (Palin & Mordecai, 1984; Palin, Mordecai, & Palmer, 1985, published by the Psychological Corporation, perform comprehensive linguistic analysis of a language sample by means of computer programs which run on both Apple and IBM systems. Interpretation of a number of ratings of performance on tasks aimed at the differential diagnosis of dysarthria is available from NFER: the Frenchay Dysarthria Assessment (Enderby, 1983). The computerised differential analysis runs on the Apple II, II plus and IIe models and the BBC B models. The Computerised Boston (Code, Heer, & Schofield, 1989) produces profiles from raw scores on the Boston Diagnostic Aphasia Examination (Goodglass & Kaplan, 1983), as well as storing data on disc. This recording and analysis system runs on IBM compatible microcomputers and is available from Far Communications.

3.4 SUBJECTIVE REPORTS AND BEHAVIOUR RATINGS AS A MEANS OF INVESTIGATING COGNITIVE DYSFUNCTION

In order to assess the effect of cognitive problems in everyday life and to measure changes in everyday life which occur following cognitive retraining, subjective data obtained by means of questionnaires, rating scales, and behavioural observations must be considered.

One problem with the use of questionnaires is that the correlation between self-report and objective testing is not always high (e.g. Larrabee & Levin, 1986; Sunderland, Harris, & Baddeley, 1983). Much better correlations are observed between relatives' reports and objective tests (e.g. Brooks, 1979; Huppert, 1989) and it is common practice to ask relatives as well as patients to fill in questionnaires prior to and following a course of cognitive retraining.

Published scales and questionnaires vary widely in the activities on which they focus, and in the degree of detail of response required. Sensitivity to change is therefore very variable. The merits of different published ADL scales have been reviewed fully elsewhere (e.g. Gresham, Phillips, & Labi, 1980; Hall, 1980; Woods & Britton, 1985). Gresham's evaluation of basic ADL scales highlights the Barthel Index (Mahoney & Barthel, 1965) as possessing the advantages of completeness, sensitivity to change, amenability to statistical manipulation and, additionally, because of its widespread use, greater familiarity than the other scales for the majority of staff. We recommend the use of this Index to rate ADL status but emphasise that the areas of activity assessed by this type of rating scale are limited to basic physical functions. In the case of the Barthel Index the areas of behaviour covered are feeding, wheelchair/bed transfer, grooming, toilet transfer, bathing, walking, using stairs, dressing, controlling bowels, and controlling bladder. The use of such rating scales is therefore of value only with patients who have very severe handicaps following brain injury.

Some scales include ratings of social and communicative behaviour. The Clifton Behavioural Rating Scale (Pattie & Gilleard, 1979) is widely used in the UK and covers these areas in addition to physical disability. It is an instrument which is quick and easy to use but has the disadvantage that, as with many of the scales that include ratings of social behaviours, it is validated on (and usually used with) an elderly rather than a brain-injured population. Furthermore the range of social behaviours covered is limited. Candidates for cognitive retraining will often be selected from a less severely impaired group and information about a wider range of activities will be required in order to determine the goals of retraining. There are fewer scales available to meet this need. The Holbrook Activities Index (Holbrook & Skilbeck, 1983) is a relatively short scale which is particularly useful in monitoring change in a less impaired group. The index was originally developed for use with patients who had suffered a stroke but is appropriate for use with a wider brain-injured population. Numerical scores can be calculated for domestic, leisure/work, and outdoor activities. A scale which has been developed specifically for the brain-injured population and which is somewhat more sensitive than those already mentioned with regard to cognitive function is the recently-developed BIRS (Brain Injury Rehabilitation Scale) (Farmer & Frank, 1988).

A more detailed and wide-ranging set of inventories developed by Katz and Lyerly (1963) focuses on the patient's adjustment and social behaviour in the community. These inventories were originally developed for use with psychiatric patients but have proved useful in assessing quality of life in a group of brain-injured patients (Klonoff, Costa, & Snow, 1986). In the Katz scales a close relative is asked to rate the patient's symptomatology and social behaviour by responding to 127 descriptive statements in terms of the frequency with which the statement applies to the patient. The patient is also asked for a self-rating on the same items. The scales provide detailed information and are sensitive measures of change but, because of their length, can be cumbersome to use, their completion requiring a good deal of commitment and cooperation from patient and relative.

"Purpose-built" questionnaires have also been developed by centres involved in the rehabilitation of the cognitively impaired patient (e.g. the Edinburgh Questionnaire, McKinlay, Brooks, & Hickox, 1986; the Newcastle Question-naire, Bradley & Welch, 1987). The advantage of such scales is that, by definition, they are developed to satisfy particular needs and can incorporate items from different indices and inventories which are judged to be of value. The disadvantage associated with their use is that normative data for the entire scale is not available. However, when the main aim is to compare scores before and after intervention this may not be a serious flaw.

The Edinburgh Questionnaire samples a range of areas of functioning including cognitive ability, involvement in social activities, and potentially problematic behavioural responses. The Newcastle Questionnaire (see Appendix IV) is divided into four sections investigating cognitive ability, affective response, involvement in social activities, and role in the family. Both the patient and a close relative are asked to complete the questionnaire.

If an unpublished questionnaire or rating scale is to be used to assess the outcome of a retraining programme it is likely that time devoted to the development of an instrument attuned to the aims of the programme and the particular needs of the group of individuals to be rehabilitated will prove well-spent. Minor additions to, or omissions from scales used by other institutions may be the only alterations required to produce an appropriate instrument. However, in some cases therapists may wish to develop an entirely new scale using existing instruments as a guide.

Subtle changes in behaviour can be recorded by means of experimentally-designed instruments. Such techniques have been used widely by Roger Llewellyn Wood and his associates at the Kemsley Brain Injury Rehabilitation

Unit who have emphasised the importance of behavioural techniques in the assessment and treatment of the brain-injured patient. For example Wood (1986) describes a time-sampling procedure in which staff recorded, at 2-minute intervals during a 30-minute session, whether or not the patient was attending to a therapy task. Wood and Fussey (1987) also used an attention-rating scale in which staff made an overall rating (poor concentration in therapy at one end of the scale, good concentration in therapy at the other).

Gordon (1987) notes that time usage whereby a patient records the amount of time spent in a targeted activity is being used with increasing frequency to measure the effectiveness of various types of rehabilitative intervention. This method has not yet been used widely with brain-damaged groups but Gordon himself has demonstrated its usefulness in establishing the effects of a visual perceptual retraining programme on the reading habits of right brain-damaged stroke patients (Gordon et al., 1985).

3.5 SUMMARY

This chapter has considered the issues involved in assessment for rehabilitation. A tailor-made retraining programme is always considered to be the ideal for the brain-damaged individual and assessment geared towards specific dysfunctions in such patients is seen as the most desirable form of assessment. However, it is recognised that the development and application of such testing techniques is so time-consuming that in clinical practice less detailed descriptions of deficit and the use of standard clinical tests, with inherent advantages in terms of normative data, would represent best practice. It is stressed that a good assessment prior to rehabilitation will measure strengths of the individual as well as deficits in functioning. It will identify factors such as denial or lack of attention which may affect the individual's ability to benefit from the rehabilitation programme. It will provide a baseline measure of functioning for later comparison of results and it will be comprehensive in terms of a range of mental functions which are assessed.

The advantages and disadvantages of large test batteries are discussed and it is concluded that, in practice, most neuropsychologists favour assembling their own test batteries for assessment of neuropsychological functioning on the grounds that the flexibility they can achieve will allow them to accommodate handicaps and limitations of response by individual patients. The features of a good test are discussed and factors such as brevity, repeatability, sensitivity, and applicability to real-world situations are emphasised. Computerisation of testing allows the therapist to note the way in which a patient interacts with a machine prior to rehabilitation. If the test is well written for microcomputer application it can allow time saving on the equivalent paper and pencil tests, and it is argued that there is no reason to suppose that a computerised test should be any less sensitive or applicable to the real world than non-computerised tests.

Following a review of the available literature the conclusion is reached that the most appropriate assessment for cognitive retraining will include both computerised and non-computerised tests. The computerised tests should lead to economies of time and facilitate uniformity of presentation and accurate recording of responses while non-computerised tests have an advantage in terms of the range of higher mental functions which can be assessed.

A review of the types of tests commonly in use over a range of higher mental functions, including attention, memory, mental speed, visuospatial ability, visuoperceptual ability, perceptual reasoning, and language functioning is provided. This section also includes descriptions of some newly-developed tests, including computerised tests and instruments of analysis.

Finally, the role of subjective reports and behaviour ratings is discussed in relation to the investigation of cognitive dysfunction. The poor correlation between self-report and objective testing is noted and the good correlations between relatives' reports and objective tests are commented upon. Such instruments are felt to be important in the evaluation of the effects of cognitive retraining on the performance of everyday activities.

It would appear that a good assessment for rehabilitation must involve both computerised and non-computerised tests, cover a wide range of higher mental functions, be able to detect strengths and weaknesses in the patient's performance, be repeatable, be applicable to real-world situations and, above all, be acceptable to the patient undergoing assessment.

4 Cognitive Systems and Their Remediation

4.1 APPROACHES TO REMEDIATION OF COGNITIVE DYSFUNCTION

Restitution of Function

The phrase "restitution of function" implies that, as a result of intervention or of spontaneous recovery, an impaired system can be restored to its premorbid mode and level of functioning. Once this has occurred abilities subserved by that system will no longer show evidence of impairment.

There is no doubt that recovery of function can occur following insult to the brain. Such recovery normally occurs spontaneously and may be explained in terms of physiological or anatomical processes. These processes are described in Chapter 1. In the main they involve disturbance of brain function in the absence of significant neuronal death. Where chronic loss of function is observed (implying neuronal death) it is debatable whether restitution of function to premorbid levels is a possibility. Follow-up studies suggest that this is rarely the case (Milner, Corkin, & Teuber, 1968; Sarno & Levita, 1971).

In spite of the fact that full restitution of function to premorbid levels, without the use of alternative strategies, may be an unrealistic target, it is nevertheless the preferred target for the majority of patients and their families. Gianutsos and Matheson (1987) argued that because the potential pay-off is great, restitution should be given a clinical priority. Wilson (1987) advocated an approach in which objectives are specified in terms of amelioration of problems rather than total restitution of function. Where restitution is the aim, the therapeutic approach typically involves repeated practice, using tasks which require the operation of the impaired system. Although there are conflicting claims as to the value of repeated practice on the same task (Newcombe, 1982), with many clinicians remaining sceptical, some abilities may improve with practice. Gianutsos and Matheson (1987) presented a brief case report describing a patient whose scanning ability improved after repeated performance of a speeded reading task. They argued that this type of approach which implies "strengthening [of a cognitive function] through exercise" may play a role in the recovery process and therefore should not be ruled out as an element in the rehabilitation programme.

Substitution of Function

The principle involved in substitution of function is one of reorganisation of the functional components of a complex ability. Thus tasks which depend upon the ability to be retrained should, following intervention, be performed efficiently but in a way which differs from the premorbid method of performance. Physiological bases for substitution are discussed in Chapter 1. An example is that of "functional redundancy." A given psychological function may be very widely represented in the brain. Thus the damaged area of the brain may, premorbidly, have been only one of many areas contributing to performance of tasks dependent upon that function. Those who support this view argue that function can be improved if these non-damaged areas can be encouraged to make a greater contribution to tasks which depend upon the psychological function in question.

Luria (1963) proposed that functions are hierarchically represented, so that performance can potentially be mediated by higher or lower level centres in the brain. Luria considered active re-learning to be of crucial importance in the achievement of this type of reorganisation. A frequently quoted example is that of the patient unable voluntarily to command the tongue movements involved in licking the lips because of an apraxic disorder secondary to brain damage. The patient could nevertheless make those movements without hesitation as an automatic response when his mouth was smeared with honey. Conversely, a patient unable to copy a sequence tapped out by the examiner had no difficulty in tapping out his age. The latter task involved a higher level conceptual ability as opposed to the lower level motor task involved in copying sequences of taps.

Substitution Versus Restitution Approaches

In practice it can be extremely difficult to identify the mechanisms which are coming into play in any given retraining task. If patients are presented repeatedly with a task which depends upon the operation of a system which has been shown to be impaired, they may benefit simply because of repeated practice. The patients may however improve performance because they are developing, consciously or unconsciously, alternative strategies for the performance of the task. Where the retraining programme explicitly teaches alternative strategies and requires that they be used in given tasks it can be claimed that a substitution approach is being taken. Once alternative strategies are used automatically and subconsciously, the patients may be unaware of the way in which they are performing a given task. As already noted, the possibility of strengthening effects of repeated practice cannot be ruled out entirely and the case can be made for rehabilitation programmes which contain a mixture of both repeated practice and alternative strategy approaches.

Training in the Use of Prosthetic Aids

The use of external aids involves a rather different approach in which the patient is trained to use items as diverse as notebooks, noticeboards, and electronic devices to resolve some of the practical problems which result from the deficit. Use of the aids may become habitual and their use may thus reduce the practical problems associated with impaired functioning. The use of such devices emerges as an important component of memory therapy, and a thorough review of this area is provided by Harris (1984). Wilson and Moffat (1984b) noted the importance of suiting rehabilitation strategies and patients' needs; the use of shopping lists, diaries, and timers can be more effective in dealing with practical problems resulting from poor memory than attempts at improving memory function through cognitive retraining. Certainly the use of such aids should be considered in the final stages of a rehabilitation programme. Even if cognitive retraining has achieved improvements in certain areas of memory functioning, they may be helpful in alleviating problems associated with residual deficits. Harris (1978) considered the use of external memory aids in the cerebrally-intact population. He noted that active cues (e.g. a timer) were preferable to passive cues (e.g. a knotted handkerchief). This point is relevant to the use of aids with the brain-damaged population. As Wilson (1984) has noted, these patients may simply forget to use the aids provided. An effective procedure has been reported by Gouvier (1982). An alarm was set to "beep" hourly. This cued the patient to consult his or her personal appointment calendar.

Prosthetic aids have also been used in the management of speech and language disorders. In cases where damage to the speech organs is so severe that no speech output is possible or volume is severely reduced, voice synthesisers, voice amplifiers, and visual display units are available as communication aids (e.g. British Telecom's "Claudius Converse Electronic Voice"; the Mardis "Orac" portable speech communication system; Datamed's "Communicator" and "Easi-Talk"). Non-electronic devices such as a communication board or notebook with picture stickers (supplied by Winslow Press) are very portable communication aids. External aids can also be of value in the treatment of aphasia. For example, packs of picture cards such as "Colorcards", available through Winslow Press can provide cues for the patient with naming difficulties. Bruce (1987) and Bruce and Howard (1987) reported the use of a microcomputer-based aid which provided a synthesised phoneme. Aphasic patients with severe naming problems were taught to use the aid to generate phonemic cues which assisted their naming ability. Chute and Hoag (1988) refined a series of programmes for a patient with a profound expressive dysphasia and severe physical limitations. Chute, Conn, Dipasquale, and Hoag, (1988) reported on the development of the program, which runs on an Apple Macintosh Microcomputer. The patient used a single switch to click-select letters from a display and thus to assemble words and phrases which were then "spoken" through the "MacinTalk" speech synthesiser system software.

4.2 BEYOND THE COGNITIVE SYSTEMS

Cognitive systems are not self-contained entities: when damaged they impact upon further areas of a patient's life, such as functional (ADL) and social activities, and are in turn themselves influenced by personality and mood factors. The easier field to discuss is that where cognitive deficits act as a contributory factor to other areas of a person's life, and a number of studies have addressed this. In terms of prognosis for ADL outcome, an early study by Ben-Yishay, Rattok, and Diller (1970) using WAIS subtest scores noted the value of cognitive tests in predicting ADL outcome. A few years later Lehmann et al. (1975) found that a subset of WAIS subtests (picture completion, digit symbol, block design), when combined, correlated significantly ($p < .01$) with functional outcome in their sample of 114 stroke patients. Whilst particular IQ subtests have been investigated, to some degree, in predicting ADL outcome, less attention has been given to the use of overall intellectual level. This is somewhat surprising, given that brief and easy to administer instruments exist for this purpose. A good example is Raven's Coloured Matrices (RCM: Raven, 1965). David and Skilbeck (1984) used the RCM in their study of 88 dysphasic stroke patients, and noted its prognostic value: patients who died within 6 months of their stroke had significantly lower ($p < .01$) RCM IQs at initial assessment.

ADL recovery has also been predicted from other cognitive tests, not just those involving intellectual level/ability. For example, Botvin, Keith, and Johnston, (1978) noted a significant correlation of 0.48 between the cognitive test scores, including mental arithmetic and memory, and outcome. Prescott, Garraway, and Akhtar, (1982), too, observed the predicted value of memory test performance at one month post-stroke. Similarly, Andrews, Brocklehurst, Richards, and Laycock (1980) found "perceptual disturbance" to be highly predictive ($p < .001$) of ADL dysfunction in their stroke patients. However, as this disturbance was assessed by impaired picture drawing, the cognitive dysfunction may have been more complex than purely a perceptual deficit.

Disturbance of perceptual abilities are often cited as barriers to good ADL recovery. Perhaps the greatest impediment to the work of physiotherapists and occupational therapists are the perceptual deficits of neglect, whether these be visual in nature, or those affecting body awareness (Skilbeck, 1983). Driving is a skill which is important for successful functioning in many occupational and home environments. Neuropsychological, particularly visuoperceptual and visuospatial, tests have been shown to be predictive of the cognitive aspects of driving (Gouvier & Warner, 1987; Gouvier, Webster, & Blanton, 1986). In a recent study Sundet, Finset, and Reinvang, (1988) found that the occurrence of apraxic disturbance was associated with a poorer ADL recovery at 6 months post-stroke in left hemisphere cases. Wade, Skilbeck, and Langton-Hewer (1989) confirmed the importance of constructional apraxia to ADL outcome in their population study involving almost 1,000 patients: failure to copy a Greek cross at initial assessment only a few days after stroke was strongly associated with poor ADL at 6-months follow-up. These authors also noted that low initial RCM IQ was associated with a poor ADL outcome at 6 months post-stroke.

Some studies are available which have examined outcome more widely than in just ADL terms. Roberts (1979), in his follow-up study of 359 patients, noted that cognitive deficits and personality changes were the principal determinants of level of employment obtained post brain injury, rather than physical disability, a finding which was supported by the research of others, including Oddy and Humphrey (1980), and Weddell, Oddy, and Jenkins (1980). Levin, Grossman, Rose, and Teasdale (1979) noted that the patients who showed a good outcome following head injury in quality of life terms, assessed by the Glasgow outcome scale (GOS) (Bond, 1975), had WAIS IQs of 85+ at about 12 months post-trauma. In addition to having lower IQs, those patients showing a poor outcome also tended to show more pronounced deficits on memory tests, and disturbances in language. Similar findings were obtained by Jennett, Snoek, Bond, and Brooks (1981). Van Zomeren (1981), using a modified GOS, observed significant correlations between choice reaction time at 5 months post-injury and outcome at 12 months after trauma for GOS scores and social factors. The latter comprised work, family life, and leisure activities. Klonoff et al. (1986), in an exploratory study, also investigated quality of life outcome (including aspects of emotional functioning, social functioning, ADL, and leisure) in 78 head-injured patients 2–4 years after injury. These authors were able to draw upon the data from a large number of neuropsychological tests. Their findings included significant correlations between outcome (as rated separately by patient, and by family) and cognitive variables (particularly motor, constructional, and memory). Finally, the return to work of 50 head-injured patients was recently examined by Bayless, Varney, and Roberts (1989), in terms of executive performance on the "Tinker Toy test" (Lezak, 1982). It is unusual for research studies to concentrate on frontal lobe performance (even though head injuries are often associated with impairment in such performance), and so the study is worthy of note. Bayless and his co-workers found that the performance of head-injured patients who returned to work were not significantly different to normal control subjects, but both of these groups performed significantly better than a group of head-injured patients who did not manage to obtain employment post-trauma.

Whereas it is clear that research has extended our knowledge of the relationships between cognitive dysfunction and outcome, it has proved more difficult to make progress in the direction of the influence of mood and personality upon recovery following acquired brain damage. Aside from cognitive impairments, rehabilitation therapists most often report (and complain!) to neuropsychologists that patients are failing to thrive and progress in therapy due to the psychological deficit of low motivation. Motivation is often defined in terms of the level of insight displayed by the patient (see discussion in 2.3 in Chapter 2). A study by Herbert and Powell (1989) investigated the relationship between level of insight and rehabilitation gain in a group of 54 patients registered at an Employment Rehabilitation Centre. They found that the clients who over-rated their abilities were more likely to make good progress. Their group contained only 7 individuals who had sustained brain injury. A replication of the study with a head-injured group undergoing rehabilitation at RAF Headley Court (Malia, personal communication) yielded no such relationship between optimism and rehabilitation gain. It appears that different mechanisms mediate insight and motivation in the brain-injured population.

Motivation cannot be regarded as purely a personality characteristic divorced from the damage which has been suffered by the brain (Mutchnick, 1988). Luria (1963) particularly linked poor motivation to the involvement of the frontal lobe, producing extensive apathy for most forms of activity. Particularly important seems to be damage to the pre-frontal region and limbic system. The damage may lead to a lack of a strategic view from the patient, and poor goal planning. Proposed, or ongoing, cognitive rehabilitation tasks (or physical therapy tasks) may then be viewed by the patient as irrelevant or unhelpful. The observed result may be generalised apathy, or hostility to suggested rehabilitation programmes. Because of this poor motivation and lack of engagement with the rehabilitation programme, many patients will perform below the optimum. They present a great challenge to rehabilitation workers who are attempting to motivate them to participate as fully as they are able. Although it is very difficult to measure, Feigenson, McCarthy, Greenberg, and Feigenson (1977) observed poor motivation towards rehabilitation in 8% of their patients, indicating that this was associated with slow ADL recovery. In spite of the fact that this is not an uncommon problem, usually direct treatment to improve motivation is not provided. For example, Wilson (1981) listed 51 problems treated over a 9-month period at a UK neurological rehabilitation centre, including only one case of treatment for poor initiative/motivation. Wood (1987) addressed this issue, pointing to behavioural research work (e.g. Wood, 1984) where reinforcement "motivators" had been provided. The area of poor patient motivation, or cooperation, with rehabilitation is an important one, and one which remains under-researched. A major effort is needed to undertake studies which will provide guidance to the rehabilitation team on managing, and reducing, this bar to optimal outcome.

Personality variables have occasionally been investigated in relation to rehabilitation outcome. In their small study of a group of 21 patients, Finlayson and Rourke (1978) failed to obtain a significant relationship between the personality variable of "locus of control" and rehabilitation outcome. This variable reflects a person's perception that their life events are under their control (internal), or are largely determined by fate or external factors (externally controlled). As such, this variable might be viewed as one determinant of motivation. Finlayson and Rourke did note, however, that patients' locus of control scores correlated with therapists' judgements of their level of motivation.

Personality and behavioural disturbances (e.g. irritability, slowness, tiredness) in the patient are particularly important to the family; for example, Brooks and Aughton (1979) found that these factors were far more distressing to the family than the patient's physical deficits, this finding being supported by McKinlay et al. (1981), and Oddy and Humphrey (1980) also noted that relatives attributed their stress mainly to behavioural disorders in the patient. Brooks (1984) has provided a good review of this area. Depression of mood is often observed following acquired brain damage. This may arise as a direct consequence of the organic damage sustained, although research on the relationship between depression and site of lesion is inconclusive (anterior left hemisphere damage may be particularly important—see Wade, Langton-Hewer, Skilbeck, and David 1985a, for brief review). Depression is also often seen as a psychological reaction to the disabilities acquired (whether these be physical, cognitive, or social) as a result of the brain damage. For example, Wade et al. (1985b), examining depression at 6 months post-stroke in a sample of 334 patients observed (conservatively) a frequency of at least 20%. Other possible psychological responses include anxiety and loss of self-esteem.

After the initial, acute phase, patients who have sustained major neurological/brain damage may be left with significant residual deficits requiring rehabilitation. Whilst participating in a rehabilitation programme, patients can become so dependent upon their therapists and family that they adopt a "sick role" beyond that necessitated by their ADL impairment. The dependency, which is to a certain degree necessary in relation to therapists and family carers, becomes distorted and exaggerated, as the patient feels that he or she has little control over outcome and life in general. Without this control the patient cannot undertake normal responsibilities (including going to work, helping around the house, etc.) and may be defined as not having to accept responsibility for "getting better" (see Wilmott, 1989, for review). When the patient with acquired brain damage is cast in the role of "sick person" by family, therapists, and the community at large, then it is not surprising that the motivation to recover is impoverished. The probability that patients will be viewed as sick/disabled is higher if they have an obvious physical sign of their neurological damage, such as hemiplegia. In this situation, they are likely to be stigmatised by the attitudes and behaviour of others towards them: the presence of physical disability may lead to negative characteristics being ascribed to the patient, such as low intelligence, or to them being ignored or pitied. Such reactions from others are devaluing and the patient's self-esteem is likely to be significantly reduced.

In addition to the physical and cognitive deficits resulting from the acquired brain damage, and the psychological trauma of coping with these, it can be seen that a neurological patient may have to cope with other psychological difficulties, such as depression and loss of self-esteem. Beyond help with these latter problems which may be offered by the clinical psychologist, or other members of the rehabilitation team, family carers are in the best position to offer psychological assistance to their relative. The family is important in helping to reinforce the positive set which the rehabilitation team should be establishing with the patient in relation to himself/herself. Family members know the patient extremely well and, after the active rehabilitation phase, are in the best position to help the patient cope with residual disability and adjust to it. For these reasons, it is helpful to engage family members as early as possible within the active rehabilitation field. Besides being able to enlist their help as part of the rehabilitation "team" and programme, continued assistance and supervision of the patient's rehabilitation may be achieved via the family in the long term. Under the best circumstances the family will be the principal agents in the generalisation of cognitive retraining tasks into real life. Care must be taken, however, to look to the psychological needs of the family as well as of the patient. The reviews offered by Brooks (1984) and Wade et al. (1985a) highlight the stresses placed upon a family by one of its members sustaining major brain damage from head injury or stroke.

4.3 A MODEL OF DISABILITY AND REHABILITATION

The Newcastle retraining programme was developed from an eclectic model of disability and rehabilitation. The model (see Fig. 4.1) favours a process-specific approach to the retraining of identified deficits but accepts the validity of certain arguments in favour of a general stimulation approach and recognises that, in clinical practice, different approaches are not necessarily mutually exclusive. The model also incorporates the psychosocial context in which the brain-damaged individual may find themselves. Finally, it takes account of effects of attending a retraining programme that are related both to the content of the programme and to the change in daily routine which results from attendance.

Overview

The model (Fig. 4.1) links acquired brain damage with both cognitive deficits and psychosocial deficits (e.g. personality changes, depression). The extent and nature of these deficits will be influenced by premorbid factors. For example, stroke is a disease of later years, often following a history of vascular changes in the brain associated with, for example, hypertension or transient ischaemic attacks. These changes, of themselves, may well have adversely affected cognitive functioning prior to the stroke (see Wade et al., 1985a, for review) and have a bearing upon the cognitive dysfunction observed post-stroke. Similarly, premorbid factors may affect the psychosocial changes associated with acquired brain damage; for instance, the occurrence of head injury is not a random event, and there is considerable evidence that people sustaining head injuries show a tendency to have a premorbid history of alcohol abuse, social abnormality, or unusual personality traits (this area is reviewed by Bond, 1984). These premorbid factors are likely to play some part in determining the psychosocial deficits noted after acquired brain damage.

The model depicts the acquisition of cognitive and psychosocial deficits as leading to an impoverished environment in which the patient now has to operate. Of itself, this impoverishment will result in a further reduction in the patient's cognitive efficiency. As indicated in the last section, the acquisition of psychosocial deficits, coupled with a poor environment, is likely to have an adverse effect upon the patient's self-esteem. Thus, disability is established in the patient by a combination of cognitive impairment and adverse social/personality consequences, which may feed back upon themselves in a "vicious circle". In the next stage of the model, where the rehabilitation system commences, a comprehensive assessment of the patient is undertaken to establish the number and level of deficits sustained and to identify which abilities are preserved. The results of this assessment may, via feedback, lead to greater insight and motivation towards rehabilitation on the part of the patient, which in turn leads to an improvement in psychosocial deficits such as irritability and depression and, ultimately, to improvement in self-esteem. This process can be assisted at various stages by the introduction of additional therapy/counselling from the clinical psychologist.

Also following from the identification of deficits and abilities should be the provision of general cognitive stimulation and, often, a retraining programme aimed at specific cognitive deficits. If effective, the latter should lead to improved cognitive function and, as described in the previous section, a better functional outcome. This part of the system may be assisted by non-specific cognitive stimulation, and a number of mutually beneficial exchanges are possible between improved cognition and improved motivation/psychosocial status. Further assessment associated with the improved cognition stage may identify residual

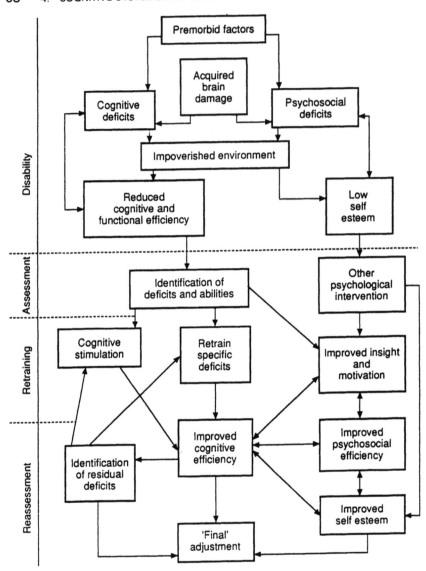

FIG. 4.1.   Model of disability and rehabilitation.

cognitive deficits, potentially leading to further cognitive stimulation and specific retraining. If these residual deficits are not considered by the rehabilitation team to be amenable to remediation, then this information is recognised in the "final" adjustment stage, along with information about improved cognitive and psychosocial functions.

Disability.   It is well-accepted that brain injury frequently leads to impaired cognitive functioning. Many reviews of the nature of cognitive deficit following different types of brain injury are to be found in the literature (e.g. Brooks, 1984; Luria 1966; Newcombe, 1982; Skilbeck, 1983). It is also widely accepted that psychosocial changes follow brain injury (e.g. Brooks, 1984; Oddy & Humphrey, 1980; Skilbeck, Wade, Langton-Hewer, & Wood, 1983). Perhaps the most obvious psychosocial change relates to employment status. Many patients do not return to work after severe head injury, for example (Brooks et al., 1987), and there are frequently dramatic changes in role for both the brain-injured patient and members of his or her family (e.g. McKinlay et al., 1981; Oddy, 1984). More subtle changes such as increased social isolation (e.g. Hyman, 1972; Oddy & Humphrey, 1980), psychosexual effects (e.g. Bond, 1976; Kreutzer & Zasler, 1989), changes in self-image such as reduction in self-confidence and self-esteem (Kreutzer & Zasler, 1989; Powell, 1986) and low motivation (Mutchnick, 1988) are also acknowledged as sequelae of acquired brain damage. It is highly probable that, following discharge from hospital, the brain-damaged patient will return to a situation in which there is less stimulation than prior to the brain damage. The patient may no longer be able to work, may play a less active role within the family, and may suffer social isolation. They are unlikely to seek out activities which are mentally stimulating in view of the tendency to manifest potentially dysfunctional responses to cognitive failure following brain injury. Prigatano (1987) discusses such responses: the catastrophic reaction and the denial of deficit. If a patient produces a catastrophic reaction they will become agitated when faced with failure on a task, and may appear dazed, unfriendly, evasive, or even aggressive. Goldstein (1952) argued that the patient's behaviour in this case is very similar to that of a person in a state of anxiety. Prigatano (1987, p. 362) made the point that "one coping strategy for many brain-injured patients may be simply to withdraw from the environment after repeated failures in dealing with it." An alternative reaction is frank denial of deficit. The patient will excuse failure on the grounds of fatigue or lack of interest in the task or may refuse to cooperate with assessment because they recognise no need for intervention. Should a brain-injured patient enter this downward spiral there is clearly little chance of deficits being retrained or effectively managed, because cognitive activity will tend to be avoided. The inability to participate usefully in social and family life will tend to lower self-esteem even further.

Rehabilitation.   The first stage in the rehabilitation of the brain-damaged patient is a thorough assessment of deficits and abilities. The methods recommended for use in assessment for rehabilitation planning are discussed in Chapter 3 of this volume. Feedback of information about test results may, in itself, improve the patient's insight and motivate them to embark upon the retraining programme. However, psychotherapy sessions or counselling may be necessary at this stage (Mutchnick, 1988; Prigatano, 1986). One caveat that should be noted here is that denial may be regarded as an effective coping strategy and part of an effort to "restore self-esteem" (Moore, Stambrook, & Peters, 1989). Nevertheless, in practical terms, it is clear that the patient who frankly denies all cognitive deficits will be unlikely to see any reason to participate in a retraining programme. Whereas a totally accurate assessment of his or her deficits may not be a prerequisite of retraining, a degree of insight into needs is necessary if the patient is to be motivated to attend a retraining establishment. If the patient errs on the side of underestimation of their own abilities, knowledge of strengths as well as weaknesses may help the patient to benefit from retraining as well as acting directly upon level of self-esteem.

The process-specific approach to rehabilitation is described by Sohlberg and Mateer (1989, pp. 22, 33):

> In the Process-Specific Approach to cognitive rehabilitation, the treatment is orientated towards targeted remediation of specific cognitive areas. It assumes that these specific areas can be treated individually. Under ... [this] approach, a constellation of related tasks, all of which target the same component of a particular cognitive process, are systematically and repetitively administered.

Sohlberg and Mateer (1989, p. 22) argued that this approach may

> be conceived of as a restorative model [although it] also advocates methods to assist individuals in compensating for residual deficits, recognising that restoration of cognitive capacity to a functional level is not always possible.

Although we are in full agreement with the latter aim, we have shifted the training approach in the Newcastle study towards a compensatory, rather than a restorative, approach. In this respect our approach resembles one of the treatment approaches developed from the cognitive neuropsychological treatment model which was described by Howard and Hatfield (1987, p. 105) as follows:

> Treatment from the perspective of the neuropsychological school is still in its early stages. Its characteristics have, however, emerged ... Treatment methods of a variety of different types can be adopted, depending on the analysis of the underlying disorder: direct relearning [of information which is "missing"], reorganisation of function [aiming to achieve the same result using different methods of processing], or facilitation of access [where there is a failure of access to intact information].

Problems may arise in sustaining the rehabilitation process as the brain-damaged patient can often move into a home environment with reduced stimulation at a time when, paradoxically, there is increased potential for cognitive gains. Discharge from hospital, where the patient has been surrounded by a fair amount of activity and where the opportunity for intensive physiotherapy, neuropsychological input, speech and occupational therapy exists, is likely to occur at the point when physical stability is attained. Secondary effects of brain injury such as the swelling or "shock" reaction described earlier will have resolved. While the patient has been in hospital the family will have adjusted their pattern of everyday life to absorb the tasks which used to be carried out by the patient and, on discharge, he or she may be cast in the "sick role" and thus take little responsibility for everyday activities, even within the home. Thus the patient does not capitalise on the physiological improvements being made during the recovery period and remains cognitively passive. Catastrophic reaction and denial of deficits may discourage the patient further from engaging in mentally-stimulating behaviour.

Evidence as to the efficacy of rehabilitative intervention which has been gleaned from animal studies has sometimes used the term "intervention" to mean provision of an enriched environment rather than specific remediation of a deficit. For the brain-damaged patient an "enriched" environment has to be one that is mentally stimulating. The notion of the value of cognitive stimulation has emerged in a number of approaches to therapy. Howard and Hatfield (1987) described the "stimulation school" in speech therapy as an attempt to elicit correct responses by any possible means. Diller (1987, p. 12 and p. 11) described the "deficiency" model which "suggests that exposure to the task will be useful" and is based on the idea that "atypical behaviour is due to an absence of proper experience". These notions support the view that cognitive stimulation has some value in rehabilitation although we would argue strongly that remediation directed at specific deficits is likely to be a more effective approach.

Psychosocial changes which result directly from attendance at a cognitive retraining programme relate to change in routine. Many of the patients in the Newcastle study reported that the need to leave the house every day, perhaps to get up earlier in the morning than they had been in the habit of doing and, in some cases, the experience of travelling without other family members, made attending the hospital seem "almost like returning to work". They reported feelings of freedom and independence and many, having established a habit of leaving the house alone, continued to take part in activities outside the home after the retraining programme was completed.

We emphasise that, following retraining, there is a need for reassessment to identify residual deficits and it is at this point that the use of external aids may be useful in increasing functional independence. Increased independence can lead directly to increased self-confidence and self-esteem. As Patten (1972, p. 31) commented, in discussing patients who have increased their memory span as a result of cognitive training in the use of visual imagery: "the patients reported here have found that they are now relying on their own memory skills rather than on those of others. The benefit from a marked increase in self-esteem that comes from being able to show off memory skills to relatives and friends should not be underestimated."

The aim of intervention is thus to halt, and then reverse, the downward spiral of disability, and to optimise the effects of gains achieved through cognitive retraining.

4.4 REMEDIATION OF COGNITIVE SYSTEMS

This section discusses representative examples from the literature relating to the training of cognitive systems using both computerised and non-computerised methods, although greater emphasis is placed on the former. The studies selected are, in the main, those which have been carried out at major centres in both Great Britain and the United States. Other studies are included to illustrate points of discussion.

It is clear that the use of computerised methods is becoming increasingly popular. In 1982, Lynch saw the potential of computerised games as a retraining tool. At that time, Lynch stated that a literature search in this area did not reveal a single relevant reference. However, some seven years later the situation is quite different. Sohlberg and Mateer (1989, p. 30) stated that "no chapter reviewing general procedures of cognitive rehabilitation would be complete without some discussion of the use of microcomputers in cognitive rehabilitation." A survey carried out in the United States (Bracy, Lynch, Sbordone, & Berrol, 1985) demonstrated that 73% of the centres surveyed that reported providing cognitive rehabilitation of head-injured patients used microcomputers in their clinical work. The use of computerised techniques has developed less rapidly in the United Kingdom. Nevertheless, a questionnaire survey, which we carried out in 1989, indicated that psychologists were experimenting with computerised retraining in many of the major centres where cognitive retraining was carried out. We received replies which answered "yes" to our question "Do you use/have you used microcomputers in a cognitive retraining programme?" from therapists at Frenchay Hospital and the Burden Institute in Bristol; the Astley Ainsley Hospital in Edinburgh; the Wolfson Medical Rehabilitation Unit, Atkinson Morley's Hospital and the Royal Hospital and Home, Putney in London; St. Andrew's Hospital, Northampton; RAF Headley Court; the Youth Disability Unit, Stoke Mandeville Hospital, Aylesbury; and the Stroke Research Unit, General Hospital, Nottingham. Computerised retraining was in the planning stages at Pinderfields Hospital, Wakefield. Psychologists in the Manchester area informed us of the use of computerised cognitive retraining programmes within the North Manchester Area Health Authority and at the Royal Manchester Children's Hospital[1]. Informal discussion with colleagues indicates that this is not an exhaustive list.

---

[1] One of the authors (VAB) has included computer-based techniques in the rehabilitation programme run at the Head Injury Unit, Ticehurst House Hospital, Sussex.

Attention

One of the most influential groups in the field of cognitive retraining is that based at the New York University Medical Centre. The research programme at the Institute of Rehabilitation Medicine began in the early 1970s and is still producing major contributions to this field of work today.

The Rehabilitation Monographs produced by the group (associated workers include Diller, Gordon, Weinberg, Ben-Yishay, Piasetsky, and Gross) record the techniques developed and the progress made by trainees (e.g. Ben-Yishay, Piasetsky, & Diller, 1978). Evaluations are sometimes in the form of single case reports but group evaluations have also been carried out. Remedial intervention directed towards a range of cognitive deficits has been carried out by this group.

Ben-Yishay et al. (1987) reported the development of the ORM (Orientation Remedial Module) battery which is used in the remediation of attention-concentration deficits. The battery comprises five exercises which train the patient to attend and react to environmental signals, to time responses in relation to changing environmental cues, to be actively vigilant, to estimate the passage of time accurately and to synchronise responding with complex rhythms. The tasks require accurate timing and synchronisation in their presentation as well as timing of responses. They were originally presented by means of electronic instruments but the battery has now been computerised and runs on the Apple IIc or IIe and IBM–XT microcomputer (described by Piasetsky et al., 1983; available from NYU Medical Centre, Rusk Institute of Rehabilitation Medicine). Results obtained with the computerised version of the battery are reported as being in line with results using the original equipment for presentation.

Ben-Yishay et al. (1987) used the original equipment and reported data from 40 subjects who had suffered severe head trauma at least 1 year (and more frequently between 2 and 4 years) previously. Training was carried out over a three-month period, 2 hours training per day, amounting to a total of 62 hours. As a group, the subjects improved their performance on each of the training tasks, with no carry-over between the tasks, up to the point where their scores were within the normal range. A stable baseline on psychometric tests, which had been administered 3 months prior to the training, had been demonstrated. Small but significant gains were observed on the standard psychometric tests when they were administered after training. For example, the mean scaled score on the WAIS Digit Span subtest increased from 9.8 to 10.4 and the mean scaled score on the WAIS Picture Completion subtest increased from 10.2 to 11.1. A subgroup was tested on the experimental tasks at 3 and 6 months follow-up. The training effects were found to persist over time. Ben-Yishay et al. (1979; 1980) also addressed the issue of generalisation. A case study was reported in which the behaviour of one patient was systematically observed and positive changes in relation to this patient's functioning noted. The patient (MS), a 17-year-old man educated to degree level, had suffered severe head injury in a road traffic accident

21 months previously. He had severe attentional deficits, being unable to maintain focused attention and being very distractible, and was almost totally disorientated. He was observed on the ward and problem behaviours were identified and quantified over a two-week period. This provided a baseline against which to judge improvement. Retraining was carried out for 2 consecutive hours each day using the original electronic version of the ORM. After 62 hours of training, problem behaviours were again recorded on the ward. MS was found to be significantly better-orientated, more alert, more able to respond appropriately to the demands of his physical environment, more realistic about his current situation and more able to reason logically. It would therefore appear that there is at least some evidence from a single-case study that attentional processes can be improved by retraining and that the effects are to some extent generalised. The study would have been improved by the measurement, pre- and post-training, of problem behaviours which were not related to attentional deficits. If behaviours unrelated to the training programme did not improve, the validity of the programme as a means of retraining attention would have been better demonstrated. In practice, it is difficult to identify behaviours which would not be affected by changes in orientation and alertness.

Attention training was administered to four patients by Sohlberg and Mateer (1987), working at the Good Samaritan Centre for Cognitive Rehabilitation in the United States. Two of these patients had suffered closed head injury, one a penetrating head injury and one an aneurysm. The 4 were all young, ages ranging from 25 to 30. As in the Ben-Yishay studies, different aspects of the attentional process were targeted, these being: focused, sustained, selective, alternating, and divided attention. A number of the retraining tasks were computerised and obtained from commercially available programs like REACT (reaction time programs, published by Life Science Associates) and Visual Reaction Stimulus Discrimination (program requiring inhibition of response to non-target stimuli, published by Psychological Software Services). Other tests used cards (e.g. multilevel card sort, Sohlberg and Mateer, 1986) or audio-tapes (e.g. stimuli recorded in background noise) and were developed by the authors as part of the APT (Attention Process Training) pack.

Attention training was carried out over a period of 10 weeks, with 7 to 9 sessions per week being provided. The attention training was part of a wider cognitive retraining programme which targeted areas of deficit other than attention at different times, and which lasted about 8 months. Improved PASAT scores following the initiation of attention training were observed in all four cases. In the two cases where pre-training scores indicated mild to moderate deficits, post-training scores were within normal limits. Where severe deficits were observed before training, scores moved into the mildly-impaired range following training. A single-case design measuring multiple baseline across function areas (Hersen & Barlow, 1976) was used to assess the effectiveness of the training. The three areas of cognitive functioning which were targeted were memory, visual processing and attention. Attentional processes were targeted first in three of the four cases. In these cases a test of visual processing was administered during the attention-training period. Scores on this test remained stable while PASAT scores (the attentional measure) improved. The fourth subject underwent visual processing training before attention training. Small gains in the attentional measure were noted during visual processing training but these levelled off until the period of attention training when more dramatic increases were seen. Sohlberg and Mateer (1989, p. 131) argued that:

> This double dissociation provides powerful support for independent improvements in specific cognitive areas with process-specific training. The clinical implication is that therapy directed toward the remediation of underlying deficit processes should be encouraged.

There is no formal evidence of generalisation to functional skills. However, during the course of cognitive training all subjects attained independent living status, two obtained sheltered employment and two competitive employment.

The multiple-baseline-across-cognitive-area design, used in this study, is recommended for clinicians who are evaluating the effectiveness of treatments, when different cognitive areas are to be retrained sequentially. The study would have benefited from more sensitive measures of generalisation to everyday skills, although the data on employment and living status is valuable in providing gross measures of functional ability. More sensitive measures would be required for more severely impaired patients, who might make significant gains in cognitive ability without making the transition to independent living status and employability.

The third study to be discussed in relation to the retraining of the attentional system was reported by Gross, Ben-Nahum, and Munk (1982). The first author has worked with the New York University Medical Centre team; the study described here was carried out at the Unit for Neuropsychological Treatment and Rehabilitation, Givatayim, Israel. Experimental tasks were not computerised although both tasks lend themselves to computerisation and one requires the use of electronic instrumentation. This is a conditional response task in which the patient responds by illuminating coloured bulbs according to certain rules. The other task involves presentation of rows of random digits or geometric figures. The therapist covers two or more of the stimuli sequentially and the patient must remember the covered stimuli and respond by naming the stimulus, which will be revealed with each successive move. This task is in fact quite difficult to administer without specially-designed equipment. A computerised version of the task forms part of the Newcastle Training Package; administration of the computerised task is straightforward compared to the non-computerised task and so far has presented no problems to either the patients or the therapists.

The evaluation carried out by Gross et al. (1982) used the above tasks for retraining attentional deficits. Four patients took part in the study. They were first assessed using a number of psychometric tests of attention and memory. Training sessions consisted of work with the tasks described above which targeted attentional deficits or of "control", training involving work on tasks not specifically designed to remediate attentional deficits. Patients were retested after the first 10 hours of training (the order of presentation of control or experimental training was alternated) and after the second 10 hours of training. The data presented suggests that both control and experimental training improved performance on the Digit Span and Digit Symbol subtests of the WAIS and the Logical Memory and Associate Learning subtest of the WMS. Improvement tended to be greater following experimental training, an exception being performance on the Associate Learning subtest of the WMS, which was better following control training.

Interpretion of these results is complicated by the small size of the sample and by the possibility of carry-over effects from control to experimental training and vice versa. The results as they stand provide some evidence for the system-specificity of training effects but also suggest that more than one cognitive system may be involved in certain tasks. For example, the Logical Memory subtest of the WMS might appear to be a straightforward memory test, yet performance on this subtest improved more after experimental (i.e. attentional) than after control (i.e. memory) training, implying that efficient attentional processes are a necessary precondition to efficient memory.

Recently, some excellent studies evaluating the effectiveness of computer-based retraining have been carried out at the Astley Ainslie Hospital in Edinburgh. Gray and Robertson (1989) reported three single cases in which attentional problems were targeted. The training tasks used were: (1) Rapid Number Comparison, in which four equal length strings of digits are displayed simultaneously for a variable period of time—the number which is repeated must be identified; (2) Digit Symbol Transfer (Braun, Bartolini, & Bouchard, 1985), which is a commercially-available version of the psychometric task in which subjects must translate rows of symbols into digits according to a code displayed on the screen; (3) Alternating Stroop, in which the patient must respond to either a colour or a colour name and must switch between the different response conditions. The program ran on an Apple IIe computer. A multiple-baseline-across-function design showed that the procedures used were effective in producing change in the targeted function, while no improvements in the control measures were observed. A randomised controlled trial, using computerised tasks aimed at remediating attentional deficits, failed to show significant differences between the experimental and control groups immediately after training (Gray & Robertson, 1988). However, at 6-month follow up, a significant group effect was observed, with the experimental group showing significantly greater improvements on a range of psychometric measures sensitive to attentional impairment (Robertson, personal communication). This result is encouraging in terms of the possible generalisability across subjects of this type of training task.

That a task be effective with patients randomly allocated to a training group is, in fact, a very stringent requirement. As previously mentioned in discussion of group versus single-case studies (see Chapter 2) the group may have different types of deficit. Additionally, extraneous factors such as different levels of motivation may reduce the likelihood of effectiveness. Since it is clinically desirable that tasks be used with a range of patients, studies where tasks are administered to a group of patients are required to provide data relating to the range of patients with which a task could be used. Analysis of individual as well as group data in this type of study could yield valuable information about the effect of variables such as age, chronicity, and level of motivation on the capacity to benefit from the treatment. Such data would help clinicians to select suitable candidates for treatment.

The next study to be described was carried out at St Andrew's Hospital, Northampton. Wood and Fussey (1987) reported on the evaluation of a computer-based attention training procedure. The procedure requires the subject to respond to a target stimulus, presented on a monitor with distractor stimuli, at the precise moment when it passes between a pair of markers which form a "gate" on the screen. The program runs on a Commodore 64 computer with a Sony Trinitron monitor[1]. Responses are made via the computer keyboard and no additional response device is required. The authors described the task requirements as: visual scanning, perceptual discrimination, judgement and anticipation and motor response.

Training sessions were 1 hour in length and held 5 days a week for 1 month (20 hours in all). Subjects for retraining were 10 patients who had suffered closed head injury or head injury with skull fracture and who were designated, on clinical criteria, as having attentional problems. Their performance was compared with a group of 10 brain-damaged controls matched for severity of injury and time since injury and with a group of 10 neurologically normal controls. A number of outcome measures were used including the Digit Symbol subtest of the WAIS, a choice reaction time task and two behaviour recordings. One of the latter recorded the amount of time the subject attended to a therapy task and the other was an attention rating scale completed by nursing and therapy staff. Staff were not aware of whether a patient was a member of the control or the experimental group. There was a gradual trend towards

---

[1]The St Andrew's Attention Assessment and Retraining Package is a set of 4 programs for the Commodore 64, comprising Attention Division, Maze Learning, Visual Vigilance and Quadrant Reaction Time tasks. It was developed for use with head-injured adults by Mark Cook. The package is not currently available to those working outside St Andrews.

improvement on the training task for the training group over the first 7 days, with performance levelling off around a 70% hit rate for the remainder of the training period. No significant differences were observed between the groups on the psychometric outcome measures. There were, however, significant differences between pre- and post-training behavioural measures for the training group whereas no such differences were found at follow-up for the brain-injured control group. These measures were not obtained for the cerebrally-intact control group who were members of the community and whose behaviour could not, therefore, be observed by ward staff. This group were included in the study as additional controls for the psychometric measures of change. This result is interesting in that it shows that attention retraining can be an effective means of changing attentional behaviour.

There is no obvious reason for the absence of gains in psychometric tests in this study. The patient group was comparable with patient groups from the other studies. Training took place over a shorter period of time than in the Ben-Yishay et al. (1987) and Sohlberg and Mateer (1987) studies (4 weeks as opposed to 3 months and 10 weeks respectively) but offered more hours of training than did the Gross et al. (1982) study (20 hours as opposed to 10). In relation to this point it is important to note that there is a practical need to establish the minimum input which will be effective in cognitive rehabilitation. Wood and Fussey (1987, p. 152), in considering the limited duration of their program, stated:

> It is an unfortunate fact of clinical rehabilitation that an hour a day is probably as long as would be available given the demands of a busy rehabilitation programme. Therefore, if demonstrable gains cannot be noted in outcome measures using the time span noted in this study, then it may be argued that such attentional retraining would not be clinically viable.

The Wood and Fussey program was the only program to use a single task. One highly speculative explanation of the results is that a variety of retraining tasks is more effective than a single task, both in terms of maintaining the subject's motivation, consolidating gains and facilitating generalisation from the training task to psychometric tasks which are subserved by the system targeted for retraining.

An alternative explanation is (as in the Gray and Robertson study, 1988, discussed previously) in terms of differing functional lesions in the patient group. A number of different types of attentional process have been identified. The retraining task, as described by Wood and Fussey, was an extremely artificial task (in that it was not clearly related to any everyday activity), and did not appear to require the operation of all attentional subsystems. Thus it may not have been an appropriate training task for all individuals in the group.

Negative results were also reported by Ponsford (1990) who described a computer-based training programme which focused on deficits in speed of information processing. Investigation of the deficits of 54 severely head-injured patients revealed deficits in divided attention which appeared to result from reduced speed of information processing. Two training tasks designed to improve information processing speed were selected from the package developed by Gianutsos and Klitzner (1981) and additional programs were written by Ponsford. Ten severely head-injured patients, 6–34 weeks post-injury, who had been judged to have attentional deficits, underwent training consisting of a total of 30 half-hour daily sessions. A single-case multiple baseline across subjects design was used. Outcome measures included psychometric measures, such as the Digit Symbol test and a letter cancellation task, and a rating scale of attentional behaviour which was completed by an occupational therapist. Although steady improvement was noted on all measures, there were no significant effects of intervention on any measure. Improvements were attributable to spontaneous recovery. As with the previous study the period of time spent in training was relatively short and Ponsford commented that more intensive training or training over a longer period could have been more effective. Unfortunately, details of performance on the training tasks themselves is not provided; one would not expect the intervention to affect the rate of spontaneous recovery significantly, if there was no on-task improvement over and above that which resulted from spontaneous recovery. A further relevant point is that, although attentional ability and speed of information processing are undoubtedly related, it may have been the case that the speed of processing training tasks was not subserved by those attentional mechanisms subserving the attentional behaviours on which the rating scale focused.

The final study is described because of the nature of the training tasks used, although it contributes little to the evaluation literature. Finlayson et al. (1987) used a computerised retraining program developed within the framework of REHABIT (Reitan Evaluation of Hemispheric Ability on Brain Improvement Training; Reitan, 1979). They described a single-case study of a young graduate treated 10 months after her head injury. Preliminary training targeted attention and orientation. At a later stage visuospatial impairments were retrained. Exercises were carried out twice weekly over a 22-week period using an Apple II microcomputer. This patient showed marginal gains in verbal and performance IQs as measured by the WAIS–R and significant improvements in performance on psychometric tests of new learning, complex problem solving ability, mental flexibility, and psychomotor skills. Since only one pre-training and one post-training psychometric assessment was made, the effects of the retraining exercises cannot reliably be separated from the effects of spontaneous recovery. The 4 attention/orientation exercises used were: (1) a complex reaction time task; (2) a task involving learning of a list of digits of increasing length; (3) a task which requires the subject to track moving targets on the monitor; (4) a task that requires the subject to keep a moving target on course for a prolonged period. In the first of these tasks (INTERCEPT) coloured rectangles appear randomly on the screen and the subject is required to manipulate the direction of a line moving across the screen, by depressing the keyboard arrow keys, with the aim of impacting on as many of the coloured rectangles as possible. In the second (SIMON SAYS) number sequences of increasing length are presented on the screen and the subject responds by typing the number sequence into the computer after a pre-programmed delay. (A similar task, without the delay before response is required, has been developed by Warburg, 1988.) The third task (SINK THE SHIP) requires the subject to hit a ship which moves from left to right across the bottom of the screen with a "bomb" dropped from an aeroplane moving from left to right across the top of the screen. The speed of the ship varies randomly from trial to trial; the speed of the aeroplane is invariant. The fourth task (DRIVER) we feel to be of potential value in retraining high level attentional and visuomotor skills. The object of the exercise is to keep a vehicle on a road that constantly shifts from side to side as the vehicle progresses from the top to the bottom of the screen. The exercise has 10 levels of difficulty, each involving progressively greater vehicle speed and narrower path width.

Visuoperceptual and Visuoconstructional Abilities

We begin this section as we began the previous section with an account of the work carried out at the New York University Medical Centre. This work was summarised by Piasetsky, Ben-Yishay, Weinberg, and Diller (1982) and more detailed information is available in the series of monographs produced by the research group (e.g. Diller et al., 1974). Three remediation packages were described. One was directed towards the remediation of visual hemi-inattention (or visual "neglect"), one towards improving somatosensory awareness (awareness of one's own body and its orientation in space) and spatial organisation, and one towards retraining pattern organisation and sequential analysis.

Components of the first package are a task which provides an "anchor" to direct the patient's gaze into the neglected visual field in order to establish compensatory scanning habits, and tasks involving scanning of the whole visual field. The second package includes a task in which patients locate sensory stimulation on their own bodies and relate the location to a position on a model of part of the human body. This package aims to train somatosensory awareness. Spatial organisation is trained by means of estimation of the length of rods. The patient must place cylinders to correspond to the estimated length of the rod and then place the rod on the cylinders; under- or over-estimates become obvious at this stage, thus providing immediate feedback. Components of the third package are tasks which present written passages or dot configurations which must be systematically scanned in order to locate specified words or form meaningful gestalts.

Weinberg et al. (1977; 1979) evaluated some of these techniques by studying two separate groups, one of 25 and one of 30 patients who had suffered right-hemisphere damage and were experiencing visuoperceptual problems. Pre-training and post-training measures on a number of visuoperceptual tasks (including line bisection, letter cancellation, copying a name and address, and oral reading) were recorded. Results on these measures were also obtained from a control group of right brain damaged patients, who received conventional occupational therapy. The training package used in the first study consisted of 21 hourly sessions on tasks directed at improving visual scanning. Statistically significant gains were found for the treatment group, with the most severely impaired patients improving most. A follow-up assessment one year after the completion of training showed that gains were maintained over time. The second study added tasks aimed at training somatosensory awareness and spatial organisation. Treatment effects were enhanced by the addition of these tasks. A small effect was observed when a group of 35 patients who had problems in performing complex visuoperceptual tasks but showed no evidence of unilateral spatial neglect were trained in spatial organisation (Weinberg, Piasketsky, Diller, & Gordon, 1982). Gordon et al. (1985) reported the use of these perceptual retraining tasks with a group of 48 brain-injured patients with right hemisphere damage who improved faster than a control group (containing 29 patients with right hemisphere damage) on perceptual measures. All patients received 35 hours of treatment.

The tasks described above were not computerised but required the use of specialised electronic equipment. Diller and Gordon (1981) described the use of a visuoconstructional training task which required little in the way of specialised equipment. The training was in the performance of the Block Design subtest of the WAIS and used the technique of saturation cueing. (In the saturation cueing technique, cues are provided which initially minimise the task requirements for the patient so that success is ensured—for example, the initial requirement may be simply to put in place only one or two blocks in the design, and cues are gradually withdrawn so that the task can be performed unaided.) Training was administered to a group of brain-damaged individuals over 10 sessions. The experimental group improved more than the control groups (who had attended conventional occupational therapy sessions) on performance of the training task and related psychometric tests (e.g. the Object Assembly subtest of the WAIS) which were administered before and after training. Generalisation to activities of daily living was also observed. The experimental group received higher ratings after training on a double-blind analysis of the occupational therapy reports prepared before and after training. Additionally, eating behaviour which requires accurate eye–hand coordination was videotaped and the tapes analysed. Again the behaviour of the experimental groups received higher ratings than the control group on this task after training. A follow-up study by Gordon and Diller (1983) focused on the subject of generalisation and showed that patients who had taken part in a visuoperceptual retraining programme read more often, and for longer periods of time, than those who did not receive this specialised retraining.

Young, Collins, and Hren (1983) used a combination of the New York University Medical Centre's tasks for training visuoperceptual and visuocon-structional skills, including the Block Design training described in the preceding paragraph. A control group of 9 right-hemisphere stroke patients received 1 hour of routine occupational therapy for 20 successive days. Two experimental groups underwent training, one training programme included the Block Design training and the other did not. Both training groups improved to a significantly greater extent than the control group, and the group whose training had included Block Design training improved more than the other training group. Measures on which significant improvement was observed included reading and cancella-tion tasks. Little generalisation to performance on psychometric tests was observed; for example, the groups did not differ significantly on any of the WAIS subtests other than Block Design following the training period.

The studies reported so far (all of which have used the New York University Medical Centre's tasks) are group studies. Experimental and control groups were composed of right brain-damaged individuals in each case, but homogeneity of the groups was not established in respect of equivalence of the functional lesions. If the same treatment is administered to patients with qualitatively different cognitive deficits it is unlikely to produce results in all cases, and the fact that positive results were obtained in this series of studies, despite the use of an experimental design which tends to decrease the likelihood of such results is impressive.

Ironically, a study in which treatments were varied according to subtypes of visual imperception provided less support for the efficacy of visuoperceptual retraining. Taylor, Schaeffer, Blumenthal, and Grisell (1971), at the Detroit Rehabilitation Institute in the USA, administered a range of psychometric measures pre- and post-intervention to left hemiplegic patients. Functional level was also rated using ADL criteria such as dressing and eating ability and ability to transfer to and from a wheelchair. Twenty-six experimental and twenty-one control patients took part in the study. Control training by physical, ADL, and occupational therapists was directed towards motor problems while experimen-tal training targeted visuoperceptual and visuospatial problems observed in individual patients. Examples of training given by Taylor and colleagues include following a route marked on a map, in a case where there was poor ability to judge spatial relationships, and visual tracking of a moving stimulus in cases of visual inattention. Tasks were not computerised. Each patient completed 20 treatment days. At post-training assessment both experimental and control groups had improved on both cognitive and functional measures. There was no significant difference between groups. Improved ADL skills in the control group were predictable in view of the intensive motor-directed training which they received. That the experimental group also improved in ADL argues for the generalisability of visuoperceptual training. It is less easy to explain improvement by the control group on cognitive measures. This study would have been improved by the addition of a no-treatment control group, and a group who received both types of treatment. The former would have controlled for the effects of spontaneous recovery and the latter would have revealed whether or not the effects of the two types of intervention were additive.

Results which were, on the whole, negative were also reported by Edmans and Lincoln (1989) working at the Stroke Unit in Nottingham. They used single-case designs to investigate the effects of perceptual training on three patients who had suffered right-hemisphere CVAs and one patient who had suffered bilateral CVAs. Unlike all the patients who took part in the New York University Medical Centre series, all four patients were assessed and treated in the early stages of recovery (first assessments 3 to 8 weeks after onset). Perceptual deficits investigated were spatial relations deficits, visual inattention, and sequencing deficits. Training consisted of practice on a wide range of non-computerised tasks, including 3-dimensional copying, scanning from left to right, and placing pictures in the correct order. The patients were assessed using an ADL scale as well as psychometric tests. In three of the four cases, improvements recorded could not be directly attributed to the treatment. In the fourth case perceptual difficulties improved to within normal limits. Reduction of visual inattention appeared to have been due to the specific treatment given but improvements in spatial abilities were not attributable to specific treatment. Improvements measured on the ADL scale occurred during baseline and treatment periods. The authors were not able to identify any characteristics that might have indicated which patients are most likely to respond to this type of treatment.

One possible explanation for the negative results, which the authors considered, is that the treatment activities were not actually affecting the abilities targeted for training. The following study is reported here because it raises the possibility that the relationship between task and rehabilitative technique (in this case cueing in a case of visual neglect) may be crucial. In their presentation of a single-case study of left visuospatial neglect, Halligan and Marshall (1989) reported that a patient's inaccuracy on a computerised line bisection task was reduced by cueing from the neglected side of space. The cue was provided by the initial position of the cursor which the patient was required to move by means of an AMX "mouse" pointer. Previous investigation of cueing techniques had provided inconclusive results and Halligan and Marshall suggested that a possible problem with earlier studies was that the cue task was not "intrinsically linked to the experimental task." Although the development of remedial techniques was not the primary aim of their study, their finding is relevant to such development. The implication is that the provision of a cue to direct the patient's attention to the neglected field may not be effective; the therapist must also consider the relationship of the cue to the task to be performed.

Programs developed by Steve Smart and Ian Robertson at the Astley Ainslie Hospital in Edinburgh have recently become commercially available (Smart, 1987). These programs have been used in evaluative studies. They run on BBC computers from the B model upward and require a Microvitec Touchtec 501 Touch Sensitive Screen[1]. A pilot study was carried out with three patients who showed left-sided visual neglect (Robertson, Gray, & McKenzie, 1988). Two of these patients had suffered strokes and one a head injury. The training period was very short by comparison with other reported studies, involving six 45-minute sessions over 3 days in 2 cases, and 7 sessions over 8 days in the third case.

The computerised tasks require systematic visual searching of the whole screen in order that a target stimulus may be located. The subject is cued visually and auditorily to use the optimal search strategy.

A single-case, multiple-baseline across-function design was used. All three patients showed improvements in test results related to the trained skill, while little change in test results unrelated to the trained skill was observed. The authors note that they did not obtain evidence relevant to the issue of generalisation to functional activities. However, the relevant measures on which the patients were tested before and after training were distinct from the training tasks (for instance, non-computerised reading and word-search tasks), and improved performance on these measures indicated that a degree of generalisation took place. The group then continued to use the computerised training tasks in a randomised controlled trial in order to investigate the extent to which treatment effects were generalisable across patients. Results were reported by Robertson, Gray, Pentland, and Waite, 1990. Subjects were identified as having significant unilateral left visual field neglect according to the Behavioural Inattention Test (Wilson et al., 1987). This test was the principal outcome measure used. The patients were randomly allocated to experimental training or control training. In the control procedure recreational computing (activities such as word games were selected in order to minimise the involvement of the impaired system) was provided for approximately the same number of hours as experimental training. There were 20 patients in the experimental and 16 in the control group. As previously noted, the programs involved the location of stimuli in both left and right visual fields. Subjects were cued to attend to the left (i.e. the neglected) visual field and to scan systematically with visual cues, and with an auditory cue "Look left" presented via a voice synthesiser. A reaction time and vigilance task were also included in the training package. The experimental group spent a mean of 15 hours in training and the control group a mean of 11 hours in recreational activity. Blind follow-up at the end of training

---

[1]Available from Microvitec PLC, Futures Way, Bolling Road, Bradford, West Yorkshire, BD4 7TU. Price £210.

and at 6 months post-training revealed no statistically significant results between groups. This result contrasts with the successes reported by the New York University Medical Centre group (e.g. Weinberg et al., 1977; 1979) and with the success reported by the same authors in their single-case studies. Robertson, Gray, Pentland and Waite (1990) mentioned, in connection with the absence of significant results, a lack of generalisability of treatment effects to a wide patient population, and the need for more intensive treatment. In relation to the latter factor we note that mean training hours for Robertson, Gray, Pentland and Waite's group was 15, as compared with 21 for Weinberg's group. Certainly, these findings argue against routine clinical use of this type of training. However, it is clear that retraining can be helpful in the remediation of visuoperceptual/ visuospatial deficits and the existence of conflicting results increases the need for a knowledge of the factors which should be taken into account in selecting patients for a particular type of retraining.

For those who wish to experiment with this type of training but prefer not to write their own software, a number of computerised training packages have been developed and are commercially available. The programs used in the Astley Ainslie studies have already been described. In the USA the programs produced by Rosamund Gianutsos and her colleagues (Gianutsos & Klitzner, 1981; Gianutsos, Vroman, & Matheson, 1983) have been used in a number of centres. These programs run on Apple machines. The software for Cognitive Rehabilitation Therapy developed by Odie Bracy and available through Psychological Software Services includes programs for the retraining of visuospatial deficits. This software runs on Apple, Atari, and IBM machines. A group based at the Cliniques Universitaires Saint Luc in Brussels (Groupe Zorglub) has recently developed a set of five programs for the evaluation and retraining of visual neglect. These programs currently run on the Apple IIe, and are being adapted to run on the Apple II+ and the Apple GS. They are supplied on a single double-sided disc and further information is available from Françoise Coyette at the address for Groupe Zorglub given in the list of suppliers in Appendix I.1.

Memory

Apart from language, which has received a great deal of attention over the past two centuries, memory is probably the cognitive system which has been most frequently targeted for retraining following cerebral damage. Its rehabilitation and retraining has been discussed in detail by Wilson (1987) and Wilson and Moffat (1984a). Retraining techniques described focus on teaching the amnesic patient to use mnemonic strategies.

The most frequently chosen strategy is that of using visual imagery (e.g. Wilson, 1987, Chs 6 and 10). Wilson noted that previous research into the ability of amnesics to benefit from the use of visual imagery has provided conflicting findings. She presented a series of case studies which show that the technique is successful in relation to learning to associate names and faces, although a group study suggested that patients with very severe memory impairments did not benefit from using the strategy in a verbal learning task.

Other mnemonic strategies include semantic elaboration, in which unrelated words are linked to form a story and a PQRST[1] technique which is used in memorising complex verbal material (for discussion see Wilson, 1987, Ch. 9). A number of examples of the successful use of these techniques may be found in the literature (e.g. Glasgow, Zeiss, Barrera, & Lewinsohn, 1977; Malec and Questad, 1983). Unsuccessful attempts to use the strategies are often reported by word-of-mouth but, unfortunately, may not be documented because of the widespread editorial policy of favouring positive findings in the selection of work for publication. Papers most frequently report individual case studies using multiple-baseline designs in order to evaluate the effects of treatment (e.g. Crosson & Buenning, 1984; Gianutsos & Gianutsos, 1979) although some group studies have been carried out (e.g. Gasparrini & Satz, 1979). The use of these training techniques involves a great deal of therapist time, often in a one-to-one setting. It is not surprising, therefore, that the possibilities of computerised training have been recognised and several reports of computerised memory retraining can be found in the literature.

Skilbeck (1984) noted the advantages (both in savings of therapist time and in flexibility of administration) of computer-aided training in the use of these mnemonic devices.

He illustrated the point with a description of microcomputer-based training in the use of the pegword system which was carried out at Frenchay Hospital in Bristol. (This system involves learning a "peg list" of rhyming numbers and words, for example "one is a bun." The first-to-be-remembered item is then linked by means of a visual image with the pegword.) Training was administered over five weekly sessions and by the fifth session the patient, an 11-year-old girl, who had suffered a head injury and associated haemorrhage of the left frontal lobe, was able to remember a list of 9 items with 100% accuracy while she was only able to remember 60 to 70% of items when using a repetition strategy.

Parente and Anderson (1983) reported two single cases, both of whom experienced memory problems following CVA. Computer programs were run in the patient's homes to train mnemonic strategies such as the organisation of material into categories and division of to-be-remembered number strings into "chunks". The authors reported improved scores on the Weschler memory scale.

---

[1]The PQRST technique requires the patient to: (1) Preview the information to be read; (2) form questions about that information; (3) read the information carefully with the goal of answering questions; (4) state the answers to the questions; (5) test for retention by asking and answering the questions again.

The most dramatic success in the field of computerised training which included memory training is reported by Bracy (1983), a prominent advocate of computer-based rehabilitation in the United States. Two case reports (one describing a patient who had sustained a CVA; the other describing a 12-year-old who had had a severe head injury) are presented. Training was very intensive (25 hours per week over a period of 2 years); however, since training used computers based in the home, a large amount of the therapist's time was not involved. Bracy reported substantial gains in IQ test scores, suggesting that there is some generalisation of training-related gains. A range of programs developed by Bracy are available commercially (through Psychological Software Services). Also available commercially are programs devised by Gianutsos and colleagues (Gianutsos, Cochran, & Blouin, 1984). In an evaluation of these programs, Gianutsos (1981) reported improvements in both long- and short-term memory following the use of the programs with a post-encephalitic amnesic patient.

Memory programs in a package developed by Claude Braun (Braun et al., 1985) emphasise the development of mnemonic strategies. A similar approach is taken by Roger Johnson, working at Addenbrooke's Hospital in Cambridge. He has written a number of programs which aim to develop mnemonic strategies such as use of first letter cues, use of visual association and organisation of to-be-remembered material into categories. Ways in which the mnemonic methods can be applied to practical situations are suggested at the end of each program. The disc is available from the author (see Appendix I.2 for address).

Computers have been used in relation to memory loss in three other ways. One is in relation to the reorientation of patients who are disorientated either because of the presence of a dementia or because they have sustained brain damage. Reality Orientation programs present and re-present information relevant to the patient's immediate situation (for example, date, location, and personal details). The programs test, and then retest repeatedly, the patient's level of knowledge. The use of these programs at Frenchay Hospital in Bristol and at Newcastle upon Tyne's Regional Neurological Centre was described by Skilbeck (1984) and Norris et al., (1985, Ch. 10).

This application originated in the field of psychogeriatrics, when it was used with confused elderly patients. Many neurological patients manifest similar difficulties in orientation to those seen in the field of psychogeriatrics. Skilbeck (1984) reported a single case study of a disorientated head-injured patient (RM). The orientation program was run on a Commodore PET microcomputer over a period of 5 weeks. RM's performance using computer-administered questions was compared with his results in face-to-face orientation training. The results showed that RM learned across trials in each single session and across sessions. Skilbeck noted, on the basis of this and other applications of the therapy, that the advantages of computerised presentation lie in reduction in the tedium of constant repetition of material for the therapist and in increased interest for the patient. According to Skilbeck (1984, p. 130–131) the findings reported "do not suggest that major differences should be expected between computer-administered and face-to-face orientation training."

Glisky, Schacter, and Tulving (1986a, b) described a rather different approach to the use of microcomputers with amnesic patients. They noted that microcomputers might serve as useful external aids for this patient group but that knowledge of a basic computer vocabulary would be a necessary prerequisite. They therefore used the computers to administer training in the use of computer terminology including basic commands (e.g. LOAD, RUN) using a technique of vanishing cues to link key words with their definitions. Thus, initially a large proportion of the letters of a word were supplied as cues and the number of letters supplied were gradually reduced until the subject could recall the word or its definition without the aid of cues. Glisky et al. (1986a) report results of this type of training with 4 patients with memory impairments. In 3 cases the impairment followed a closed head injury, in the fourth it followed viral encephalitis. All patients were at least 2 years post-trauma. Sessions were conducted twice weekly and 8 learning trials per session were administered. At the end of 8 sessions the number of words correctly produced following training using the vanishing cues method ranged from 60% to 100% of the full list of 15 words.

The authors noted that the amnesic patients learned more slowly than a control group and were less efficient in using their newly-acquired knowledge in a "transfer" test in which slightly different descriptions of the words were provided. Nevertheless, there is clear evidence that learning and transfer of knowledge did occur in the amnesic group. That a training program of this type should be microcomputer-based is entirely appropriate since the long-term aim is to acquire the knowledge and skills necessary for unsupervised use of a personal computer. In this respect Glisky et al's approach differs from that adopted by the majority of therapists working in the area of cognitive training who aim to improve underlying cognitive skills, and who measure success in terms of performance on psychometric tests and/or ratings of performance in ADL. For the latter group improvement on the computerised training task is a means to an end whereas for Glisky's group efficient performance of the computerised task was an end in itself.

The use of computers, or any electrical or electronic gadget, as an external aid to memory presupposes that the memory-impaired individual has sufficient capacity for new learning to be able to interact effectively with the aid. Wilson et al. (1989) investigated the performance of neurologically-impaired patients (amnesic due to CVA in 55 cases, severe head injury in 37 cases plus a small group brain-injured through other causes) in learning a new technological skill (how to operate an electronic memory aid).[1]

---

[1]Toshiba Memo-Note 60.

They noted that the acquisition of such a skill may involve procedural learning (that is, implicit learning of how to do something rather than the explicit recall of information), which is known to be intact in some cases of severe amnesia. They collected data from 100 brain-damaged patients and 50 control patients. All members of the control group, but only 59% of the experimental group learned the task within three trials. They then correlated performance on the experimental task with other measures of memory to see whether it was similar to a procedural learning task, a spatial memory task, a visual task, a verbal task, or an amalgam of all of these. On the basis of their investigations, they concluded that acquiring a new technological skill requires a combination of memory skills and is not an example of a purely procedural task. Because their results indicated that brain-damaged patients with memory difficulties had considerable difficulty in learning the new skill, they stressed the need for careful training in the use of external memory aids.

A third use of microcomputers to alleviate the problems of memory loss is reported by Vroman, Kellar, and Cohen (1989). The study is unusual, both in the rationale for computerised memory training and in the target population, many of whom had been diagnosed as suffering from dementia.

The project was carried out at the Bellevue Hospital Centre's Geriatric Outpatient clinic in New York. The patients, all of whom were over 60 years of age (range 62–89 years) and reporting memory problems, attended weekly sessions for an initial period of 15 weeks (they were allowed to continue beyond this time if interested in doing so). Thirteen men and 30 women completed the training programme. The computer software used in sessions was that developed by Gianutsos and colleagues (1984), mentioned earlier in this section. Patients were encouraged to use mnemonic strategies such as visual imagery and semantic elaboration to improve performance on the tasks. In this retraining programme (as in that carried out by Glisky et al. 1986a, b) mastery of the task was the goal, and measures of task performance were used to evaluate outcome. The authors justified their use of memory retraining in terms of enhancement of metacognition. Metacognition is a term used to describe an individual's awareness of how his or her cognitive processes function. They argued that, because patients reflect upon the demands of different tasks and develop and practice strategies during sessions, the use of each strategy may gradually "generalise to other tasks in daily life". Patients were also helped to "identify intact areas of functioning and to rely more heavily upon these areas when approaching a task". Unfortunately, evidence that this occurred in their patient group is anecdotal. It contradicts the prevalent belief regarding generalisation, which is that brain-damaged patients with memory problems need to be taught to apply strategies in a range of different settings (Wilson, 1987). Vroman et al. presented three illustrative individual case reports, which indicated improvement in memory as measured by increased scores on the training tasks rather than by independent measures of memory. Improvements on task scores were noted in all 3 cases, even in the case of an 80-year-old woman who had been diagnosed as having a progressive dementia. The other patients did not have clear organic basis for memory impairment. This study is not reported because it is not regarded as making any significant contribution to the literature on the evaluation of effectiveness of memory retraining. The data presented is limited and there are enormous difficulties in interpreting data from a group which mixes patients without organic disorders with patients diagnosed as suffering from degenerative conditions. The study's value lies in the supportive evidence it provides for the acceptability of computer-based memory training for an elderly group. Patients with, and without, organic disorder were able to improve levels of task performance, and were reported as finding the training "challenging and rewarding". Many patients opted to continue with the programme after the 15 weeks of training which comprised the initial programme.

Language

Issues raised by the use of microcomputers in the rehabilitation of language-disordered patients were discussed in a series of papers published in the journal *Aphasiology* (Vol I) in 1987. The introductory and final papers were written by Richard Katz (Katz, 1987a,b) who had already published an introduction to the subject of microcomputers in aphasia therapy the previous year (Katz, 1986). Katz (1987a) noted that the primary role of computers at that time was the "supplementary treatment of visual skills, especially reading comprehension and, to a lesser extent, writing" and that (Katz, 1987b) "most commercial software replicates frequently used activities from work books and other sources of supplementary treatment activities." Software limitations and the failure to make full use of the potential of the microcomputer have been noted in connection with memory retraining (O'Connor & Cermak, 1987) and were emphasised in relation to aphasia therapy by Katz (1987a), Enderby (1987), and Seron (1987b), who argued that clincians should work towards developing "programmes that are beyond the capabilities of the clinician and thus not comparable with current clinical practice." Areas mentioned by Seron in which the computer was likely to be more efficient than the clinician were in the measurement of speed and accuracy of response and accurately timed presentation of material. He also commented on the limitations of the computer in terms of difficulty in responding to unpredicted events and inability to interpret events which occurred in therapy in the light of expert neuropsychological knowledge. Relevant to the consideration of the need for software designers to capitalise on the strengths of microcomputers is an interesting study investigating different kinds of feedback in relation to speech therapy, which was carried out by Kinsey (1987, and in press). Eighteen patients who were aphasic following cerebrovascular accident took part. Each was exposed to three different experimental conditions. These were: (1) therapeutic task and feedback administered by a speech therapist; (2) therapeutic task and feedback administered via a microcomputer (a BBC Master); (3) therapeutic task administered by means of a computer but feedback given by the therapist. Observation of speech therapists in clinical sessions, carried out prior to this study, indicated that they were often unwilling to state explicitly that the patient was in error, although their responses implied that this was the case. The preliminary data from the study suggested that the clear and consistent feedback provided by computer was more helpful to patients working on linguistic tasks than conventional feedback given by the therapist.

In an earlier study Kinsey (1986) compared performance on computer-administered versions of standard speech therapy tasks with performance on the tasks when administered by a speech therapist. The group of 12 aphasic subjects, all with unilateral dominant hemisphere lesions, acted as their own controls, the order of performance of the computer- and conventionally-administered tasks being systematically varied. Kinsey found that, once patients had become familiarised with the computerised mode of presentation, whether the task was administered by computer or by a speech therapist made little difference to the time taken to reach target levels of performance.

An investigation carried out by Burton, Burton, and Lucas (1988) showed that the majority of aphasic patients in their sample responded well to the computer and enjoyed using it, although elderly and more severely language-impaired patients were more apprehensive and needed additional help. This investigation looked at patients' attitudes to the use of the computer in a much more systematic way than that reported by Vroman et al. (1989) in connection with memory retraining in elderly patients. Burton et al. used questionnaires and rating scales to obtain data from patients working at a number of different speech therapy centres. No restrictions or directions as to selection of patients was given to the speech therapists participating in the study.

An important theme raised in the series of papers in *Aphasiology I* in 1987 is that of the need for evaluation of software designed for the purposes of remediation of cognitive deficit. Katz (1987a,b; 1989) cited a number of studies which suggested that computerised techniques had been helpful in the treatment of language disorders. Seron, Deloche, Moulard, and Rousselle (1980) and Deloche et al. (1983) developed microcomputer presentations of standard therapy tasks directed towards training spelling to dictation and written naming tasks in patients with language impairment following CVA, head injury, or tumour excision. Responses to dictated words or pictures of objects were typed into the computer by patients. Computerisation provided an added dimension as regards feedback. Incorrect letters did not appear on the screen thus avoiding "visual reinforcement of false choices" (Seron, 1987a). Results showed a significant reduction in the number of words mis-spelled in this task as well as in the selection and sequencing of letters.

Mills (1982), working with the Veterans Administration in Michigan, used an Apple II+ microcomputer with a Mount Computer Supertalker to provide auditory comprehension practice for an adult who was aphasic following a CVA. Line drawings of objects were displayed on the screen and an auditory command such as "Find the cat" was simultaneously presented via the speech digitiser. The patient responded by pressing a key corresponding to the number of the drawing he wished to select. Improvement on the task and on auditory comprehension subtests of the PICA (Porch Index of Communicative Ability; Porch, 1967) was recorded throughout training. Katz and Nagy (1982; 1983; 1985), working with the Veterans Administration in Los Angeles, California, used a microcomputer to improve reading comprehension. Tasks were developed for an Apple II microcomputer and included a tachistoscopic word-recognition task to help develop word recognition and tasks requiring the patient to match words to pictures. They presented a number of single-case reports of patients with language disorders following vascular events in the majority of cases. Katz and Nagy (1984) also used the Apple II to help patients learn to spell commonly-used nouns. Line drawings of objects were presented on the monitor and the subject was asked to type in the names of the displayed objects. The computer provided immediate feedback in this task and selected and presented cues when the patient was unable to respond correctly. Katz and Nagy reported improvement on the computerised tasks and on non-computerised reading or spelling tasks in each case.

These studies have been criticised by Loverso (1987) who argued that claims for the effectiveness of these training procedures were undermined by the failure to provide more than one pre-treatment and one post-treatment measure. Although observed improvements cannot be unquestionably attributed to the treatment task in these studies (because the possibility of spontaneous recovery cannot be ruled out), the evidence presented tends to support the claim that the treatments were effective. A study by Scott and Byng (1989) controlled for spontaneous recovery. The authors used a multiple-baseline-across tasks design with a patient who had developed an acquired dyslexia following a head injury and who had difficulty in distinguishing homophonous words (i.e. words which sound identical such as "bawled" and "bald"). The therapy programme "Homotrain" was presented on a BBC Model B microcomputer. The patient was required to select the correct word to complete a sentence from a set of distractors which included the homophone. The patient improved in her ability to recognise and comprehend homophones and the authors demonstrated that the improvement was attributable to the training task because no significant improvement occurred in tasks which had not been directly trained in the programme (e.g. writing homophones).

A rather different approach to the use of microcomputers in aphasia therapy is in the provision of phonemic cues to help overcome word-finding difficulties. Colby et al. (1981) built a portable microcomputer for this purpose. The aphasic patients (who had suffered CVAs or head injuries) pushed keys in response to prompts from the computer when attempting to retrieve a word. A series of questions (e.g. "Do you remember the first/last letter of the word?") were displayed for the patients to answer. The computer then displayed a list of "probable" words based on the information known. The use of a computerised aid which provided a synthesised phoneme (the first phoneme of the word) is described in a single case study of the use of such a device by Bruce, 1987. In this study, mentioned earlier in the chapter, the patient's naming ability improved significantly following training and there was evidence that the improvement had generalised to unseen, as well as treatment, material. Bruce and Howard (1987) investigated the use of the computerised aid with five stroke patients who were able to indicate the initial letter of words which they could not produce. The microcomputer used was an Apple II which provided recorded digitised speech of 9 selected consonant phonemes in response to pressure on the key marked with the corresponding letter in the keyboard display. All subjects had five treatment sessions using the aid. During treatment sessions they used the aid in a picture-naming task. All the patients benefited from training; 4 of the 5 were significantly better in naming with the aid, and improvement generalised to names which had not been involved in the treatment. The authors concluded that this type of cueing was a promising approach to the treatment of word retrieval difficulties in aphasia.

The use of computer-based training in computing skills with the aim of using the computer as a mnemonic aid (Glisky et al., 1986a,b) has been discussed in the section of this chapter devoted to the rehabilitation of memory. An analogous use is reported by Dean (1987) who described a project undertaken at Queen Margaret College in Edinburgh. One of the ways in which computers were used in this project was to investigate the aphasic patient's ability to manipulate artificial as opposed to natural language. Dean presented brief case histories of three patients (2 had sustained CVAs, the aetiology is not stated in the third case) who were taught to write computer programs, the production of a program itself being the target for the patient in each case. It is interesting to note that in one of these cases "spin-off" effects on written natural language skills were observed.

Multi-system and Holistic Approaches

The majority of experimental investigations of the efficacy of retraining techniques target a single cognitive system or component of that system for retraining. A number of authors have recommended precise delineation of each patient's deficits and the development of an individual set of tasks (e.g. Byng & Coltheart, 1986; Gross et al., 1982; Howard & Hatfield, 1987). There is, however, a problem inherent in such an approach. This is that, although discrete deficits occurring in isolation are reported in the literature, clinicians will be aware that the majority of patients referred to them present with a number of deficits which give rise to a range of difficulties in their everyday lives. Isolated deficits are the exception rather than the rule. This is particularly noticeable when dealing with a population who have sustained closed head injury. Brooks (1984, Ch. 4), reviewing cognitive deficits in this group, notes that "severe head injury leads to marked and persistent deficits in various areas of cognitive functioning" and cites studies revealing impairments in learning and memory, intelligence, language, and perception.

In a case where multiple deficits are present, which system should be retrained first? Some clinicians (e.g. Finlayson et al., 1987; Harrington & Levandowski, 1987) have made the assumption that cognitive systems are hierarchically ordered and that there are "foundation skills' which are, to use the description provided by O'Connor and Cermak (1987, p. 273), "inherent components of higher cognitive functions" such that improvement in foundation skills is "important in enabling the patient to perform more complex operations." The notion of hierarchical function is attributable to Luria (1973) who described three "basic functional units". The first unit is involved in regulating level of arousal and wakefulness, the second in receiving, analysing, and storing information, and the third in programming actions and regulating behaviour. More complex activities are based upon these basic or "foundation" processes. Although Luria did not favour a strict localisationist approach, these "functional units" were associated with particular areas of the brain (arousal and wakefulness with the brain stem and other subcortical areas, reception and analysis of information with the temporal, parietal and occipital lobes, and programming and regulation with the frontal regions of the cortex), rather than with a neuropsychological model of the way in which the brain functions. Although at a gross level the notion of hierarchy makes sense (for example, a patient who is unable to maintain a wakeful state will be impaired on any activity they are asked to perform), there are strong arguments for the modularity of cognitive systems (Ellis, 1987; Fodor, 1983; Schwartz & Schwartz, 1984). A module is a separate system, capable of independent functioning, but interconnected with other systems. Both the range of selective impairments and dissociations of function documented by cognitive neuropsychologists (Marshall & Newcombe, 1984, p. 67; Shallice, 1979, p. 186) and the ability of normal subjects to perform two complex tasks without detriment to either (Allport, 1980) support the notion of modularity and provide evidence against the hierarchical view.

In cases of multiple deficit, where gross attentional or learning deficits are not present, there is therefore a case to be made for simultaneously targeting a range of cognitive systems. Each retraining session may include work on a number of different tasks, each directed towards retraining a different cognitive system, or tasks may be designed which draw upon a number of different abilities. In the latter case, retrained skills will be practised in tasks where that skill must be used in conjunction with other skills. Where gross attentional or learning deficits are present it makes sense to deal with these deficits as a first step.

The multi-system approach was adopted in the Newcastle Study (described in Chapter 6 of this volume). Therapists considering this approach may find the software available from the Burden Neurological Institute in Bristol useful. The "Cognitive Rehabilitation Suite" comprises 56 programs designed to stimulate a range of cognitive systems in recovering head injury patients. The discs run on all BBC models and are supplied free of charge to non-profit-making organisations (see Appendix I.2 for address).

Useful information regarding the commercially available package developed by Bracy (1983) was reported by Ethier et al. (1989a,b). The main focus of the research carried out by this group working in Montreal was the learning process itself. They used a selection of programs, running on six Apple microcomputers, with a group of 22 head-injured patients, one year or more post-injury. Detailed analysis of the scores obtained at each training session (two 2-hourly sessions twice weekly over a period of 6 months) enabled them to reach the following conclusions:

1. There do not seem to be counter-indications to the use of the exercises; deterioration of performance was observed with only one exercise which the authors recommend should not be used.

2. Improvement was elicited by the majority of the training tasks but variations in the extent of the improvement were observed. When speeded exercises were used patients benefited more from the more complex exercises but the reverse was true for non-speeded exercises where greater gains were obtained with simple tasks. More improvement was manifested on untimed than on speeded tasks. We give examples of specific exercises shown to be effective in eliciting on-task gains in Chapter 8 (Figs 8.2 and 8.3) of this volume.

3. A plateau was usually reached after 6 or 7 trials of a given exercise and it is recommended that practice is limited to 6 or 7 trials per session.

4. It appeared slightly preferable with the majority of tasks to space practice over a number of sessions rather than to mass the practice within a single session.

5. Severely and less severely impaired patients seemed to benefit equally from most of the exercises.

A number of post-acute brain injury units have been set up, (mainly in the United States) in recent years. Burke, Wesolowski, and Guth (1988), working in the USA, noted that at the time of writing there were about 600 head injury rehabilitation programmes running, while in the early part of the decade fewer than 10 could be identified. Many of these units take a "holistic" approach to rehabilitation. They are concerned with the social, emotional, and behavioural adjustment of the brain-injured individual, and aim to promote the highest possible level of independent functioning on discharge. Cognitive retraining is frequently an important part of the programme in such a centre; input may be highly structured and frequently targets a range of cognitive systems. For example a multi-system approach was adopted in the neuropsychological rehabilitation programme run at the Presbyterian Hospital in Oklahama, USA (Prigatano, 1986). The programme, which is still in operation, is intensive and broad-based. Patients attend for 6 hours a day, 4 days a week for 6 months. Approximately one hour a day is spent in cognitive retraining (a total of 96 hours). Most of the remaining time is devoted to psychotherapeutic intervention of different types—group psychotherapy with an analytic bias and group cognitive therapy. Time is also set aside for social interaction and independent work. The systems targeted for cognitive retraining include attention, perception, learning and memory, abstraction, problem-solving and information-processing speed. Patients work in small groups of two or three with a staff member who may be a clinical psychologist, occupational therapist, or speech therapist. Training tasks are not computerised.

In order to evaluate the effectiveness of the programme, psychometric tests were administered before and after training to a group of 18 head-injured subjects and to a control group. The patients had all sustained severe traumatic head injury. Chronicity ranged from 6 to 81 months in the experimental group. The control group, matched on gross neurological sequelae, received no treatment. There were modest but statistically-significant improvements in the training as compared to the control group in certain measures. These measures were the WAIS Performance IQ, the WAIS Block Design Scale Score, and the Wechsler Memory Quotient. There was no significant difference between training and control groups as regards Verbal IQ. A number of measures other than psychometric measures were used in the evaluation of effectiveness. The Katz–R Adjustment Scales were completed by relatives to assess effects on personality functioning. The patients who had attended the rehabilitation programme showed more improvement than the control group. Reports by relatives indicated lower ratings on helplessness, degree of social withdrawal, signs of general psychopathology, and restlessness or hyperactivity. An impressive finding (to the British reader) is that of 50% return to gainful employment (full or part-time) or course of education following rehabilitation. Thirty-six percent of the control group returned to work or study. As Jackson (1989) has pointed out rates of return to work after head injury are much higher in the USA than in the UK and Prigatano et al. (1986) were dissatisfied with the 14% difference between treated and untreated groups. Their programme was redesigned after the results of this evaluation were known and now includes a work trial and the teaching of job maintenance skills.

Although there are difficulties in interpreting the results of a broad-based study such as this in terms of mechanisms of improvement and relative contributions of different types of intervention, there is clear evidence that the overall outcome is positive. There is scope for ensuring that improvements in cognitive function generalise to everyday activities since the programme includes sessions devoted to social and occupational skills. A question relating to this type of provision which remains unanswered is that of the minimum period after which intensive and broad-based rehabilitation is effective. Is a 6-month rehabilitation period necessary? Jackson (1989) noted a tendency for the NHS in Great Britain to aim for "rapid turnover and short sharp shock rehabilitation". Yet, he argued "the experience of the Kemsley Unit at Northampton Hospital had taught us that a lengthy time is necessary to establish new patterns of behaviour in the brain injury survivor which ameliorate their personality and cognitive deficits." The point was reiterated by Peter Eames of the Burden Neurological Hospital (Eames, 1987) who noted that "studies of the impact of rehabilitation (though still all too few) suggest that the longer this continues, the greater is the level of independence which can be achieved."

A similar broad-based approach is adopted by therapists at the Head-Injury Recovery programme run at Coastline Community College, California, described by Harrington and Levandowski (1987). This is an even longer (2-year) course with a large cognitive retraining component. Social and emotional adjustment are also targeted. The authors do not give information about the exact number of hours spent in cognitive retraining, but about 25% of each day spent at the college was devoted to this activity. Systems targeted in a series of modules were orientation, concentration, and psycho-motor skill, perceptual processing, perceptual cognitive integration, logical reasoning, and problem solving. A final "transitional community" module involves application of learned skills including work experience. Cognitive retraining utilises both classroom instruction and "computer-assisted instruction". Eighteen head-injured adults were included in the evaluation of the programme. The psychometric measure was the Luria–Nebraska Neuropsychological Battery (Golden, Hammeke, and Purisch, 1981). Results for the group were analysed and small but significant improvements were noted on all except the tactile scale of the Luria–Nebraska. An individual analysis of results revealed that not all subjects improved on all scales although the majority improved on at least four measures.

The design of this study does not allow firm conclusions to be reached regarding the programme, since the authors did not repeat pre- and post-training assessments, nor did they provide a control group. The authors themselves noted that the design did not permit them to state that the improvement measured was due entirely to the training programme, and that further assessment of effectiveness "would be improved by matching subjects with a control group" and assessing each group in a " 'blind' or anonymous fashion". The programme is interesting in the emphasis which was placed on utilising cognitive skills, targeted early in the programme, in social and community situations, including work experience. Further evaluation of the programme would benefit from the inclusion of measures of social adjustment and level of performance in activities of daily living. Because the stated aim of the programme is to "maximise each individual's potential for independent functioning", it is surprising that no measures of independent functioning were reported.

Conder et al. (1988) described a further comprehensive head injury programme running at the Medical College of Virginia. This is a multi-disciplinary program created to meet the needs of a 40-bedded rehabilitation unit serving patients with a diagnosis of head injury, cerebrovascular disease or other neurological disorder. The authors provided protocols for each of the specialist teams. Disciplines involved included nursing, speech therapy, physiotherapy and psychology. Cognitive retraining is one of the primary targets for the neuropsychological team and computerised training exercises are heavily utilised. The cognitive systems targeted are attention, discrimination, orientation, memory, and reasoning. Computer exercises range from simple games through specialised programs aimed at specific cognitive subsystems (e.g. colour recognition and matching, auditory matching of tones) and the development of functional skills (e.g. telling the time) to complex word games, logic puzzles, strategic games (e.g. Blackjack), and reasoning tasks. Patients also learn word processing skills as part of the program. As well as spending time working at tasks specifically directed towards improving cognitive deficits, patients are placed in environments thought to be conducive to improving deficits (for example, where low arousal is a problem patients are treated in what is described as an active environment, with "other people present, sunlight, music, talking, one-to-one interaction"). Behavioural programs are also part of the regime. For example, when a patient is disorientated he or she receives verbal reinforcement for arriving for a session at the right place and the right time. A broad-based program of this type ensures that the maximum time possible is dedicated to potentially therapeutic interventions, but increases the difficulty of evaluating different elements of the program, because improvement could be due to cognitive, behavioural, or environmental interventions. Conder et al. (1988) did not present any evidence relating to the effectiveness of the program (presumably because it had only recently been implemented). Nevertheless, their protocols provide an extremely useful guide for clinicians developing intensive rehabilitation programmes in residential units.

The results of a pilot study carried out at the University of California Medical Centre were reported by Ruff et al. (1989). This study compared the efficacy of two types of rehabilitation programme with 40 head-injured patients, one year or more post-injury, randomly allocated to experimental or control training. Pre- and post-training neuropsychological assessments with a repeated pre-training baseline to isolate spontaneous improvements were used in the evaluation of effectiveness. Each group received 20 treatment hours a week over an 8-week period. The study is of particular interest because of the nature of the two types of treatment. Control treatment was by no means a "placebo treatment". Both experimental and control groups received a daily psychotherapy session. The experimental group worked on exercises, mainly computer-based, designed to improve attention, spatial integration, memory, and problem solving. The memory and problem solving modules included advice on the use of compensatory strategies. The control group worked on computerised videogames and attended sessions targeting coping skills, health issues, independent living skills (e.g. budgeting, job application, reading, writing, and arithmetic) and discussion forums in which issues of role-change and self-image were discussed.

Statistical analysis of neuropsychological test results demonstrated significant improvements for both groups. The experimental group achieved greater relative gains on certain measures of memory and an error reduction for visual selective attention. It is unfortunate that no measure of improvement in ADL was included in the study, particularly as so great an emphasis was placed on psychosocial adjustment in the control group training. It is interesting to note that training which did not specifically target cognitive systems, although it was clearly cognitively stimulating, led to gains on psychometric tests. All therapeutic activities described appeared to be valuable and it is possible that merging of both types of therapeutic input in a single broad-based programme could produce additive effects.

In connection with the fulfilment of social and occupational needs of brain-injured patients, which may be an aim of specialised brain injury rehabilitation units, the British organisation Compaid should be mentioned. This charity provides access to, and training in the use of computers for severely disabled (including brain-damaged) adults. Computers are not used for cognitive retraining in the Compaid program; the scheme aims to relieve "frustration and apathy through fulfilment of potential" and to improve job prospects. Patients can be familiarised with recreational, educational, and word-processing applications, with software for graphics, and with systems for account-keeping and general office management. Further information can be obtained from the Compaid Advice Centre in Kent (see Appendix II for address).

Other Systems

This chapter has not attempted to present an exhaustive survey of all techniques available but has discussed the major areas of intervention. Remediation of cognitive systems other than those discussed is possible. As task complexity increases, the likelihood of involvement of more than one system in the performance of a single training task also increases. An example of such a task is DRIVER (Finlayson et al., 1987) which involves visuospatial, motor coordination and self-monitoring ability, in addition to attentional skills. Processing speed is an area in which computerised training tasks are particularly valuable and there are a number of programs available which have as their primary goal improvements in speed of processing (e.g. The Reaction Time

Program prepared by Robertson and Smart, 1988). Non-computerised tasks for training systems impaired as a result of frontal lobe damage (e.g. problem-solving and reasoning skills) are discussed by Ben-Yishay et al. (1978) and Craine (1982). Many of the more complex computerised games including some of those described by Lynch (1982) may prove valuable in the retraining of "frontal" systems. However, many complex games require too high a level of skill in these areas at the start of play. They are thus unsuitable for patients with moderate or severe deficits and specially-designed programs are required in order that the more severely impaired patient may participate in this type of retraining. Commercially-available packages developed for the purpose of retraining by Laatsch (1983) and Bracy (1986) contain programs developed specifically for the remediation of problem-solving skills. These programs offer simpler instructions, less cluttered screen, less complex task demands, and clearer feedback than many games programs, while requiring problem-solving ability in order to make appropriate responses.

4.5 SUMMARY

The majority of evaluative studies discussed indicate that gains in intellectual function as measured by psychometric tests and even improvements in the quality of everyday life can result from efforts directed towards retraining impaired cognitive systems. However, there are too many questions which remain unanswered for us to assume in our present state of knowledge that the efficacy of cognitive retraining has been proven. One problem with the existing literature is that not all studies are designed in such a way as to allow the unequivocal attribution of improvements to the treatment. Two very different types of design are suitable for evaluation studies. In the group design, a control group is included in order to measure spontaneous recovery and non-specific or "halo" effects of treatment. In the single-case design, multiple baselines across time and task are used to take account of these variables. The relative merits of the two types of design are discussed in Chapter 2 of this volume. Choice of design depends upon the question which the research sets out to answer or on the context of the evaluation. Both group and single-case designs may be used to demonstrate that treatment can work. If the concern is to establish how the treatment works then the single-case design is indicated, since without precise specification of the locus of the lesion within a functional model, the nature of the deficit and the mechanism by which improvement takes place cannot be understood. Single-case designs are invaluable in establishing beyond reasonable doubt that measured improvement is attributable to the treatment, again because of the tight specifications of both the nature of the deficit and the demands of the training task. This can also be established in a well-designed group study, but group studies are more susceptible to the effects of extraneous variables. The group study is indispensible when clinical questions on patient management are posed. Such questions relate to the best use of therapist time, the relative merits of different training packages, and the nature of service plans for this patient group. Within the UK health service as it is at present it is not feasible, even if it is desirable, to design and administer individual treatment programs for every neurological patient referred. In the clinical setting there can be ethical problems with requiring patients to attend for repeated testing in order to establish a baseline. The expense and inconvenience of repeated journeys to hospital may overstress a family system already coping with enormous problems in caring for a brain-damaged family member. Should available time be devoted to cognitive retraining with the limitations imposed by shortage of time and staff, or would the time be better spent in counselling the patient and his or her relatives in order to facilitate adjustment to deficits? The group design is also most useful, if appropriate correlational analysis is carried out, for establishing which patients are most likely to benefit from treatment. A series of single-case studies could also be used to answer this question, providing negative as well as positive results are reported. The editorial policy of many journals tends to favour positive rather than negative findings, and studies which meet with success are much more likely to be published. We simply do not know how many well-designed but unsuccessful attempts at retraining have been made. Discussion with colleagues in other centres suggests that negative results in evaluative studies using both group and single-case designs are by no means a rarity.

There is an argument for the use of the statistical techniques of meta-analysis (Fitz-Gibbon, 1984; Glass, McGaw, & Smith, 1981), in this field; as yet no such study has been undertaken. Meta-analysis is described as the application of statistical methods to the summarisation of research results. It is concerned not only with the presence of significant effects but with the size of the effects. The first step in such an analysis is an exhaustive literature search and all studies, including those with methodological weaknesses, are included. The methodology used, sound or otherwise, becomes one of the variables to be coded, on the basis of explicit criteria, prior to final analysis. The techniques of meta-analysis are complex but powerful enough to deal with complex data in which studies using widely different experimental designs and outcome measures can be interpreted, and which, according to Fitz-Gibbon (1984), facilitate "judgement of the substance as opposed to the statistical significance of the findings".

A further problem with the existing literature is the paucity of evidence relating to generalisation to activities of daily living. Although information on the effects of a well-specified training programme on performance of tasks closely related to the training task is theoretically interesting, the aim of rehabilitation, in the clinical setting, is to improve the patient's ability to function in everyday life, not to improve performance on what might be regarded as "laboratory" tasks. Measures of employment status, activity levels, functional independence, and psychosocial adjustment can (and we would argue, should) be included in all clinically-based evaluations. Because of the difficulty of relating performance on real-life tasks to information processing models, the inclusion of such measures may pose a problem for researchers working within the cognitive neuropsychological framework. The need to demonstrate unequivocal treatment-specific effects may also conflict with the development of training tasks which facilitate generalisation of skills. For example, in the study reported by Scott and Byng (1989) a patient's ability to recognise and comprehend homophones was improved by training. Treatment-specificity of the improvement was demonstrated by the absence of improvement on a closely-related task (writing homophones), which had not been trained. The methodological argument here is sound. However, from a more practical point of view, it would surely have been of greater benefit to the patient if a training task with more far-reaching effects could have been designed.

In the currently-available literature, the use of psychometric measures alone is the most frequent method of evaluating retraining programmes. Although significant results have been reported in many studies, the size of the gain in psychometric test scores may be very small. We do not know what effect these gains are likely to have on the ability to function effectively in everyday life. It is conceivable that a small gain may enable the brain-damaged patient to reach a threshold at which wide-ranging improvements may be noted. Small gains may also be important in restoring a patient's confidence in his or her ability to perform mental operations. On the other hand, it may be the case that small gains have a negligible effect on everyday functioning. Studies like those of Gordon et al. (1985), which investigated the effects of cognitive gains on everyday performance, are of crucial importance.

Although effectiveness is, at present, the most pressing question addressed by experimental studies in cognitive retraining, studies which do not address this issue can provide data on issues of feasibility and patient acceptability which are valuable to the clinician planning a retraining programme.

Finally, what of the computerisation of retraining programmes which has been the focus of this chapter? Specific advantages and disadvantages will be discussed in the following chapter. It is sufficient to note here that examples of both computerised and non-computerised training programmes have been reported as effective, and that examples of both have yielded no significant effect. There is as yet no clear indication in the literature as to whether computerised programmes tend to be more effective than non-computerised ones and the decision to select the computerised or non-computerised mode may, in our present state of knowledge, be made on the basis of practical considerations.

5

Microcomputers in Cognitive Retraining

Examples of the application of computers to cognitive retraining have been described in the previous chapter. In this chapter we look at some of the issues relating to the use of computers in this field and weigh up the advantages and disadvantages.

5.1 ADVANTAGES

Scope and Complexity

Use of a computer enables the therapist to develop tasks that could be extremely difficult to administer in non-computerised form. Reaction time tasks, for example, require timing in milliseconds. Timing to this degree of accuracy is impossible to achieve by means of a stopwatch. Even if reasonably accurate timing is achieved (some stopwatches record to one hundredth of a second) the therapist's attention would tend to be absorbed by the timing operation and would be less effective in supporting and/or instructing the patient in the training task. Response timing sometimes needs to be at the millisecond level in order to detect subtle cognitive recovery over time (e.g.Skilbeck, 1990; van Zomeren, 1981). Precisely-timed presentation is also easy to achieve with computerised tasks.

Gianutsos (1980) is one of many writers who have commented on the value of presentation of stimuli for a fixed duration. Graphics facilities permit presentation of changing displays. For example, in a memory task designed by Bracy (1987) (Psychological Software Services listed in Appendix I.1) the computer randomly generates a trail through a maze of rooms. The visual display changes to simulate passing from room to room. Changing displays can be useful in providing cues in training, as well as in maintaining motivation by stimulating interest. Thus, in Robertson and Smart's (1987) programme for the retraining of visual neglect different sectors of the screen are outlined in sequence, in order to help the patient to adopt a systematic visual scanning strategy. Displays which change interactively are also extremely important in retraining tasks. For example, one of Richards' (1986) therapy games (entitled "Numeric Invaders") involves "firing" at numbers which descend from the top of the screen requiring a fast and spatially coordinated matching response. The patient is informed of a "hit" by disappearance of the target number which is replaced by another. In general the computer can perform a much more complex sequence of operations than can the individual therapist interacting with a patient. Of course there are some things which the computer does not do particularly well. If the therapist needs to train a patient in the auditory rather than the visual mode, program choice is very limited. Some computers do not have voice-simulation facilities, and those that do may produce a very artificial sound which is unlikely to be processed in the same way as the human voice. Developments are underway in the area of voice simulation but resolution of problems, especially as regards computer systems at the lower end of the price range, has not yet been achieved. Similarly, responses are frequently limited to the visuomotor mode, although a range of response devices are available within this mode. The increased variety of these devices is particularly helpful when working with a patient with a physical disability. The disability might be extremely severe, but as long as the patient can blink, blow, has some limb movement, or can turn their head then these movements can be fed through an available response device to interact with the microcomputer. Suck/blow air switches, voice-activated switches, and a range of pressure switches can also be utilised according to the patient's preserved physical activity, and electrode eye movement devices are probably the most sophisticated. Of particular value has been the development of the Concept Key Board which can act as one large pressure-sensitive pad or may be partitioned into a large number of different sections to match the number of responses desired. An infinite number of overlays are possible to fit with a desired response matrix. Parmar and Lawlor (1990) have described some of the above response devices in more detail. Computers with voice recognition facilities are not widely available.

Feedback

Computers are able to give accurate and rapid feedback and have no qualms about informing the patient of an incorrect response! The tendency for therapists to "wrap up" negative feedback has been mentioned in Chapter 2. If a patient is to improve performance, a knowledge of number of errors and of where these errors have occurred is essential. A further advantage of computerised presentation is that visually-presented feedback can be presented in verbal or non-verbal form if the patient is better at absorbing material of one, or other, type. Continuous auditory feedback can be used to inform immediately of a correct or incorrect response. Typically a "beep" or 3 or 4 ascending tones signify a correct response while an incorrect response is met with a "raspberry"! It has been suggested (Miller, 1984) that a patient working with a computer feels less humiliated by their mistakes than would be the case if they were working in direct contact with a therapist. A similar point is made in respect of the aggressive patient by Johnson and Garvie (1985) who cited the case of a young man who tended to respond angrily to correction by a therapist but who adopted an entirely different attitude to computerised feedback, tending to find his errors amusing when they were fed back to him via the computer.

Ability to Motivate

Clarity of feedback and a reduction in the patient's self-consciousness in relation to errors may be two of the reasons for the capacity of computerised programmes to motivate the patient. That computers are highly motivating has been noted repeatedly in published papers, in discussion with colleagues, and in our own experience of the use of computerised retraining programmes. Johnson and Garvie (1985) described a highly distractable patient who would settle and work quietly at the computer for periods of half an hour or so, and Parmar and Lawlor (1990) stressed how their clients with a mental handicap became highly motivated to learn when microcomputers provided the medium. Gianutsos (1981) pointed out that tasks may be attractive because they are programmed in game format. A more sophisticated discussion of this issue was presented by Finlayson et al. (1987) who based their account of the computer's capacity to motivate on a theory of "intrinsically motivated instruction", initially advanced by Malone (1981) who studied the appeal of different forms of computerised instructional games for a group of school children. Malone postulated three crucial elements, these being "challenge, fantasy and curiosity." He defined challenge in terms of goals set (the presence of a goal in a game being a most important factor in determining game popularity), and performance feedback provided. The element of fantasy related to the ability of the learning task to evoke mental images, while task variables such as novelty and difficulty level could be manipulated in order to affect the element of curiosity. The ease of manipulation of the variables associated with this model is increased by the facilities which the use of a computer makes available. Goals can be clearly stated by means of standardised presentation of instructions with illustrative examples. Malone noted that good computer games often have several different levels of goals. A game with more than one level of goal is more likely to appeal to a wide range of subjects, since players whose outcome is certain at one level of goal may still be challenged by another level of goal. The suitability of the computer for the provision of feedback has already been noted. Graphics can be used to increase the probability of the formation of a mental image. The variables of novelty and difficulty level are discussed in the following section.

Flexibility

Although the writing of the original program may be time-consuming, the production of multiple forms of computerised tasks can be a quick and straightforward operation. In certain cases the program can include a random-isation procedure which automatically produces variation of the task on each occasion it is used. In other cases different data sets can be selected with ease. Similarly, variation of level of difficulty can be achieved with the minimum of extra effort once the original program is complete by altering presentation time, amount and complexity of material presented, delay between presentation and response, and time allowed for response. In certain tasks it may be appropriate for the subject to proceed at their own pace, in others performance under time pressure may be important.

Computers can be programmed to adjust level of difficulty and select alternative forms of a task without the therapist's intervention if this is appropriate. For example, in a task which requires the subject to memorise a passage and respond to questions about the passage, the occurrence of a very high number of errors could be taken to indicate that the subject should move to an easier level of the task. If the number of errors is within a middle range, repetition of the same version of the task at the same level might be indicated. Few or no errors could be taken to indicate that the subject should move to a more difficult version of the task. Number of errors is a simple criterion on which to base choice of task. The computer can be programmed to select tasks on the basis of a range of additional criteria including speed of response, variability of response, type of error response, and presence or absence of responses on an inappropriate key, which would suggest poor comprehension of task instruc-tions. It can also be programmed to respond to a request for help by providing additional instructions or to re-present material if the subject has been distracted from the task. Weiss and Vale (1987) provided a useful review of the principles and history of adaptive testing. Computerisation of an entire retraining session is a practical possibility although it is often judged to be most appropriate for there to be a certain amount of interaction with the therapist during the session.

Ease of Overlearning

It has been observed that for many brain-injured patients to learn, information must be presented repeatedly. Giles and Fussey (1988) stated that it is "directed and persistent rehabilitation" that achieves results, and noted that it tends to be overlearned skills which are initiated spontaneously in settings other than the one in which the skill was taught. The ease of provision of multiple versions of tasks and the ease with which difficulty level can be manipulated renders the computer an appropriate tool in attempting to ensure that overlearning of a skill takes place.

Autonomy in Learning

The increased independence during retraining sessions which computerisation makes possible is potentially advantageous for both subject and therapist. The constant presence of the therapist may tend to encourage a dependent attitude or attention-seeking behaviour on the part of the retrainee. O'Connor and Cermak (1987) noted the positive value of computer intervention in providing "a sense of antonomy they [the patients] might not achieve when learning is constantly supervised by another person." Certainly the use of a computer allows variation along this dimension during the course of retraining. It may be appropriate to have high therapist–trainee contact at the beginning of the retraining process and to reduce therapist contact as training proceeds.

Computerised sessions can also lead to large savings in therapist time. Since a high ratio of patients to therapists presents problems for many professionals in the field this is a significant advantage. However, Norris et al. (1985), discussing the use of microcomputerisation in clinical practice, cautioned that "it is difficult to work out exactly how much time can be saved by using a computer ... It is no good concealing the fact that the initial stages do take up a lot of extra time and can be distinctly frustrating ...". In our experience the use of computerisation does free the therapist from the task of constant supervision. Even when the therapist remains in the room with the trainee to organise the changes from task to task and offer comments that reinforce the feedback provided on the screen he or she is free to spend the time while the subject is working on the computer in other activities providing these do not require undivided attention. It is also possible for a therapist to work with two or three patients simultaneously providing two or three computers and copies of software are available!

Incidental Learning

After a series of sessions working on the computer and, in some cases, observation of loading the printing routines, the majority of subjects become familiar with the range of functions which the computer performs and express an interest in acquiring a microcomputer for their personal use. The procedures for loading and running games programs on a home-based computer are easier to acquire when a subject has had experience of interacting with a computer, and subjects sometimes feel confident enough to attempt to learn programming skills if they acquire their own computers.

Data Storage and Analysis

Evaluation of the effects of retraining is facilitated by the computer's data storage and analysis facilities. Scores on tasks presented over a number of sessions can be recorded on disc and subjected to statistical analysis without the need for the therapist to record scores or re-enter data into a computer for analysis. The microcomputer is capable of storing large quantities of data and can store the results of a group of subjects which can then be analysed in terms of group effects. Thus both the progress of individual subjects and of the effectiveness of the retraining programme can be evaluated with ease once a comprehensive system has been designed. West (1990) has offered an excellent introduction to statistical analysis of data held on microcomputer. A caveat is that individual discs can be damaged and information lost. It is good practice to back up storage discs and many would recommend that two back-up discs are made for each disc in current use.

5.2 DISADVANTAGES

Inappropriate Use of Programs

If cognitive retraining software is readily available, then the possibility of its use by those who do not have expertise in the area is increased. This could lead to failure to match retraining programmes with specific deficits, absence of integration of cognitive retraining into a wide programme of rehabilitation, and lack of evaluation of the effects of retraining. These effects will have implications for the outcome of the interventions; they will tend to reduce the effectiveness of the retraining programme. They are not, however, essentially threatening to the well-being of the brain-damaged patient or their family. More worrying aspects of use of programmes by unqualified individuals concern lack of awareness of models of adaptation or of the affective disorders which may follow trauma. Insensitive explanation of the expected effects of the retraining programme, inclusion of depressed individuals who have unrealistic expectations of the programme, and failure to facilitate readaptation to residual deficits following retraining could all lead to increased distress for both patient and carers. Use by unqualified individuals could also lead to a reduction in the flexibility with which the retraining course is carried out if there is a lack of careful monitoring throughout the programme. Thus, the subject may lose motivation through working at too easy a level or become frustrated by the continual presentation of tasks at which they are failing. The sensitivity of the brain-injured individual to perceived failure can lead to the development of "learned helplessness", a state in which the individual feels powerless to act upon their environment in a way that will promote positive change.

The American Congress of Rehabilitation Medicine has laid down standards for the use of cognitive retraining programmes with brain-injured individuals. The areas of concern were listed by Kurlychek and Levin (1987) as follows:

Appropriate training and supervision
Patient admission criteria
Development of program protocols
Performance of adequate assessment
Documentation and program evaluation.

The adoption of a similar code of practice in this country would help to safeguard brain-injured patients against inappropriate interventions which could have a detrimental effect upon their recovery of function and adjustment to residual disability. Recommendations for the design of software for computer-based assessment are in existence in the UK, prepared under the auspices of the British Psychological Society (Bartram et al., 1987). The section that deals with hardware and operating systems contains recommendations as to the use of a standard operating system that are also applicable to the development of rehabilitation software. The authors stipulated (p. 87) that the operating system selected should be one which: (1) is widely used; (2) supports a good range of programming languages and allows these to be linked; (3) has a rich directory structure; (4) permits networking.

Operational difficulties

Johnson and Garvie (1985) drew attention to the difficulty which a brain-injured individual may have in remembering which response keys are available for use in a given task or in learning to press a sequence of keys. In many cases the "Return" key must be pressed to enter a response and if this is forgotten the subject may have no idea why the computer is failing to respond to an entry. In practice such problems can be easily overcome by the selection of appropriate response devices and care in writing subroutines that deal with data to be input by the user. Keyboards with fewer keys which are more widely spaced and more clearly labelled than those on a standard keyboard are useful. An example of such a keyboard is that provided with the Bexley–Maudsley Automated Psychological Screen (Acker & Acker, 1982). This keyboard has 9 widely-spaced buttons labelled with the figures 1 to 9. A number of different overlays are available; these provide alternative labels for the keys and cover keys that are not to be used in a particular task. The need for the "Return" key to be pressed can be eliminated by the use of appropriate commands in the program (for example, in BBC Basic the use of the "Get" command). Other useful programming procedures are to clear the computer's keyboard buffer before each input and to disable keys that are not required in the program.

Johnson and Garvie (1985) also commented on the difficulties which can result from physical limitations occurring in association with brain-injury. As described earlier in this chapter, alternative devices and careful programming can minimise or eliminate problems arising from both physical and cognitive difficulties.

Software Deficiencies

The need for careful programming to take account of specific difficulties that may be encountered by the brain-injured individual means that commercially-available programs may be unsuitable for use with this group, and that the programming will have to be undertaken by the therapist. This is particularly true in relation to many of the commercially-available games programs, which include too many choice points or too complex a sequence of responses, and are thus unsuitable for use in cognitive retraining. Even those programs that are written specifically for this purpose may have limitations, presumably because of a lack of expertise in programming on the part of the therapist. O'Connor and Cermak (1987) noted that, in spite of the range of options associated with the use of a microcomputer, "potential applications seem to outstrip the practical applications", and that there seems to be a temptation to computerise existing tasks rather than to develop new tasks which make full use of the computer's potential. Kemp and Earp (1990) warned that the quality of commercially-available software is often extremely poor, and that a process of evaluation needs to be undertaken to identify the most appropriate high-quality programs available. These authors advocated a check that the software is compatible with the disc format of the user's machine, and as to whether it requires a colour monitor or peripheral devices to run. The ease of installation and general running should also be checked. In terms of quality of construction, the user also needs to know that all software options are operative, and that the program will not "crash" if a required peripheral device is not attached to the microcomputer, nor if the patient produces a non-valid response (either accidentally or as a deliberate response). Users need to be sure that the supporting documentation for the software is adequate and that the program is helpful in use (e.g. by offering "help" options, and by being menu-driven).

Generalisation of Learning from Computerised Tasks to Everyday Life

The ultimate aim of cognitive retraining must be to increase the patients' functional independence; gains in the training tasks themselves are a means to this end. An issue which has concerned therapists working in neurological rehabilitation is the extent to which computerised tasks differ from everyday tasks. It has been argued that if there is no strong relationship between the two the likelihood of generalisation of learning from laboratory tasks to everyday performance is reduced. This is of course also a problem for many non-computerised therapy tasks but the issue has received more attention in relation to computerisation. The issue of generalisation is discussed at length in Chapter 2. The arguments will not be restated here but the importance of encouraging generalisation of gains on training tasks by means of real-life "homework" tasks cannot be overemphasised. We conclude the discussion in Chapter 2 by pointing out that in the ideal rehabilitation programme, cognitive retraining sessions should run in parallel with training in specific skills in order to maximise transfer of cognitive gains to real-life settings.

However, careful design of computerised tasks can at least ensure that training tasks and day-to-day tasks problematic for the patient make demands on the same cognitive skills. In 6.3 in Chapter 6 we note the result of an experiment designed to investigate the ecological validity of two of the training tasks used in the Newcastle Cognitive Retraining Programme. Highly significant correlations were obtained between scores on one of the computerised tasks and a real-life task, although no such correlations were found for the other task. Furthermore, computerisation can facilitate simulation of complex everyday tasks such as driving and when used in this way the computer can reduce rather than increase differences between tasks.

5.3 DESIGNING A MICROCOMPUTER-BASED COGNITIVE RETRAINING PROGRAM

This section discusses the steps to be taken to design an effective program once a patient has been identified as a suitable candidate for retraining and draws attention to issues which the therapist will need to consider at each stage.

Step 1 Establish Which Areas of Cognitive Function are to be Targeted

The first action on the part of the therapist will be to arrange a discussion session with patient and carer, with the aim of finding out which activities of everyday living are causing problems because of inefficient performance. It is sometimes the case that patient and carer are not in agreement about problem areas. In this case it may be helpful to ask both to record cognitive failures independently for a period of about a week. When the records are consulted then agreement may be easier to reach. It is important that the patient is in agreement that the area to be targeted for cognitive retraining is indeed an area of deficit if he or she is to remain well-motivated throughout retraining. Once a list of problems is agreed, analysis of the problems by a psychologist will be required in order to identify the cognitive systems that subserve the tasks which are difficult for the patient to perform adequately. A formal assessment using clinical tests should then be carried out. The aims of this assessment are described fully in Chapter 3. It should provide additional confirmation of the presence of the deficits that have been reported, and identify spared abilities, which may facilitate the development of alternative strategies, as well as providing a baseline against which future assessments—some of which will be carried out after the retraining programme has been completed—can be compared. If a number of subsystems appear to be impaired, decisions must be made in relation to the simultaneous or consecutive retraining of different types of deficit, and if consecutive retraining is selected, the order in which different cognitive systems are to be retrained must be established.

The desirability of targeting severe attentional difficulties in the early stages of the retraining programme has been noted in 2.3 in Chapter 2. It has been claimed (by Ben-Yishay et al., 1987, p. 166) that attentional disturbances may "mask and/or prohibit access to the patient's residual intellectual abilities and critical faculties", and Harrington and Levandowski (1988) argued that "attending behaviour' is the most basic "thinking skill". A distinction between primary level and higher level cognitive functions has been proposed by Luria (1973). Luria's work forms one basis for Harrington and Levandowski's classification. In fact, the notion of a succession of progressively more abstract internal representations is not a recent development. In his fascinating discussion of the historical development of models of the mind Marshall (1982) noted that such a schema has been attributed to Aristotle, who reached conclusions regarding the fractionation of the mind and the existence of primary faculties in 384–322 BC!

Ben-Yishay et al. (1987) viewed the attentional system as a complex system which can itself be subdivided, and proposed that the different attentional subsystems are organised hierarchically (the most basic being alertness, followed by maintenance of concentration and selective attention/ability to discriminate), although there is a high degree of overlap of the component attentional functions. According to the analysis undertaken by Ben-Yishay and his colleagues, increasing complexity of function is associated with a greater need to rely on internal, as opposed to external, cues, the need to maintain concentration for longer periods, and increasing demand for higher-level processing of information (e.g. decisions must be made on the basis of the attended material).

Fig. 5.1 presents a proposed hierarchy of cognitive systems. However, as noted in discussion of the multi-system approach to retraining (Chapter 4, section 4) the notion of hierarchy must be considered in conjunction with evidence for the modularity of cognitive systems. The proposed hierarchy of cognitive systems shown in Fig. 5.1 is based on analyses of task difficulty as well as the recognition of the importance of basic attentional processes and sets out the order in which attentional systems may reasonably be targeted for remediation without suggesting a rigid, biologically-based hierarchical arrangement.

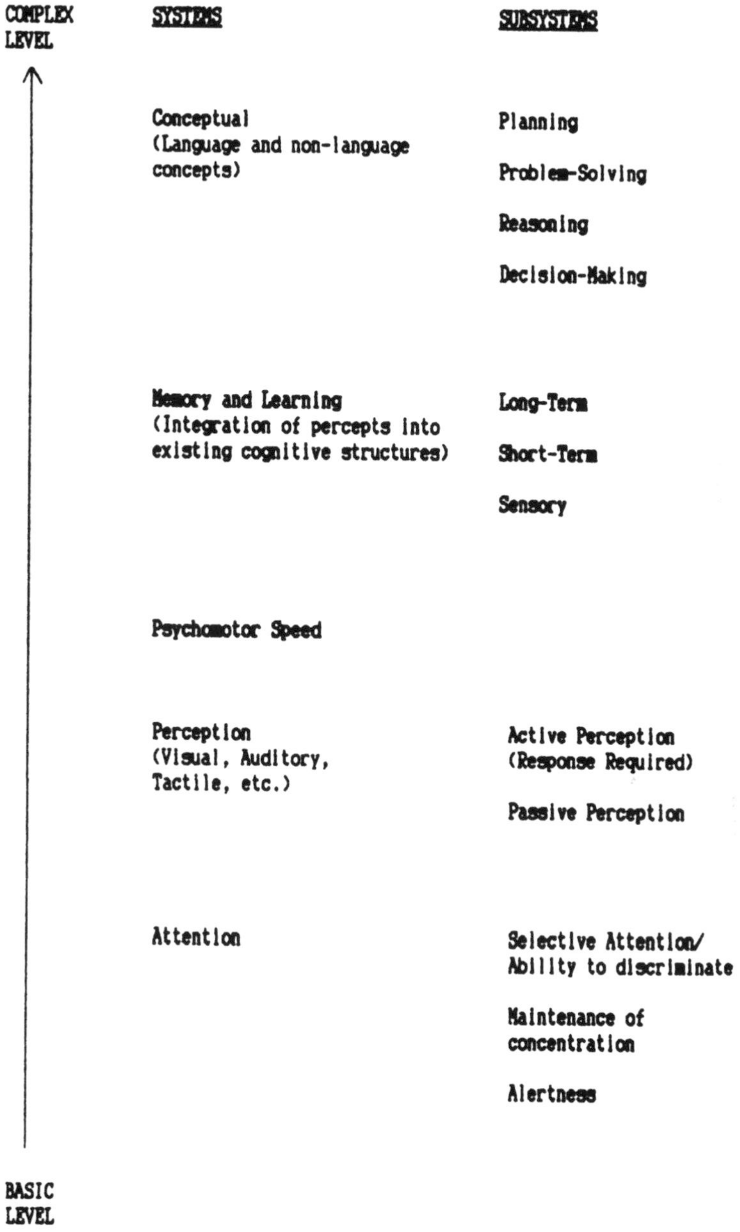

COMPLEX
LEVEL

SYSTEMS

SUBSYSTEMS

↑

Conceptual
(Language and non-language
concepts)

Planning

Problem-Solving

Reasoning

Decision-Making

Memory and Learning
(Integration of percepts into
existing cognitive structures)

Long-Term

Short-Term

Sensory

Psychomotor Speed

Perception
(Visual, Auditory,
Tactile, etc.)

Active Perception
(Response Required)

Passive Perception

Attention

Selective Attention/
Ability to discriminate

Maintenance of
concentration

Alertness

BASIC
LEVEL

FIG. 5.1. A proposed hierarchy of cognitive systems.

Step 2 Design Task

The task may be designed to be as closely analogous as possible to the task that has been reported to present problems in everyday life. Alternatively the training task may differ from the problematic everyday task, while drawing upon the same underlying cognitive abilities. The majority of psychologists working in neuropsychological rehabilitation adopt the latter approach, arguing that the basic processes identified as impaired in the course of psychometric assessment must be trained before the more complex operations involved in functional skills. As Kurlychek and Levin (1987) noted, the direct skills training approach derives from the tradition of behavioural psychology, rather than neuropsychology or cognitive psychology. Nevertheless, the computer does make possible certain types of simulation task which would be almost impossible to design in non-computerised form. Simulation of cognitive abilities required in driving is one such example. Computerisation allows the provision of feedback about visuoperceptual judgements, estimations of distance, and so on, in a true-to-life situation. That is, if erroneous judgements are made the subject's vehicle will "crash". However, although the programming of such tasks is possible, programs of this type suitable for use by head-injured persons are not currently available.

Ideally a series of tasks would be developed. Tasks performed early in retraining would target underlying cognitive abilities, and tasks presented later in the retraining programme would encourage the application of these abilities in tasks which are closer to real-life tasks.

Step 3 Computerise task

Select a commercially available program, or write a program. The latter option is more likely to result in the development of a program which is closely matched to the requirements of a particular department. It may be time-consuming to write, especially if there is no competent programmer in the department. However, the acquisition of programming skills may prove extremely useful for the therapist who undertakes to write the program, and if the end result is an effective and widely-applicable retraining task then time spent may be worthwhile. The BASIC language is extremely easy to learn and to use, and will probably be the language chosen by the newcomer to programming. BASIC varies slightly from one make of computer to another but many commands are identical whichever computer is used. Books on BASIC are easy to obtain. Most books on specific programming languages include a section on programming principles, which will explain the importance of preparation of a flow chart before starting to write the program, the use of "de-bugging" techniques to ensure an error-free program, and the desirability of developing a parsimonious elegant programming style.

Step 4 Plan Duration of Training Sessions and Length of Programme

Provision of conditions which will maximise the patient's ability to benefit from retraining sessions is obviously the primary concern. However, the amount of time the therapist has available and other demands which may be made on the computer must be taken into account. Where more than one computer is available in a department it may be appropriate for the therapist to supervise two trainees simultaneously. Finlayson et al. (1987) cited evidence from experimental psychology, which predicts that short, frequent sessions will be more effective than long infrequent sessions. In practical terms, daily rather than weekly sessions are indicated. Hourly or half-hourly sessions are most commonly reported in the literature and sessions of this length are more likely to fit in with the organisation of work in a psychology department than are longer sessions. It is clear from the review of retraining programmes presented in Chapter 4 that the duration of programmes varies considerably—from about 8 weeks to about 2 years—and there is no clear evidence of an effect of length of programme on outcome. This is another area in which further evidence from research is awaited. Until such evidence is available decisions relating to duration of programme may tend to be made on the basis of practical considerations like length of waiting list. It is important to remember that for each individual admitted to the retraining programme time must be made available for describing the programme to patient and carer and discussing possible outcomes. It is also probable that the therapist will be asked to counsel the patient and his or her relatives during the programme, especially if crises in the family occur.

5.4 SUMMARY

This chapter outlined the advantages and disadvantages of using microcomputers in cognitive retraining. Amongst the former is the fact that the microcomputer allows the development of tasks which would otherwise be very complicated to administer to patients. Microcomputers offer good control over timed presentation of stimuli, and can produce rich visual displays. The provision of immediate and relative feedback is easy via microcomputer, and the available evidence suggests that their use can enhance task motivation. The flexibility inherent in computer programs facilitates changes in task difficulty to suit individual patients. It was noted that patients can gain a sense of autonomy from reduced therapist input. Microcomputers also offer excellent data storage and analysis facilities.

The disadvantages of using microcomputers in cognitive retraining are fewer and relate to low-relevance or poor quality software, or the inappropriate selection of software by an inexperienced user. The remainder of the chapter concentrated upon the principles and steps involved in designing a cognitive retraining programme for the microcomputer. The discussion covered selection of impaired cognitive functions for retraining, design of the computer task, choice of commercially-available program or that produced in-house, and planning both length of sessions and the duration of the retraining programme. The chapter also included a proposed hierarchy of cognitive systems.

6

The Newcastle Study: Background, Subjects and Method

6.1 BACKGROUND

Awareness of the long-term problems of acquired brain damage has increased dramatically over the past decade (McKinlay & Pentland, 1987). There is now a substantial literature relating to the cognitive, emotional and behavioural sequelae of the major neurological conditions, in particular those associated with head injury (e.g. Brooks, 1984; Wade & Langton Hewer, 1987a). The number of patients with disabling neurological diseases is by no means insignificant. Wade and Langton Hewer (1987b) estimated that an average Health Authority of 250,000 people includes 5,000 with disabling neurological disease, 1,500 of whom require daily assistance, and the provision of rehabilitative care is a matter of concern in Health Districts throughout the UK. Estimates of incidence and prevalence in a number of countries indicate that these high figures are in line with those of other developed countries. For example, Harrington and Levandowski (1987) report an estimated incidence of 7.5 million head injuries per year in the USA, of which 500,000 persons are hospitalised. In Sweden, according to Nordstrom, Messeter, Sundbarg, and Wahlander (1989), head injury is noted to be "the major cause of death and persisting disability below the age of 40." Meier et al. (1987) devote a section of their book on neuropsychological rehabilitation to the international development of rehabilitation programmes, contributors reporting from the USA, Scandinavia, Europe, and Japan. In the UK a number of reports have been commissioned to identify the services available to brain-injured individuals and their families (e.g. South East

Thames, 1987; Southampton General Hospital, 1988). The majority of these reports have highlighted the inadequacies of existing service provision and, in some cases, this uncomfortable recognition of unmet need has led to further reports specifying forms of care required (e.g. South East Thames, 1990; McMillan, Brooks, McKinlay, Oddy, Tyerman, & Wilson—A working party of the British Psychological Society, 1989). In Chapter 8 we discuss these recommendations and outline an adequate and comprehensive service which could be organised and provided within the existing arrangements for the provision of care.

Rehabilitation is not only a matter of concern to health service providers. Voluntary organistions such as Headway (established in 1979) have done a great deal to increase public awareness of need and to organise for themselves facilities which are not provided by the local Health Authority. Insurance companies and solicitors, involved with the settlement of claims following accidents for brain injury, also concern themselves with the nature and provision of rehabilitation, because better outcomes can lead to lower settlements.

In the current climate in health provision within the UK, with reorganisation of services and the way in which services are financed being of immediate concern to health service professionals, there is a pressing need to identify those groups most likely to benefit from rehabilitation and to select the most cost-effective means of improving the levels of personal and economic independence of individuals within these groups.

The Newcastle study was a two year project, which commenced in October 1987. Its primary aim was to obtain information relating to the clinical effectiveness of a microcomputer-based training package and to answer a broad question which had arisen in the context of long-term and short-term planning of services to the brain-injured population within the catchment area of the Northern Regional Neurological Centre. In the short term, a limited amount of psychologist-time had been made available for work with this group. Computer facilities and the expertise to design a computer-based cognitive retraining programme were available so that running of such a programme was a practical possibility. In the long term, consideration was being given to the inclusion of a cognitive retraining module within a comprehensive rehabilitation programme.

The arguments relating to the use of standard versus individually-tailored training packages have been presented in 2.2 in Chapter 2 and elaborated in 4.5 in Chapter 4. The use of a standard package in a clinical setting leads to economies of time which enable several patients to be retrained in the time that would be required for the treatment of a single patient if an individual programme were designed. The use of a computerised package leads to further economies of time (see discussion in Chapter 5). There is, however, little value in running such a programme if there is no evidence of its effectiveness. There have been, as already noted, relatively few evaluations of training packages using a group as opposed to individual case design, carried out in the UK. No evaluation of a broad-based programme focusing on cognitive functioning alone and targeting a range of cognitive deficits has been reported in the literature, although the evidence relating to comprehensive therapeutic programmes which have contained a cognitive module is available (e.g. Prigatano, 1986). We were aware that a number of other centres were considering running a programme of this type and that information relating to effectiveness would also be useful for colleagues working in other parts of the UK.

The amount of therapist contact time which could reasonably be allocated to an individual patient both in the short and long term was estimated and taken into account in developing the programme. The structure of the programme was strongly influenced by practical considerations relating to service delivery. It was envisaged that the study would represent a first step towards the development of a programme which could be widely used in busy hospital departments with the many brain-injured patients requiring remedial intervention in respect of cognitive deficits. The content of the programme was theoretically based, the tasks being developed following identification of the cognitive systems subserving functional skills which patients found themselves unable to perform efficiently. The development of the computer programs themselves is described in 6.4 in Chapter 6.

"Effectiveness" was interpreted broadly, with the emphasis on patient/carer satisfaction. It was, however, stipulated that some evidence of improvement in the patient's ability to function effectively in everyday life would be required before a decision to include a retraining module in the comprehensive rehabilitation programme was made.

6.2 SUBJECTS

Patients were referred to the programme by neurologists and neurosurgeons and also by general practitioners who were circulated with information about the programme. The experimental group was composed of 23 patients who had sustained cerebral damage not related to a progressive condition. The patients were accepted into the retraining programme only if it was clear that they were sufficiently motivated to complete an exacting 24-session course. A major consideration was geographical location and for many people it was not possible to travel long distances for retraining. Another group of potential patients who met all the criteria for selection could not be used in the study because their denial of symptoms suggested to them that no treatment was required. Finally, there was a group of patients who would have been suitable on clinical grounds but, unfortunately, their personal traumas had so damaged the structure of their lives that it was practically impossible for them to engage in a rehabilitation programme, e.g. a head-injured mother who had four children, being looked after by her husband who was at the same time trying to hold down a full-time job. The constraints on the population and the need to cover a wide range of factors including age, time since brain damage acquired, and estimated premorbid IQ convinced us that a simple design for the study could not be achieved. We argue that there is a need to reconcile the desirability of a group study, which would aid generalisation to clinical real-life situations, with a high degree of intragroup variability which leads to the case study approach. The approach we have followed is to focus upon the group as far as possible (which implies partial groups, to be realistic in situations where some subjects produce ceiling/unimpaired scores at pretraining assessment or start of training), coupled with case examples (including matching with control subjects for pre- and post-assessment neuropsychological data) where these illustrations help to understand change over time.

Table 6.1 provides profiles of the patients involved in the study including details of the type of damage sustained.

The majority of patients had suffered closed head injury and cerebral damage was diffuse. All cases of closed head injury had been classified as severe. Another group had sustained cerebro-vascular accidents. One patient had cognitive deficits following herpes encephalitis and another had experienced episodes of decompression sickness. The time since injury varied from 4 months to 6 years, the mean time since injury being 25.5 months. The group contained 19 males and 4 females and ages ranged from 20 to 66 years, mean age being 33 years (sd 12.5). The project targeted an age range of 16 to 70 years. These age cut-off points were adopted in order to make it less likely that the interpretation of results would be complicated by effects of stage of life-span development. Apart from these age limits and the exclusion of those with degenerative conditions, the only additional requirements were that auditory comprehension should not be so severely impaired as to make comprehension of task instructions impossible and that the patient should be well motivated in respect of the program. That the former requirement was met was established during a trial session provided as part of the assessment procedure for patients who showed evidence of auditory comprehension deficits. Since comprehension may be improved by contextual information and the use of gesture this method of selection was felt to be more appropriate than the use of cut-off scores on comprehension subtests within a formal battery of diagnostic tests of aphasia.

The difficulties of establishing the extent to which a person is motivated have been discussed in 2.3 in Chapter 2. In a clinical interview with the patient and carer(s) we elicited information about awareness of deficits and expectations of retraining. Denial of deficits or expectations of a complete return to premorbid levels of functioning were regarded as dysfunctional and in 2 cases patients worked with a psychologist outside the neuropsychology specialty with the aim of developing more realistic attitudes to their problems. Retraining commenced after these sessions were completed. Patients and their carers were informed of the practical details regarding attendance and both patient and carer were asked about their willingness to meet these requirements. Apparent unwillingness to

TABLE 6.1
Profiles of the Experimental Group

Case no.	Age	Sex	Neurological condition	Site of lesion	Time since onset (mnths)	Premorbid occupation	Estimated premorbid IQ
1	23	M	Encephalitis	Diffuse	12	University student	119
2	44	M	CVA	R. frontal parietal	4	Brewery labourer	112
3	20	M	CHI	Diffuse	5	Art student	115
4	36	M	CVA	Diffuse	60	Hairdresser	122
5	36	M	CHI	Diffuse	6	Engineer	120
6	23	M	CHI	Diffuse	60	Unemployed	90
7	23	M	CHI	Diffuse	6	Driver/ Labourer	95
8	40	M	CHI	Diffuse	11	Self-emp. driver	95
9	63	M	CVA	R. parietal	11	Self-emp. plumber	105
10	22	F	CHI	Diffuse	20	Unemployed	84
11	28	M	CVA	ACAA	72	Ship-builder	96
12	27	M	CHI	Diffuse	6	Unemployed	Not Available
13	24	M	CHI	Diffuse	i) 33 ii) 20	Armed forces	96
14	38	M	Decomp. sickness	Diffuse	14	Deep-sea diver	108
15	66	M	CVA	Diffuse	48	Freight manager	111
16	33	M	CHI	Diffuse	26	Armed forces	81
17	48	F	CHI	Diffuse	35	School-crossing patrol	95
18	29	M	CHI	Diffuse	17	Unemployed	101
19	24	M	CHI	Diffuse	57	Armed forces	108
20	36	F	CHI	Diffuse	9	Careers officer	116
21	21	F	CHI	Diffuse	13	Kitchen designer	102
22	24	M	CHI	Diffuse	12	Turner	98
23	22	M	CHI	Diffuse	50	College student	110

CVA—Cerebrovascular accident
CHI—Closed head injury
ACAA—Anterior communicating artery aneurysm

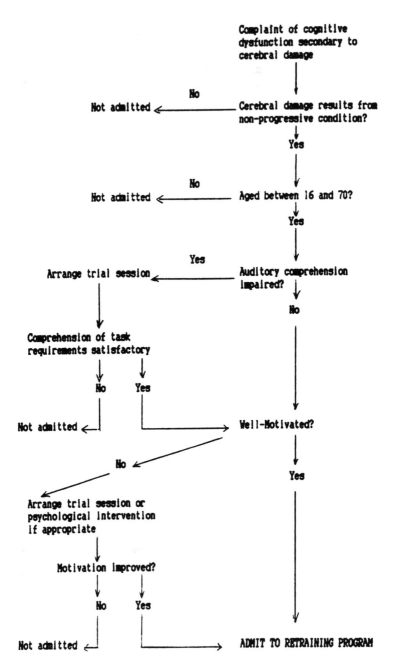

FIG. 6.1. Criteria for admission to the cognitive retraining program.

make the required time commitment was explored before admission to the program. A trial session was arranged for patients who were uncertain about their ability or willingness to interact with a computer. Figure 6.1 provides a schematic representation of the factors taken into account when admitting patients to the study.

The group had a fairly wide variety of employment backgrounds and premorbid IQ (estimated by means of the Nelson Adult Reading Test; Nelson, 1982) ranged from 81 to 122 (mean IQ, calculated for the 22 subjects for whom NART data was available, = 103.6, sd 11.3).

The control group was composed of five patients (mean age = 40.2; sd = 11.8). As explained in the following section, random allocation to the experimental or control group proved impracticable. The control group was therefore made up of those patients who had been deemed to be suitable for inclusion in the experimental group on all selection criteria, including motivation, but for whom insuperable practical difficulties (relating to travel or family arrangements) precluded attendance. Profiles of the control group are provided in Table 6.2. Mean IQ for the group was 105.6 (sd = 7.5).

6.3 DESIGN AND PROCEDURE

6.3.1 Design

A number of outcome measures were used both in relation to effect on cognitive status, measured psychometrically, and effect on affective and psychosocial variables, measured by means of questionnaire data. The inclusion of the latter measures enabled the investigation of issues relating to generalisation of improvements in retrained skills. Pre- and post-training data of both types was analysed for the group in terms of the occurrence and direction of change.

TABLE 6.2
Profiles of the Control Group

Case no.	Age	Sex	Neurological condition	Site of lesion	Time since onset (mnths)	Premorbid occupation	Estimated premorbid IQ
1	23	F	CHI	Diffuse	17	Shop assistant	96
2	54	M	CHI	Diffuse	56	Printer	103
3	53	M	CHI	Diffuse	239	School porter	105
4	34	M	CHI	Diffuse	3	Tel. engineer	105
5	37	M	CHI	Diffuse	18	Postgrad. student	119

Two control measures were incorporated into the design in order to ensure that any observed improvements in scores or rating were not due to the effects of spontaneous recovery. The first was repeated testing for both pre- and post-training psychometric assessment. Although recognising that the ideal design would include a large number of repeated assessments, our sample included subjects who travelled considerable distances in order to attend sessions and, in practical terms, it was not possible to ask them to attend more than a single repeat assessment before and after training because of the expense and inconvenience of the journey for both subjects and their families. Statistical texts tend not to state definitively the number of trials required to establish a stable baseline; Kazdin (1982) included an example of a single-case study of a behavioural intervention in which only three baseline measurements were taken. In the Newcastle Study comparisons of the two pre-test and the two post-test assessments assisted in the interpretation of the significance of change scores.

The second was the inclusion of a small control group. We had originally intended random allocation of subjects to experimental and control groups of comparable size. A problem arose in that patients were all keen to enter the experimental group and their relatives were keen for them to do so. In many cases, patients were not willing to undergo assessment if they were not to participate in the retraining programme. Because the project was time-limited we were not able to guarantee participation in the programme at a later stage. The eventual composition of the control group has been described in the preceding section. Examination of the demographic characteristics of patients in the experimental and control groups enabled us to form a small number of matched pairs which proved useful in interpreting the outcome data, although it should be noted that this was done on a *post hoc* basis.

We were also concerned to use data from our brain-injured group to identify which patient characteristics affected the outcome of treatment. The proposed sample size was not large enough to include blocking variables in the design in order to evaluate block-by-treatment interactions. Additionally, current knowledge in this area does not permit the identification of factors which are clearly important in relation to outcome of retraining. It is reasonable to assume that those characteristics which influence spontaneous recovery may also influence the outcome of remedial intervention, but this no more than an assumption. We therefore collected demographic information for each subject to enable us to undertake a certain amount of exploratory data analysis in order to establish whether characteristics such as age might prove to be important in affecting the outcome of treatment.

In certain cases individual case results are reported to illustrate points of discussion and to enable the reader to form a more detailed picture of the nature of the cognitive deficits which may occur in this patient group and of possible responses to remedial intervention.

A further area of interest was performance on the training tasks.

TABLE 6.3
Cognitive Assessment for Rehabilitation Training

Test	Rationale/cognitive system involved
1. PASAT (paced auditory serial addition test) (Gronwall & Sampson, 1974)	Measure of attention
2. Digit Symbol (Wechsler, 1955)*	Measure of processing speed
3. AMIPB Information Processing Task A (Coughlan & Hollows, 1985)	Measure of processing speed
4. E Cancellation (Diller et al., 1974)	Measure of visual neglect
5. Computerised Line Bisection (Skilbeck, 1984)	Computerised measure of visual neglect
6. Rivermead Memory Passages (Wilson et al., 1985)†	Measure of verbal memory (meaningful material)
7. BMAPS–Little Men (Acker & Acker, 1982)	Computerised measure of right/left orientation
8. AMIPB Visual Learning (Coughlan & Hollows, 1985)	Measure of visual memory
9. Rivermead Route Learning (Wilson et al., 1985)†	Measure of topographical memory
10. Rivermead Message (Wilson et al., 1985)†	Measure of prospective memory
11. Rivermead Belonging (Wilson et al., 1985)†	Measure of prospective memory
12. Rivermead Appointment (Wilson et al., 1985)†	Measure of prospective memory
13. Finger Tapping (Reitan & Davison, 1974)	(i) Measure of manual dexterity and speed (ii) All tasks required key press response; some tasks required speeded motor response. Improvement in this ability may occur incidentally.
14. Rey Auditory–Verbal Learning Test (Rey, 1964)	(i) Measure of verbal memory (independent items) (ii) Possibility of improvement generalising from conversational memory training

* Parallel forms of the Digit Symbol test of the WAIS were produced by rotating the digit symbol pairings.

† Individual items from the Rivermead Behavioural Memory Tests.

6.3.2 Procedure for the Experimental Group

Pre- and Post-training Assessment. Two pre-training assessments were carried out, the first 3 weeks before and the second immediately before the start of the program. The assessment used a range of psychometric tests selected with the aim of testing all the areas targeted by the retraining program plus a test in which performance is subserved by a non-targeted ability which was included as a control measure. The tests used and the rationale for using them are shown in Table 6.3. Individual tests listed are described fully in Chapter 3.

Subjects and carers were also asked, before commencing retraining and after completion of the program, to complete questionnaires covering the subject's cognitive function, emotional state, role in the family and ways of spending time. Ratings of state before and after the subject's accident or illness were requested on the pre-training questionnaire. A copy of the subject's retraining questionnaire is provided in Appendix IV of this volume. The carer's version of the questionnaire was identical apart from changes in the wording of questions so that they referred to the relative of the person completing the form.

TABLE 6.4
Programme for Rehabilitation Assessment and Training Sessions

Assessment	*Schedule for experimental group*	*Schedule for control group*
Wk 1	Referral	
Wk 2	Pre-training assessment	
Wk 5	Second pre-training assessment	
Wk 6	Commence training. Pre-tests on training packages	Relaxation session. Tape provided with information as to use.
Wk 7	1 × 1hr session per day	
Wk 8	1 × 1hr session per day	
Wk 9	1 × 1hr session per day	
Wk 10	2 × 1hr session per week	
Wk 11	2 × 1hr session per week	
Wk 12	2 × 1hr session per week	
Wk 13	1 × 1hr session per week	
Wk 14	Post-tests on training packages	
Wk 15	Post-training assessment	
Wk 18	Second post-training assessment	

Retraining Sessions.   The program covered a 9-week period. Each subject attended for 24 hourly sessions. These were held 5 days a week for the first 3 weeks, twice a week for the second 3 weeks and once a week for the final 3 weeks (Table 6.4 provides a timetable of events). Work during each session focused on four of the six retraining tasks, with up to four repetitions of the task being completed in each session. The rate at which subjects proceeded to a higher level of task difficulty was varied according to the severity of their impairment in a given area and the speed at which gains in performance on each of the tasks occurred. Clear feedback on number of items correct and speed of response was provided by the computer after the completion of each task. Additionally, the training supervisor drew the subject's attention to important aspects of the results (for example, the existence of a speed/accuracy trade-off) and gave encouragement or suggested the use of alternative strategies where appropriate.

The development by the individual undergoing retraining of alternative strategies in performing the task was regarded as an important component of the program. Subjects were asked by the training supervisor about the way in which they were performing the task. Subjects frequently reported that they had experimented spontaneously with different approaches to the tasks. If they did not report this and no improvement in scores on training tasks were noted within three sessions, the training supervisor suggested an alternative strategy or strategies for each of the training tasks. Suggestions were made on the basis of the subject's known residual strengths and their preference for different types of strategy. Examples of strategies suggested are as follows:

ROADRIGHT
1. Use distinguishing feature of body or clothing to help remember which is the right and which is the left side.
2. Imagine self walking up the road and turning during the memorisation stage.
3. Trace out route with finger when recalling it and making decisions about right and left turns.
4. Code the turns in the route verbally.

MEMCHAT
1. Form a visual image of the information. The image might be realistic or bizarre.
2. Try to relate new information to information already stored in memory. For example, if you know someone of the same name as the character in the story picture events happening to that person.
3. Respond to the information presented to make it more interesting and memorable. For example if you are trying to remember that a second-hand car cost £200, you might think that this is a very low price and that the car could have some serious fault.

VISCAN
1. Say aloud "Look left" to remind you to turn into the neglected field.
2. Always start searching for the illuminated key on the neglected side.

ATTENTION
Rehearse the digits to be memorised aloud.

SPEED
No specific strategies were suggested for this task. The training supervisor drew attention to the speed/accuracy trade off. The aim was to attain a satisfactory balance between the two.

PROMEM
1. Use visual imagery (bizarre or realistic) to help link time and task.
2. Set the different tasks into chronological sequence and imagine yourself doing them at different times in the day.
3. Use verbal mnemonics to link time and task (e.g. rhyming, first letter cues).

6.3.3 Procedure for the Control Group

The control group underwent assessments identical to the experimental group including psychometric testing and completion of questionnaires. The four assessments were carried out at the same time intervals (i.e. a 9-week period interposed between the second and third assessment and a 3-week period between the first and second and the third and fourth assessments). Following the second assessment session subjects in the control group attended a 45 minute session in which they were familiarised with a relaxation technique. This involved using key words like "calm" and "relaxed" and visual imagery as a means to becoming relaxed. This procedure was felt to be more appropriate than the relaxation by contrasts method in view of the fact that a number of subjects had a hemiparesis and thus had difficulties with muscle control. At the end of this session each subject was given a copy of the audio-tape which was used in the session. They were advised to use the tape (which lasted about 20 minutes) on a daily basis for the first 3 weeks and thereafter to use it whenever they felt it would be of value.

6.4 THE RETRAINING PROGRAMS

6.4.1 Design of Programs

The complaints of cognitive failure made by brain-injured individuals seen in the Psychology Department were recorded over a period of 3 months prior to commencement of program design. We noted that the majority of patients who had suffered strokes or head injuries reported multiple rather than isolated problems. The practical problems which were repeatedly reported to us by this group of patients were the starting points in the design of the programs. They are listed in Table 6.5. They include problems with remembering various different types of material (routes, conversational content, things to be done), with concentration and with speed of mental processing.

The problematic tasks were then analysed in terms of the cognitive processes used to perform the tasks satisfactorily. In some cases the cognitive systems which subserve a particular task may vary between individuals or situations. For example, finding one's way to a particular place can be achieved with the aid of verbal memory because one is relying upon a set of verbally-encoded instructions (e.g. "turn left at the traffic lights, then take the second right after the post office . . ."). Alternatively, one may rely entirely upon a visual image—a "mental

TABLE 6.5
The Design of the Retraining Programs

Reported practical problem	Cognitive systems involved	Retraining task
Difficulty in finding/ remembering way	1. Right/left orientation 2. Visual memory/learning 3. Verbal memory	ROADRIGHT Identifying left or right turns in a route. Remembering the route.
Difficulty in following conversation	1. Verbal memory 2. Attention (alertness, sustained & selective attention)	MEMCHAT Remembering conversational material – general themes & details. Immediate & delayed recall.
Loss of part of visual field, walking into doorways, etc.	1. Visual scanning 2. Visual search	VISCAN Timed visual scanning task.
Difficulty in concentrating	Attention: (a) Alertness (b) Sustained attention (c) Selective attention (discrimination)	ATTENTION Memorising changing digits. Requires continuous updating and interference resistance.
Being unable to think/respond quickly	Psychomotor processing at speed	SPEED Timed information processing task.
Remembering to do things	1. Prospective memory 2. Verbal memory	PROMEM Memorising task & time when it must be performed. Immediate & delayed recall.

map"—which is stored in visual memory. Similarly, "difficulty in concentrating" is a non-specific complaint and problems of this type may arise from deficits in one or all of the sub-systems listed. The nature of the individual cognitive systems is discussed in some detail in Chapter 3 of this volume. The cognitive systems playing a major role in the performance of the tasks are listed in Table 6.5. Other systems may be involved in the tasks to a lesser degree.

The systems most likely to be deficient having been identified, training tasks requiring the operation of these systems were developed in the context of tasks which were as closely as possible analogous to the tasks reported as being problematic. All six tasks were computerised. Four of the programs ran on the Commodore 64 and two on the BBC B. The program VISCAN required a special keyboard which was developed in the Department of Medical Physics at Newcastle General Hospital and the accompanying program was written by a technician in this department. Responses in the PROMEN program were made either on the original BBC B keyboard or on a concept keyboard linked to the BBC B. The other programs utilised the keyboard supplied with the BMAPS package (Acker & Acker, 1982). Each program had a number of different levels of difficulty and multiple versions of the programs were available within each level of difficulty.

6.4.2 Description of Programs

ROADRIGHT

This program was written for the Commodore C64. The system used a Commodore 1541 disc drive and Commodore 1701 colour monitor. A route between two "houses", represented by a red and a blue square, is shown on the monitor. The route has 1 to 4 turns in it according to the level of difficulty which has been selected. Figure 6.2 shows an example of a route.

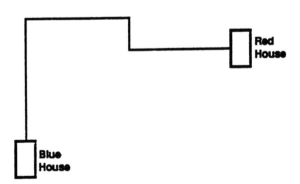

FIG. 6.2.   An example of ROADRIGHT route (3 turns).

In the Orientation section of the program the route remains visible on the monitor. The subject is told to start from either the blue or the red "house", via the monitor, and asked "Is the first turn a right or a left turn?" The same question is asked for each subsequent turn in the route. Responses are made via the BMAPS keyboard using an overlay so that all keys except 1 and 9 are covered. The overlay marks key 1 (at the far left of the keyboard) "left" and key 9 (at the far right of the keyboard) "right". The number of correct responses and response times are measured. Total correct responses and mean response time are displayed on the screen at the end of the exercise. In the Orientation and Memory condition, the route is displayed on the screen for any length of time selected by the therapist. The subject is asked to memorise the route and is then required to respond to the questions about right and left turns once the route has disappeared from the screen. The level of difficulty is thus increased by increasing the number of turns in the Orientation condition and by increasing the number of turns and/or by decreasing the time by which the route is displayed on the screen in the Orientation and Memory condition.

MEMCHAT

This program was also written for the Commodore C64 and used the peripheral devices described in the previous paragraph. To-be-remembered material was displayed in visual-verbal form on the monitor. Material was designed to resemble as closely as possible the type of information which might be given in conversation, and particularly in conversation with a recent or casual acquaintance. There are 3 levels of difficulty. At the first level a single idea is conveyed in a single sentence (e.g. "Fred used to be a painter" or "Jan lives in London"). The difficulty level is increased by increasing the amount of information to be remembered. The material presented at level 3 comprises a short story of the type that might be told in light conversation. An example is shown below.

Part 1
Simon Smith came back from work on Tuesday and found his front door wide open. In every room drawers and cupboards were open and his belongings thrown over the floor. He wondered what had happened. Then he realised that his house had been burgled.

Part 2
He checked to see if anything was missing. Nothing had been taken except £15 in cash which he had left on the mantelpiece. He decided not to telephone the police. He poured himself a large whisky, then he started to tidy up the house.

The material remains on the monitor for as long as the subject wishes. When they feel that the material has been memorised a key press displays a question and a multiple-choice answer set of 6 possible responses on the monitor. The subject responds by pressing the numbered key on the BMAPS keyboard corresponding to the correct answer. A delayed recall condition follows the immediate recall condition. In this case, the questions and response sets reappear without representation of the to-be-remembered material. The number of correct responses in the immediate and delayed conditions are displayed at the end of the exercise.

VISCAN

This program was written for the BBC B microcomputer with BBC dual disc drive and Microvitec CUB colour monitor and requires a special response keyboard made up of a bank of 64 keys, each of which can be illuminated. Program and keyboard were developed in the Regional Department of Medical Physics at Newcastle General Hospital (details from Dr Phillip Lowe, see Appendix I.2 for address). The keys are sequentially illuminated in random order. The subject is required to press each illuminated key as rapidly as possible; once the key is depressed the light goes out. The key remains illuminated, if not depressed, for a length of time which is pre-set by the therapist. Number of keys depressed within the pre-set time and response time for each key are displayed on the monitor at the end of the exercise. The response times for each key are represented graphically, using different colours for different time bands so that subject and therapist can see at a glance whether keys in one or more quadrant of the keyboard are being depressed more slowly than keys in others.

ATTENTION

This program was written for the Commodore C64. A matrix of 28 digits (4 lines of 7) is displayed on the monitor. A moving patch of colour hides 1, 2, or 3 digits. The patch moves from left to right and from top to bottom through the matrix. The subject's task is to remember the next digit to be uncovered and to depress a key on the BMAPS keyboard corresponding to that digit. Level of difficulty is increased by increasing the number of digits covered at any one time and by interposing a delay between the movement of the patch and the response so that the subject must maintain concentration for periods of time which increase in length. The number of correct responses is displayed at the end of each exercise. The number of "order" errors is also displayed when 2 or 3 digits are covered. An order error occurs when the response is the digit next but one or next but two to be uncovered.

SPEED

This program was written for the Commodore C64. It is subtitled "The Price is Right". Five prices appear on the monitor, each within a band of colour. The subject is told that there are prices of particular items (books, cars, houses, and so on). The task is to identify either the cheapest or most expensive item of that type or the second cheapest or most expensive item of that type. An example is the following display:

Which is the cheapest car?
£7500   £7950   £8240   £6750   £9600

The subject responds by pressing the correct key on the BMAPS keyboard. An overlay for the keyboard identifies each key with a colour which corresponds to each of the bands of colour on the monitor. Responses must be made as rapidly as possible. Level of difficulty is increased by increasing the number of digits to be processed. Level 1 uses single digit prices and Level 5 uses 5-digit prices. Response times, mean response time and number of items correct are displayed at the end of the exercise.

PROMEM

This program was written for the BBC B microcomputer with BBC dual disc drive and Microvitec CUB colour monitor. A digital clock appeared in the top left-hand corner of the monitor's screen. In the centre of the screen a statement of a task and the time when it is to be performed is displayed for the length of time pre-set by the therapist (e.g. "At 5.00 pm I must remember to take my tablet.") Immediate recall is tested using multiple-choice response sets. The second stage of the program requires delayed recall which follows a filled delay in which the subject is required to watch moving patterns on the monitor. In the final stage of the program the subject is asked to watch the digital clock in the corner of the screen and to stop the clock when it displays a time at which a task is to be performed. Stopping the clock triggers the appearance of a multiple-choice response set and the subject must select the task to be performed. The number of correct responses in each condition is displayed at the end of the exercise. Responses are made via the BBC B keyboard except in cases where interaction via this keyboard proves difficult. In these cases a concept keyboard is used.

6.4.3 Ecological Validity of the Training Tasks

A criticism which has sometimes been made in relation to computerised tasks is that they bear little relationship to real-life tasks and that this may reduce the likelihood of generalisation of learning from laboratory tasks to everyday performance. An investigation was carried out in the department (Boorman, 1989) which compared performance on the retraining tasks MEMCHAT and ROADRIGHT with performance on analogous behavioural tasks. The aim was to establish whether or not there was evidence of involvement of the same cognitive processes in the training and behavioural tasks. Highly significant correlations were obtained between the real-life verbal memory task and the scores on the MEMCHAT training task. This was not the case with the real-life orientation task and the training task ROADRIGHT, where no significant correlations were obtained. This was explained in terms of level of task difficulty, since the computerised task required mental rotation while the behavioural task did not. The study is described in detail in Appendix III of this volume.

These findings have important implications for the design of cognitive retraining programmes in terms of both the practical effectiveness of the training and of the tasks used to measure improvement. Tasks which appear to depend upon the same cognitive mechanisms may not do so. Studies along the lines of the one described above can be used to ensure that training tasks do, in fact, involve abilities which underpin practical tasks important to the individual patient. A related observation is that psychometric tests which appear to be analogous to training tasks may also tap different abilities. A thorough analysis of the tasks used in training and in testing and, ideally, a preliminary study investigating the relationship between levels of performance on the two tasks should ensure that the same cognitive mechanisms subserve training and assessment tasks.

6.5 SUMMARY

We have discussed the background to a study evaluating the effectiveness of a computerised retraining program which was designed to provide information required in the planning of services for the brain-injured, within a regional neuropsychology service. The subjects participating in the study and the experimental procedures used have been described in this chapter. The results are presented in the following chapter.

7

Results of the Newcastle Cognitive Retraining Programme (NCRP) Study

This chapter covers results obtained from the NCRP which was outlined in Chapter 6. Data were provided by 23 patients who undertook the retraining programme.

7.1 SUBJECTS

Subjects in the experimental group are described in detail in Chapter 6, including their individual characteristics in relation to age, time since their brain damage was acquired, and determination of premorbid IQ (Table 6.1). This NCRP group had a mean age of 32.6 years (range: 20–66) with a standard deviation of 12.5 years. On average they entered the study 25.5 months after their brain lesion (range: 4–72 months; sd: 21.1), and their mean estimated premorbid IQ was 103.6 (range: 81–122; sd: 11.3).

7.2 COGNITIVE RETRAINING DATA

7.2.1 Introduction

In this section data obtained from the microcomputer training programs themselves are considered. The tasks employed in the study are described in Chapter 6. In this chapter, in 7.2.2, group data are examined, with analyses of change during training being centred upon task scores of subjects at their first and last training sessions, using t-test and Chi^2 procedures.

TABLE 7.1
Improvement in Scores During Training

	1st Session		Final Session				
Variable	mean	sd	mean	sd	n	t value	sig.level
ATTENTION:							
Low information load:	25.2	2.8	27.9	0.5	20	4.25	p<.001
Medium information load:	20.6	17.2	23.6	6.2	20	<1.0	n.s.
High information load:	14.9	14.1	19.4	6.7	20	<1.0	n.s.
SPEED							
Total Correct:	23.1	1.9	24.1	1.8	20	1.71	n.s.
Response Time:	7.2	2.7	6.1	2.8	20	1.27	n.s.
VISCAN:							
Total Correct:	60.6	7.7	63.5	1.3	19	1.62	n.s.
Response Time:	1.2	1.8	0.9	1.6	20	<1.0	n.s.
PROMEM:							
Total Correct:	11.6	3.0	16.0	4.9	20	3.43	p<.01
Immediate Recall:	4.9	0.3	4.7	0.6	20	2.00	p<.05
Short Delay Recall:	3.1	1.3	4.4	1.3	20	3.16	p<.01
Long Delay Recall:	2.2	1.4	3.7	1.9	20	2.84	p<.01
Correct Time and Task:	1.8	2.0	3.1	2.1	20	2.01	p<.05
Right Time/Wrong Task:	1.0	1.4	1.5	1.6	20	1.05	n.s.
Right Task/Wrong Time:	0.5	0.7	0.3	0.7	19	<1.0	n.s.
Repeated Items:	0.2	0.5	0.2	0.7	19	<1.0	n.s.
MEMCHAT:							
Small, Total Correct:	17.3	3.9	18.8	1.5	21	1.65	n.s.
Small, Immediate Recall:	9.2	1.7	10.0	0.2	21	2.14	p<.05
Small, Delayed Recall:	8.1	2.8	8.8	1.4	21	1.03	n.s.
Small, Repeated Items:	0.2	0.5	0.1	0.2	20	<1.0	n.s.
Medium, Total Correct:	16.0	2.9	18.3	2.1	21	2.94	p<.01
Medium, Immediate Recall:	8.4	1.0	9.4	1.0	21	3.24	p<.01
Medium, Delayed Recall:	7.6	2.3	8.9	1.3	21	2.25	p<.05
Medium, Repeated Items:	0.3	0.5	0	0.2	21	2.55	p<.02
Large, Total Correct:	15.5	4.5	18.1	2.3	20	2.30	p<.05
Large, Immediate Recall:	8.0	2.1	9.3	0.9	20	2.55	p<.02
Large, Delayed Recall:	7.7	2.4	8.9	1.5	20	1.90	n.s.
Large, Repeated Items:	0.5	0.9	0.5	2.0	20	<1.0	n.s.
ROADRIGHT:							
Orientation, Total Correct:	13.0	2.9	13.8	2.2	16	<1.0	n.s.
Orientation, Time:	12.0	4.5	8.8	8.5	16	1.29	n.s.
Memory, Total Correct:	16.8	19.0	16.3	2.9	16	<1.0	n.s.
Memory, Response Time:	12.0	7.8	10.2	6.5	16	<1.0	n.s.

Later in this chapter, in 7.2.3, case study material is presented to illustrate the extremes of response to the training regime. Finally, 7.2.4 offers some general discussion on the findings obtained from examination of the training task data.

7.2.2 Group results

Table 7.1 presents the relevant mean, standard deviation, and t-test data for the experimental subjects. As this table shows, significant improvements in scores were observed on a number of the program variables over the training period, even though the subject group was heterogenous with regard to underlying pathology and time since cerebral insult.

Using the MEMCHAT program, 12 indices of subjects' performance were examined, relating to the three levels of information to be remembered, whether recall was required immediately or after delay, and total correct recall (see 6.2 in Chapter 6). Table 7.1 indicates that 8 of these index variables show significant change during training, there being a tendency for the accuracy of processing of smaller amounts of information to be less likely to change over the training period. This evidence of significant improvement in memory performance during training was paralleled by results obtained from another training programme addressing memory functioning—PROMEM (6.2 in Chapter 6). Using this program a majority of the variables measured, including immediate and delayed memory performance, reflect significant improvement during the training period.

Results from programmes focusing upon other types of cognitive performance were slightly less impressive when examined by t-test analyses. Neither of the speed variables examined, reflecting speed of decision making and accuracy, indicated significant improvement during training. Similarly, VISCAN, which is based upon visual reaction time according to spatial position of stimulus, yielded only non-significant t-test findings. The attention information processing training programme yielded evidence of significant change on 1 index (out of 3).

The data displayed in Table 7.1 provides strong evidence of improvement during training, based upon t-test analyses. However, given the heterogeneity of the experimental group in terms of underlying pathology, time since damage, and age, it can be argued that the contribution of t-test evaluations will be constrained by the range of performance of subjects within the group; this tends to inflate standard deviation. The data were, therefore, also examined in relation to the direction of change in variable scores between first and final sessions. Single-sample Chi^2 analyses were employed, given the hypothesis that, in the absence of any training effect, the probabililty of a subject's scores changing in a "poorer" or a "better" direction is equal. With one degree of freedom this type of analysis may only be utilised for cases where the expected frequency in each of the two cells is at least 5 (Siegel, 1956). Table 7.2 summarises the results of examining the training program variables using this method. Expected figures vary in the table according to the number of subjects showing scores which remained unchanged during training (these scores were omitted from the analyses; the principal reason for unchanging scores was production of a response at the "ceiling" of the programme variable at the first training session).

Table 7.2 shows strong, consistent evidence of improvements in performance on PROMEM and attention variables. Approximately 50% of MEMCHAT

TABLE 7.2
Chi-square Analyses of Changes in Training Scores Between First and Final Sessions

Variable	Expected Frequency	Observed Frequency	Chi² Value	Sig. Level
MEMCHAT:				
Small, Total Correct:	7.0	11	4.57	p<.05
Small, Delayed Recall:	6.0	8	1.33	n.s.
Medium, Total Correct:	10.0	16	7.20	p<.01
Medium, Immediate Recall:	7.5	13	8.07	p<.01
Medium, Delayed Recall:	8.0	13	6.25	p<.02
Large, Total Correct:	8.5	12	2.88	n.s.
Large, Immediate Recall:	7.5	11	3.27	n.s.
Large, Delayed Recall:	5.0	7	1.60	n.s.
PROMEM:				
Total Correct:	9.0	16	10.89	p<.001
Immediate Recall:	5.0	9	6.40	p<.02
Short Delay Recall:	8.0	14	9.00	p<.01
Long Delay Recall:	9.5	15	6.37	p<.02
Correct Time and Task:	7.5	14	11.27	p<.001
SPEED:				
Total Correct:	7.5	12	5.40	p<.05
Response Time:	10.0	14	3.20	n.s.
VISCAN:				
Response Time:	9.0	18	18.00	p<.001
ATTENTION:				
Low information load:	8.0	16	16.00	p<.001
Medium information load:	8.5	14	7.12	p<.01
High information load:	10.0	18	12.80	p<.001
ROADRIGHT:				
Orientation Time:	7.0	13	10.29	p<.01
Memory, Total Correct:	7.0	13	10.29	p<.01
Memory, Response Time:	7.5	11	3.27	n.s.

indices yielded significant gains during training, and SPEED and VISCAN also offered supportive results. Use of the Chi^2 method of analysis produced a slightly larger number of significant findings than did the t-test approach.

7.2.3 Case Study Material and Clinico-pathological Aspects

Within the experimental group receiving the NCRP, 2 neuropathological "subgroups" contained sufficient subjects to make it possible to consider their data separately—head-injured (HI; n = 17) and stroke (ST; n = 5), as shown in Table 6.1. A major practical question regarding the use of microcomputer CRP is whether outcome varies according to neuropathology; for example, are computer retraining programs effective with head-injured patients, but not with stroke patients?

Initial t-test analysis confirmed that there were no significant differences between the 2 diagnostic groups with regard to time since acquired brain damage (t <1; ns), or with regard to NART-predicted premorbid IQ (t = 1.709; ns). Comparisons of the 2 subgroups undergoing CRP, using t-tests yielded no evidence of differences between HI and ST subjects on the attention program variables at the beginning or end of training, with the exception of the condition in which 3 digits are to be remembered (see 6.3.2 in Chapter 6). In the latter condition, the HI subgroup both started training at a higher level (t = 2.528; p <.05) and had a higher final point on completion of training (t = 2.177; p <.05). However, the mean improvement in score during training was virtually identical for the two groups (7.4 for HI, 7.8 for ST; t <1; ns). The gains during training are presented in Fig. 7.1.

No significant differences between the 2 subgroups were observed, either at the beginning or end of training, on the PRICE RIGHT or VISCAN program variables. Similarly, 8 PROMEM variables were examined at the start and end of training, with nearly all yielding non-significant t-test comparisons for the ST and HI subgroups at both the first and final training session. The HI subgroup did, however, score significantly higher (t = 2.879; p <.02) at the start of training, and at the final session (t = 2.546; p <.05) in terms of "total correct" score. Fig. 7.2 illustrates this point. Again, though, there was no significant difference between the HI and ST subgroups in terms of improvement in total score (t = 1.050; ns).

The MEMCHAT program included the largest number of variables (23) on which HI and ST subjects were compared at the beginning and end of the training. As with other training programs, the large majority of t-test comparisons yielded only non-significant values. On 2 variables, total number correct (medium difficulty) and delayed recall score (medium difficulty), the HI sub-group scored significantly higher at the start of the training (t = 4.229; p <.001 t = 4.27; p <.001, respectively). Fig. 7.3 reflects these differences.

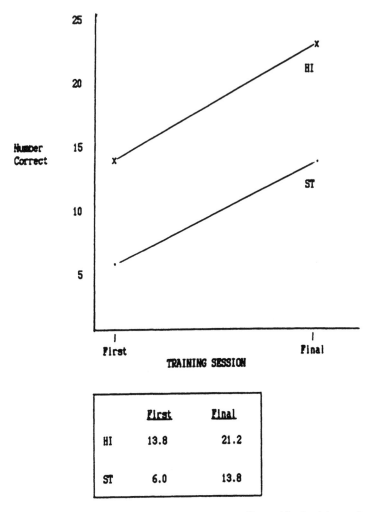

FIG. 7.1.   Changes in ATTENTION (Difficult) scores between first and final training session, for head-injury (HI) and stroke (ST) subjects.

However, these significant differences are no longer present at the end of training, and it can be seen from Fig. 7.3 that the reason for this is the "catching up" of stroke subjects during training to the relatively stable scores across CRP of the HI subjects. With regard to "total correct" score, ST subjects show a significantly greater improvement during training (t = 4.560; p <.001). A similar finding is noted for the delayed recall variable (t = 5.077; p <.001).

The ROADRIGHT program findings are consistent with those presented above, in that no significant differences between the HI and ST groups are observed, either at the start or end of training.

The data considered in this section, therefore, offer no convincing evidence that the NCRP microcomputer retraining is differentially suitable for patients who have suffered a head injury or a stroke—both are able to benefit significantly from entering the program.

Within the subgroup of five ST patients there is no single subject who offers ideal case study results for the training experience. However, in a number of ways, subject 15 (EH) offers a good example. He was close to the average age of stroke patients at 66 years, and the issue of any continuing spontaneous recovery did not arise in his case, as EH suffered his stroke 4 years prior to entering the

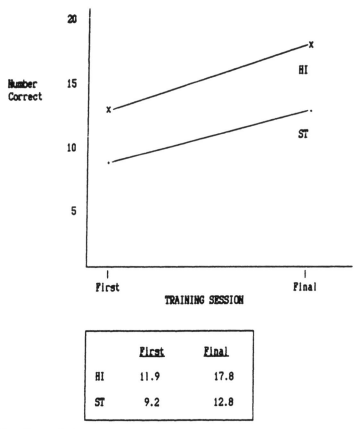

	First	Final
HI	11.9	17.8
ST	9.2	12.8

FIG. 7.2.   Changes in PROMEM, total correct scores between first and final training session, for head-injured (HI) and stroke (ST) subjects.

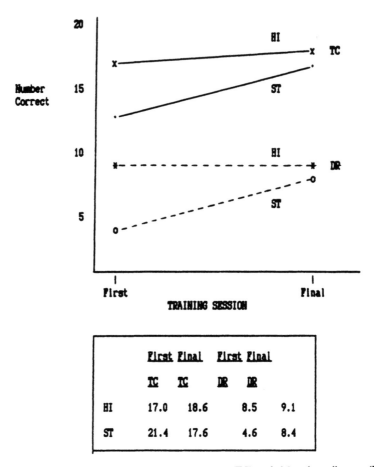

FIG. 7.3.   Changes in MEMCHAT total correct scores (TC) and delayed recall score (DR), medium difficulty, for HI and ST subjects between first and final training session.

NCRP. The rating of his improvement in cognitive functioning between beginning and end of training (gauged from the cognitive section of the questionnaire; see 7.4 in Chapter 7) was the highest of any patient in the study. His carer's rating of his cognitive gains was, similarly, the largest noted from any carer. The subjective ratings obtain support from the objective retraining data. Patient EH showed a number of good gains on PROMEM indices, as Fig. 7.4 demonstrates.

It is not clear why patient EH (case 15) showed the greatest improvement of the ST subgroup on the PROMEM index "total correct". Table 7.3 includes data on the ST subjects for a number of background variables. It can be seen that case

15 was the oldest of the stroke patients in the group, and that at 4 years post-stroke he was obviously not gaining assistance from continuing spontaneous recovery. There is no obvious determinant of PROMEM improvement from the background variables of age, premorbid IQ, and time since brain damage. Perhaps the most important factors operating are the extent and severity of stroke suffered by the patient.

Case 15 did not show large gains on the MEMCHAT "total correct" score during training, although as Table 7.3 shows, his performance was close to the ceiling of the task at the beginning of CRP in 2 out of the 3 conditions (the maximum score for any exposure level is 20). Table 7.4 does indicate that the ST subjects generally showed good improvement between first and final CRP session, except where the initial scores were already close to the maximum at the

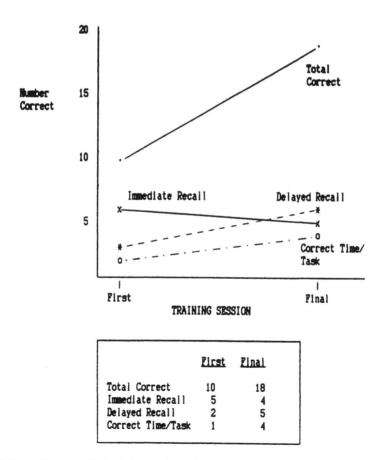

	First	Final
Total Correct	10	18
Immediate Recall	5	4
Delayed Recall	2	5
Correct Time/Task	1	4

FIG. 7.4.   Changes in PROMEM scores for patient EH between first and final training session.

TABLE 7.3
MEMCHAT Total Correct Score for ST Subjects

| | Information Load | | | | | |
| | Small | | Medium | | Large | |
Case No	First	Final	First	Final	First	Final
2	20	18	15	19	12	20
4	12	18	11	15	15	13
9	15	17	11	18	10	N/A
11	12	15	11	18	15	14
15	19	20	14	18	19	20

First shows score at first training session
Final shows score at final training session

start of training. The table shows there was a strong general tendency for ST subject scores to approximate the task's ceiling by the end of training, thereby indicating that the largest improvements are shown by the patients whose initial scores were poorest. Again, inspection of Table 7.3 does not suggest that improvement relates to age, IQ or time since lesion acquired.

ATTENTION is the NCRP program with the highest information processing demands, and as such would be expected to correlate negatively with age (see 6.3 in Chapter 6 for description). Table 7.4 reflects this, with the two older patients (cases 9 and 15) scoring poorly in the most difficult condition (three digits). Table 7.5 also shows that subjects attained the test's ceiling (maximum score 28) in the easier, one digit condition by the completion of CRP. It is clear from the figure that the difficult three digit condition remained a very demanding task for ST subjects, even at the end of training.

TABLE 7.4
ATTENTION Total Correct Scores for ST Subjects

| | Sequence to be Recalled | | | | | |
| | One Digit | | Two Digits | | Three Digits | |
Case No	First	Final	First	Final	First	Final
2	27	28	22	18	15	17
4	26	28	8	27	3	16
9	26	28	11	23	2	6
11	28	28	20	28	4	21
15	20	28	18	14	6	9

First shows score at first training session
Final shows score at final training session

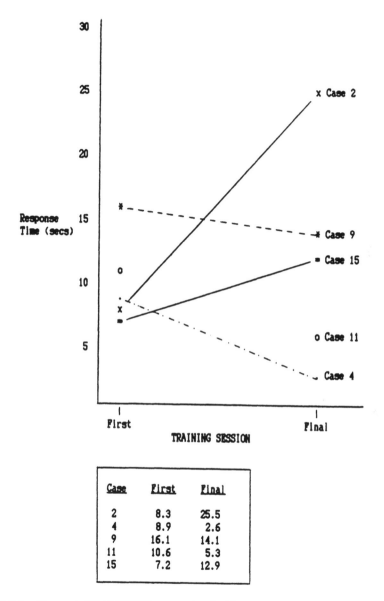

Case	First	Final
2	8.3	25.5
4	8.9	2.6
9	16.1	14.1
11	10.6	5.3
15	7.2	12.9

FIG. 7.5. Changes in ROADRIGHT memory time for ST subjects between first and final training session.

The remaining NCRP tasks of ROADRIGHT, VISCAN, and SPEED all include response time measurement. The ST subjects often showed little subgroup consistency on these measures: Fig. 7.5 presents the data for each patient in relation to ROADRIGHT memory time, and it can be seen that there is no general trend towards improvement (increased speed), nor is there a tendency for patients' final session scores to converge. Cases 4 and 11, who were the youngest subjects, showed the fastest final response times, although case 2 (third youngest) provided the longest final time.

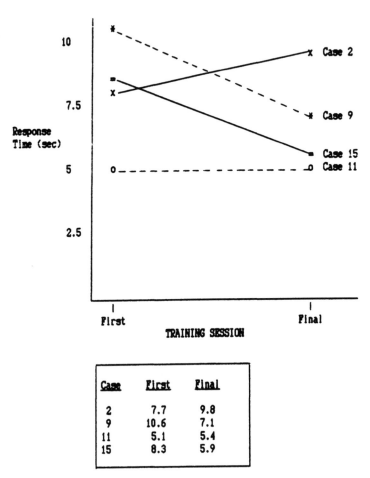

Case	First	Final
2	7.7	9.8
9	10.6	7.1
11	5.1	5.4
15	8.3	5.9

FIG. 7.6.   Changes in SPEED response time for ST subjects between first and final training session.

The response time variable from SPEED (Fig. 7.6) showed a similar lack of consistency in terms of there being no good evidence of improvement in performance during training.

The orientation response time from ROADRIGHT, however, (Fig. 7.7) did show a pattern of improvement during CRP. This task differs from the others considered above, in that it measures spatial decision making time, rather than drawing upon an information-loaded task (SPEED) and memory (ROAD-RIGHT memory time).

Results from the Orientation condition suggest that this aspect of the ROADRIGHT task was too easy, in that all subjects obtained the maximum number correct, or close to this level, at the first training session. However, some ST subjects showed marked improvements during training in terms of number correct on the memory component of the ROADRIGHT (Fig. 7.7a). Again, no predictors of improvements are apparent in Fig. 7.7a in terms of age (although

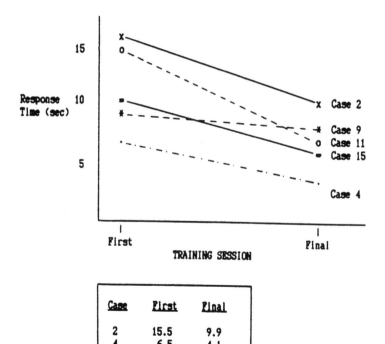

Case	First	Final
2	15.5	9.9
4	6.5	4.1
9	9.1	7.6
11	15.5	7.1
15	10.0	6.4

FIG. 7.7.   Changes in ROADRIGHT orientation time for ST subjects between first and final training session.

the older patients—cases 9 and 15—started training from a low position), premorbid IQ, or time since brain damage acquired.

The experimental group contained 17 subjects who had suffered a head injury, and 5 head-injured subjects were recruited to act as control subjects. Tables 6.1 and 6.2 reflect the wide range of time since brain damage, age, and premorbid IQ amongst the subjects. For "control" purposes, time since brain damage acquired was viewed as the most important matching variable, although age and IQ were also seen to be relevant, as was level of pre-training neuropsychological assessment performance. Later in this chapter, in 7.3.3, reference will be made to control subjects, according to the most relevant matching variable at a particular point. Control subject 1 (C1) showed reasonable match with case 10, C2 with case 17, C3 with case 8, C4 with case 5,

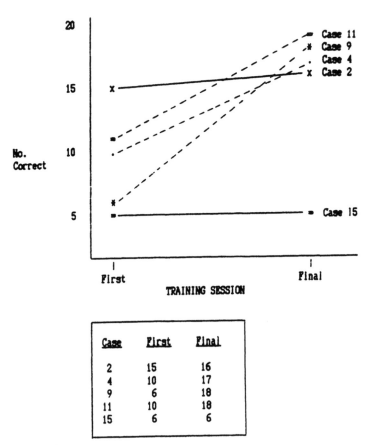

Case	First	Final
2	15	16
4	10	17
9	6	18
11	10	18
15	6	6

FIG. 7.7a. Changes in ROADRIGHT memory correct for ST subjects between first and final training session.

TABLE 7.5
PROMEM Total Correct and Short Delay Scores for
HI Subjects

	Score			
	Total Correct		*Short Delay*	
Case No.	*First*	*Final*	*First*	*Final*
3	12	15	3	3
5	16	21	3	6
6	11	11	2	2
7	15	20	3	5
8	10	23	3	6
10	13	10	3	3
12	13	23	3	6
13	12	23	4	6
17	9	16	3	4
18	15	21	3	6
19	20	21	8	5
20	10	19	4	4

First shows score at first training session
Final shows score at final training session

and C5 with case 18. Other subject matches will be mentioned below as appropriate.

Seven HI subjects and their carers completed questionnaires pre- and post-training, with 6 patients feeling that their cognitive functioning had improved during training, with 5 of their carers also perceiving these gains. Table 7.5 provides information on the HI subjects at the start and finish of training in terms of PROMEM total correct and short delay scores (the pattern was very similar for the other PROMEM variables and showed significant improvements during training—LD and CTT; see Table 7.1). Table 7.5 shows a variety of response by the HI subjects to the PROMEM tasks. Subjects 8, 13, 12, 18 and 5 showed the better gains, with subjects 6, 10 and 3 performing more poorly.

Pearson correlation coefficients did not indicate significant relationships between PROMEM and total correct score at first and final training sessions with age ($r = -0.44$; $r = 0.24$, respectively), time since brain damage (0.16; -0.31) or premorbid IQ (0.26; 0.39).

Given that the number of MEMCHAT variables which could be examined is large, further analysis concentrated upon the total correct score in the three information conditions, as was the case with ST subgroup (Table 7.3). Table 7.6 presents the data for the HI subgroup and shows that for a number of patients (e.g. 3, 12, 13 and 19) the MEMCHAT program appears to have been inappropriate—for some patients their scores were at, or close to, the ceiling of the test in each of the three information conditions at the start of training.

TABLE 7.6
MEMCHAT Total Correct Score for HI Subjects

| | Information Load | | | | | |
| | Small | | Medium | | Large | |
Case No	First	Final	First	Final	First	Final
3	19	20	17	20	19	20
5	20	20	17	20	18	18
6	4	16	13	12	5	19
7	20	20	18	20	16	20
8	19	20	20	19	15	20
10	18	19	14	17	4	15
12	20	20	19	19	20	19
13	20	19	18	20	20	20
17	19	19	20	19	14	16
18	19	20	19	20	18	20
19	20	20	20	19	20	20
20	20	20	15	20	19	20

First shows score at first training session
Final shows score at final training session

Considerable individual variation in scores and change in score is apparent from inspection of Table 7.6. The highest gains during training in the large information processing condition had been achieved by patients 6 and 10. As these patients were 60 months and 20 months post head injury, respectively, their improvements are not likely to be due to continuing natural recovery. In fact, there was a sizeable, but non-significant, correlation (0.38) between improvement in score in the large information processing condition and time since brain damage was acquired. There was also a significant negative correlation (-0.71; $p < .01$) between premorbid IQ and improvement in score in this condition. However, this effect stemmed from the fact that there was a significant correlation (0.72; $p < .01$) between score at the start of training and premorbid IQ. With the effect of initial score partialled out, the correlation between improvement in score and premorbid IQ then drops to a negligible level (-0.12). Thus, the meaningful relationship is between premorbid IQ and score at the start of training, with higher IQ subjects starting with a significantly better score. However, this initial advantage does not persist at the end of training (data in Table 7.6 suggest that this may be due to the test's ceiling being a limiting factor), given that the correlation between final session score and premorbid IQ is much lower (0.36).

To a smaller degree than MEMCHAT, some test ceiling effects were apparent during ATTENTION training, particularly in the one digit condition (see Table 7.7). In the most difficult (three digits) condition, the HI subjects generally

TABLE 7.7
ATTENTION Total Correct Score for HI Subjects

| | Sequence to be Recalled | | | | | |
| | One Digit | | Two Digits | | Three Digits | |
Case No	First	Final	First	Final	First	Final
3	24	28	22	23	16	15
5	24	28	16	28	12	28
6	28	28	4	15	6	11
7	23	27	15	23	18	26
8	26	28	17	28	18	24
10	24	28	13	5	9	17
12	27	28	28	28	26	28
13	26	28	25	27	10	27
17	27	28	17	19	4	8
18	26	28	7	27	9	22
19	28	28	12	27	18	22
20	26	28	11	28	13	26

First shows score at first training session
Final shows score at final training session

provided good evidence of improvement during training, patients 5, 13, 18, and 19 showing large gains. Unlike the MEMCHAT findings, HI subjects with higher premorbid IQs produced only marginally better ATTENTION three digits scores at the initial training session (0.37; ns). Again, no evidence that initial score related to the time since brain damage occurred was noted; in fact, patients with larger post-lesion periods obtained marginally lower initial training scores in the three digits ATTENTION condition (–0.41; ns). Nor was the amount of improvement during training related to the time since brain damage (–0.22).

Table 7.8 provides data on HI patients' response times on the ROADRIGHT and SPEED retraining tasks (unfortunately, some subjects did not undertake training on all ROADRIGHT subtasks). As with the ST subjects (see Fig. 7.7), the HI subjects generally showed marked improvements in response time across training on the ROADRIGHT Orientation Task, with more mixed results for the ROADRIGHT memory time and (particularly) the SPEED response time. However, changes in SPEED response time, and initial session SPEED response time, showed only negligible correlations with age, time since brain damage, and premorbid IQ.

Non-significant correlations were also noted from these variables with ROADRIGHT memory time, in relation to both improvement during training and initial score. However, ROADRIGHT orientation time at first session score showed a significant correlation with age (0.77; $p < 0.1$), and even having partialled out the effects of first session score, it shows a noteworthy (0.63; ns)

TABLE 7.8
ROADRIGHT and SPEED Scores for HI Subjects

| | ROADRIGHT | | | | SPEED | |
| | Orientation Time | | Memory Time | | Response Time | |
Case No	First	Final	First	Final	First	Final
3	9.7	8.5	12.7	7.3	8.7	7.5
5	9.3	5.3	3.1	5.3	5.5	5.2
6	—	—	—	—	5.2	6.4
7	—	—	—	—	4.1	2.8
8	17.1	6.4	6.3	4.0	5.3	3.9
10	7.5	6.5	8.4	6.3	10.6	7.3
12	5.6	3.2	6.3	4.8	3.0	3.7
13	—	—	7.3	8.3	5.9	4.0
17	17.9	7.6	—	—	7.9	5.9
18	13.9	6.5	15.4	6.7	8.5	4.6
19	—	—	—	—	4.7	3.2
20	15.9	7.3	33.4	21.9	4.9	3.0

First shows score at first training session
Final shows score at final training session

relationship with improvement in ROADRIGHT orientation time for the HI subgroup: Whereas older subjects show larger initial orientation times, they also tend to show a greater improvement in speed of response during training.

7.3 PRE-TRAINING AND POST-TRAINING NEUROPSYCHOLOGICAL ASSESSMENT DATA

7.3.1 Introduction

As described in Chapter 6, the NCRP included pre- and post-training assessments of subjects in both experimental and control groups. A large number of variables were available for examination, and consideration of only a subset of the data is possible in this chapter. As in 2.2 in Chapter 2, examination of the data was based upon t-test and Chi^2 analyses procedures (see 7.3.2 in this chapter). Case study illustrations are provided in 7.3.3, and discussion of the assessment data is offered in 7.3.4.

7.3.2 Group Results

Visuospatial Assessment.   This was centred upon the BMAPS "little men" (LM) task, cancellation tasks, and line bisection measures (see Chapter 3).

There are a large number of scores provided by the "little men" test; group scores for all of these have not been examined. Examination of change in little

TABLE 7.9
"Little Men" Scores at Each Assessment Point

Variable	Pre-training 1		Pre-training 2		Post-training 1		Post-training 2	
	Mean	SD	Mean	SD	Mean	SD	Mean	SD
LMUF:	5.2	2.3	6.3	2.0	7.2	1.6	7.2	1.2
LMDB:	4.4	2.5	4.6	2.2	5.2	2.1	5.7	2.1

men scores focuses particularly upon those two measures of accuracy of performance which involve the greatest degree of mental rotation (little man upright, facing subject [LMUF] and little man upside down, facing away from subject [LMDB]). Table 7.9 presents some of the little men data at the various assessment points. Using t-test analyses, the experimental group's LM scores were compared at these assessment points. No significant values were observed. However, Chi^2 analyses yielded interesting results, as shown in Table 7.10.

Whilst no significant changes are apparent between the two assessment sessions pre-training, LMUF shows a significant improvement during training, which continues to strengthen at subsequent follow-up. The LMDB variable does not change significantly during training, although significant gains are apparent by the second post-training assessment.

Neither the cancellation tasks nor the line bisection tasks yielded evidence of significant improvement in scores following training, using both t-test analyses and Chi^2 analyses.

Information Processing Assessment. The contributing tasks in this area were WAIS digit symbol and Coughlan IP procedures (see Chapter 3 for description). Although t-test values did not indicate significant changes in digit symbol scores

TABLE 7.10
Change in "Little Men" Scores between Assessments

	Comparison					
	Pre-training 1/ Pre-training 2		Pre-training 1/ Post-training 1		Pre-training 1/ Post-training 2	
Variable	Chi^2	Sig	Chi^2	Sig	Chi^2	Sig
LMUF:	2.88	n.s.	8.00	***	12.25	****
LMDB:	<1	n.s.	2.28	n.s.	5.56	**

** $p < .02$
*** $p < .01$
**** $p < .001$

across training, Chi^2 analyses (Table 7.11) pointed to no change between pre-training assessments 1 and 2, although significant improvements were observed between the pre-training 1 and post-training 1 assessments. This significant gain fell slightly by the second post-training assessment. Coughlan IP tasks measure speed of processing and accuracy. These measures were only employed at pre-training 1 and post-training 1 assessments. Again, t-test evaluation of change was non-significant, though Chi^2 analyses of scores indicated significant improvements (Table 7.11) following training in both IP speed and IP adjusted speed (adjusted to remove the "motor" component).

Memory Assessment. This included Rey AVLT and Coughlan learning tasks (see Chapter 3). The t-test data provided in 7.12 offers little evidence of Rey AVLT improvement following training. Chi^2 analyses (Table 7.13) suggests significant gains in final learning level of list A (a trial A5) following training, although Table 7.13 suggests significant change was beginning prior to training. Initial learning (first trial of list A and list B) appears unchanged across the training period.

Motor performance. This was assessed using the Halstead–Reitan tapping test. Neither t-test analyses, nor Chi^2 examination, suggested significant gains in pure motor performance as a result of undergoing the NCRP.

7.3.3 Case Study Material and Clinical Pathological Aspects

Visuospatial Assessment. Pre-training assessment 1, post-training 1, and post-training 2, t-test comparisons of HI and ST subgroup performance on the LMUF and LMDB variables (see Visuospatial Assessment in 7.3.2 in this

TABLE 7.11
Change in Information Processing Scores between Assessments

| | Comparison | | | | | |
| | Pre-training 1/ Pre-training 2 | | Pre-training 1/ Post-training 1 | | Pre-training 1/ Post-training 2 | |
Variable	*Chi²*	*Sig*	*Chi²*	*Sig*	*Chi²*	*Sig*
Digit Symbol:	<1	n.s.	4.50	*	3.60	n.s.
I.P. Speed:	N/A		7.36	***	N/A	
I.P. Adjusted:	N/A		5.33	*	N/A	

    * $p < .05$
   ** $p < .02$
  *** $p < .01$

TABLE 7.12
Change in REY AVLT Scores during Training

Variable	Pre-training 1/ Post-training 1	Pre-training 1/ Post-training 2
	t.	*t.*
Trial: A1:	<1	1.161
A2:	1.014	<1
A3:	1.095	<1
A4:	<1	<1
A5:	<1	<1
A6:	<1	<1
B	1.548	<1
%Proactive Interference	<1	<1
%Retroactive Interference	<1	2.018
Hits	<1	<1
False+	<1	<1

All results non-significant

Chapter) yielded no significant results. Table 7.14 provides the mean and standard deviation data for the subgroups. For the LMUF variable the HI subgroup showed a significant improvement between pre-training 1 and post-training 1 assessments (t = 2.508; p <.02), and between pre-training 1 and post-training 2 assessments (t = 2.974; p <0.1), though examination of changes in the LMDB scores for the subgroup for these two intervals yielded non-significant results (t <1; t = 1.348, respectively). For the ST subgroup, only the pre-training 1–post-training 1 changes for the LMDB variable produced a t value above 1.0 (t = 1,567; ns).

As with the results discussed earlier in this chapter, in 7.3.2, uncritical inclusion of all scores in t-test analyses is not warranted, given that some subjects

TABLE 7.13
Change in REY AVLT Scores between Assessments

Variable	Pre-training 1/ Pre-training 2		Pre-training 1/ Post-training 1		Pre-training 1/ Post-training 2	
	Chi^2	Sig	Chi^2	Sig	Chi^2	Sig
Trial A1:	<1	n.s.	−1.870	n.s.	<1	n.s.
A2:	<1	n.s.	<1	n.s.	<1	n.s.
A3:	<1	n.s.	<1	n.s.	<1	n.s.
A4:	<1	n.s.	1.463	n.s.	<1	n.s.
A5:	1.977	n.s.	4.365	*	1.348	n.s.

*p<.05

TABLE 7.14
Pre- and Post-Training Scores for HI and ST Subjects on the LMUF and
LMDB Variables

Assessment	LMUF: HI			LMUF: ST		
	Mean	SD	n	Mean	SD	n
Pre-Train 1:	5.0	2.3	14	6.3	2.9	4
Post-Train 1:	7.0	1.9	14	7.3	1.3	4
Post-Train 2:	7.1	1.3	14	7.5	0.9	4
	LMDB: HI			LMDB: ST		
	Mean	SD	n	Mean	SD	n
Pre-Train 1:	4.1	2.5	14	4.5	2.7	4
Post-Train 1:	4.9	2.1	14	7.0	1.7	4
Post-Train 2:	5.3	2.2	14	6.0	1.6	4

were at, or close to, test ceiling performance pre-training. In the case of the LMUF and LMDB variables, the maximum possible score is 8.

Unfortunately, case matching of those subjects whose pre-training assessments were 5 (or less), and who were assessed at each of the two post-training follow-ups does not suggest that the experimental subjects improved more than the control subjects: Although they did not receive training to improve their visuospatial skills, control subjects showed gains, as illustrated in Table 7.15.

This latter finding suggests a major task-learning component in undertaking this LM test. No significant correlations between age, time since brain damage, or premorbid IQ with pre-training score or change in score were noted.

TABLE 7.15
LMDB Scores for Selected HI, ST and Controlled Subjects

Case No.	Assessment Point		
	Pre-Training 1	Post-Training 1	Post-Training 2
3 (HI)	3	3	3
6 (HI)	2	7	3
8 (HI)	4	4	6
12 (HI)	4	8	7
4 (ST)	5	8	7
9 (ST)	2	8	5
11 (ST)	3	4	4
C1	5	6	8
C2	0	0	3
C3	0	4	4
C4	3	4	2

Subjects selected if initial score was ≤5 for the LMDB variable

Information Processing Assessment. On the digit symbol test age scale scores for the ST subgroup came very close to being significantly better than the HI subjects at the pre-training 1 assessment (t = 2.076; ns), and ST subjects performed significantly better at both post-training 1 (t = 2.590; P <.05) and post-training 2 (t = 3.03; P <.01). Although the control subgroup (C) was not significantly different to the HI subgroup, it performed more poorly than the ST subjects even at pre-training 1 (t = 2.693; P <.05).

Figure 7.8 illustrates the changes in digit symbol scores for these subgroups at the three assessment points, suggesting a similar pattern for HI and C subjects, and a non-significant improvement (t = 1.590; ns) for the ST subgroup between pre-training 1 and post-training 2. Although not significant, a sizeable correlation (0.46) was noted between change in digit symbol score and premorbid IQ in the combined HI and ST subjects. Only a negligible correlation (.02) was obtained between time since brain damage and change in score. Within the HI subgroup the highest gain in score (5 scale points) was noted for case 7 (23-year-old male, 6 months post head injury, premorbid IQ of 95), although all of his improvement appeared to dissipate by the post-training 2 assessment. Smaller gains were also noted for patients 3 and 8 in this subgroup, and within the ST subgroup cases 4 and 9 showed the best gains (see Fig. 7.9). Fig. 7.9 depicts the unpredictability of change over the training period, and subsequently.

Coughlan information processing tasks were only assessed at pre-training 1 and post-training 1. Consistent with the digit symbol findings, the ST subgroup performed significantly better than the HI subgroup (t = 2.259; P<.05) at pre-training assessment on the "IP adjusted" variable. However, ST subject scores remained stable during the training period and the HI subjects improved, so that by the post-training follow-up the difference between the two subgroups was non-significant (see Fig. 7.10). The control subject scores showed a non-significant drop between the two assessment points, as shown in Fig. 7.10. The data in this figure indicate noteworthy gains in the HI subgroup's "IP adjusted" scores following training. Unlike the digit symbol results, no evidence of a positive relationship between premorbid IQ and change in "IP adjusted" score was noted in patients undergoing training. Similarly, non-significant findings were also obtained in relation to age and time since brain damage acquired. Subjects 12, 13, and 17 within the HI subgroup showed the highest "IP adjusted" scores after training, these subjects having an age range of 24 to 48 years, a time since brain damage range of 6 to 35 months, and average IQ. For the ST subgroup, case 4, a 36-year-old patient with a premorbid IQ of 122 and a time since acquisition of brain damage of 5 years, obtained the most impressive results.

The Coughlan IP motor speed variable produces similar results, as shown in Fig. 7.11. For the 3 control subjects on whom data was collected, the scores for 2 (C2, C3) remain virtually unchanged between the 2 assessment points and for

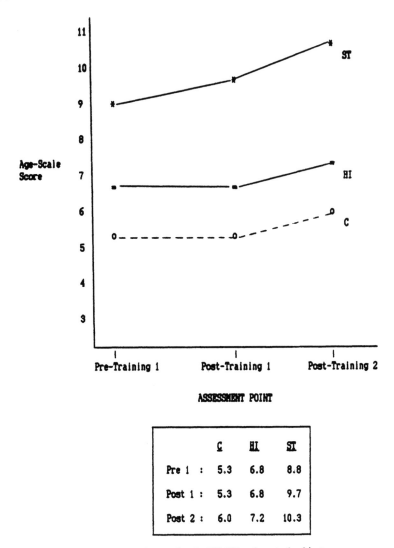

FIG. 7.8.   Changes in digit symbol score for the ST, HI and control subjects.

the other (C5) the patient's responses were slower at the second follow up. As Fig. 7.11 reflects, all but one of the 8 HI subjects tested at both follow-up points showed improvements in motor speed across training. Of the three ST subjects, the scores of one (case 9), remain virtually unchanged, and the other two (cases 5 and 15) showed some gains.

A noteworthy, though non-significant, negative correlation (–0.40) was found between pre-training 1 IP motor speed score and age for the combined HI

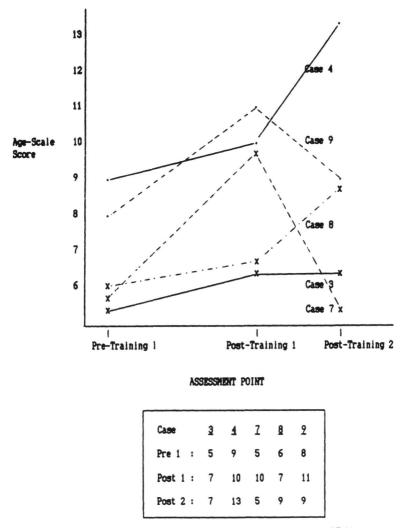

FIG. 7.9.   Changes in digit symbol score for individual cases of HI (x) and ST (.).

and ST subgroups. However, only small correlations were seen between the pre-training motor speed score and the time since brain damage (–0.05) and premorbid IQ (0.20). Correlations of age, time since lesion, and premorbid IQ all yielded low correlations with change in motor speed score between the 2 follow-up points. Matching on time since brain damage, age, and premorbid IQ for C2—case 17 and C3—case 8 yielded the plots depicted in Fig. 7.12: C subjects showed small reductions in speed between the two follow-up points, with the two HI cases improving their motor speed during this interval.

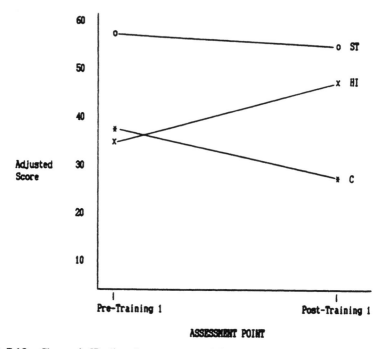

FIG. 7.10.   Changes in IP adjusted scores across training for HI, ST, and C subjects.

7.4 QUESTIONNAIRE DATA

7.4.1 Introduction

Prior to training, ratings were obtained from patients and carers with regard to the patients' premorbid functioning and current status. After the cognitive training programme both respondents completed the questionnaire again on the basis of "current" status. The questionnaire itself is reproduced in Appendix IV. Also provided in that appendix, in Table IV.1, are the percentage responses of both subject and carer in each category, for each questionnaire item. Examination of Table IV.1 suggests a number of interesting features, covering the degree of rating agreement between patients and carers, and their perception of improvements in functioning, or not, following the NCRP.

7.4.2 Patient and Carer Ratings

The two respondent groups were in close agreement in tending to view patients' premorbid condition in a very favourable light. For example, within the 11 items constituting the "memory and concentration" section of the questionnaire, no

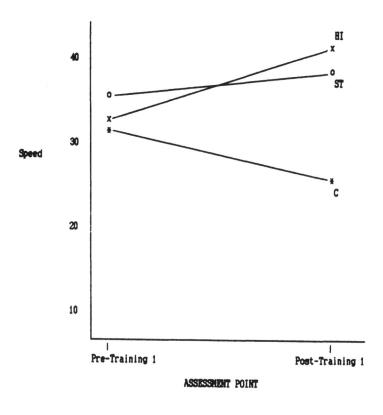

	Pre 1	Post 1
HI	32	41
ST	35	39
C	32	26

FIG. 7.11.   Changes in IP speed scores between follow ups for HI, ST, and C subgroups.

carer rated their patient relative as poor, and only 2 (out of 20) patient respondents viewed themselves as poor on any item in this section. A similar, though not as extreme, pattern of recollection for the premorbid position was also obtained from patients and carers on the "feeling" section items. These perceptions might just be viewed as understandable retrospective distortions, were it not for the fact that a much less "rosy" picture is presented by patients' and carers' perceptions in relation to the section on how patients used to spend their time in the premorbid period. Items in this section include reference to

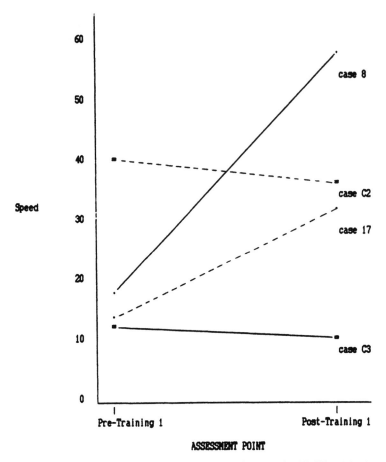

FIG. 7.12.   Changes in IP speed scores between follow ups for matching HI, ST and C subgroups.

washing up, housework, and repairs/jobs around the house. It seems to us, therefore, that the above pattern of judgement does not reflect an idealised perception of the patient by either patient or carer.

The overall group correspondence for patients and carers across the questionnaire items in relation to premorbid function is very close, with rating frequency differences usually being within 5%–10%, and only 8 of the 50 items showing differences of 20%. Agreement between the two respondent groups for frequency ratings immediately pre-training is also heartening (Table IV.1), though a tendency is noted for the carers to view their patient relative as performing more poorly in relation to "memory and concentration" items. Clear differences are apparent between the ratings of the two groups with regard to the "feelings" items of irritability and tactfulness, with reduced patient insight perhaps being a contributory factor to the differences observed. Most subsequent items show close agreement between the two groups. Again, perhaps with the benefit of greater insight, the carers' group rate the position post-training less positively than do the patients. For example, on all "memory and concentration" items, except one, the carers' group perceives the patients as performing at a lower level than do the patients themselves. A similar, though less marked, pattern is seen for the remaining questionnaire items.

The most interesting question is whether patients and carers perceive that the patients have changed following the NCRP. This can be investigated by examining shifts in the pattern of ratings across the training period. One convenient method for this is to calculate the changes in percentages of patients rated in the "poorest" categories within each respondent group, for each item, on the basis of data presented in Table IV.1. This method is the most meaningful in terms of judging the perceived practical effects of changes in level of cognitive functioning in that ratings outside these categories indicate that the patient or carer considers the level of cognitive functioning in the area under consideration to be average or above average or that he or she does not experience frequent occurrences of cognitive failure in the area. Thus, shift is of most significance for patients rating their abilities within the poorest categories since these are the patients who perceive themselves as having problems which seriously affect day-to-day functioning and, for these patients, final ratings outside these categories represent significant functional gain. Using this approach, Table 7.16 specifies all items where the changes in the number of patients rated as being in the poorest category was 20%, or greater. It is clear from this table that the patient group perceives that greater positive changes had occurred. However, the correlation of patients' and carers' rated changes across all 50 items (Spearman Rank Correlation; Siegel, 1956) yields a significant value ($R = 0.395$; $p < .01$, 1-tailed) reflecting similarities in the ratings provided by the two groups.

Using these poor category patients, Table 7.16 shows that, relatively, "memory and concentration" items provide the greater evidence of perceived improvement during the training period. One apparent anomaly is that carers felt that their relative's ability to think more quickly became poorer over the training period. A possible explanation for this finding is that it represents patients behaving less impulsively, though such a suggestion is purely speculative. Beyond the memory and concentration items, the positive changes noted by patient and carer groups on items relating to mood change and drive are consistent with changes often noted as patients improved post-trauma.

A more formal examination of the changes across the NCRP period can be made using a 1-sample Chi^2 test (Siegel, 1956). The significant results obtained using this test are displayed in Table 7.17. Again, it is obvious from this table that rated improvements in memory and concentration items are prominent and that the patient group perceived greater, and more frequent, changes than did the

TABLE 7.16
Percentage Reduction in Patients Rated in Poorest
Category

	Respondent	
	Patient	*Carer*
Memory and Concentration		
1. Rate Memory	29%	10%
2. Forget to do things	20%	21%
3. Forget lists	20%	3%
4. Family/Friends	40%	17%
5. Conversation track	22%	12%
6. Concentrate	13%	26%
7. Think quickly	–6%	–33%
Feeling		
8. Worry	20%	11%
9. Mood change	26%	29%
10. Drive	31%	21%
11. Cheerful	29%	9%
12. Speak up for self	46%	13%
Spend Time		
13. Repair jobs	31%	–5%
14. Travel public	16%	–22%
15. Visit friends	30%	–9%
16. Pub/club	21%	8%
17. Hobbies	8%	23%
Self and Family		
18. Help outside house	5%	29%
19. Make understand	40%	23%

carers. Figures 7.13a, b, c and d provide illustrations of the changes in ratings across the premorbid-post-training period and demonstrate the generally more "optimistic" perception of the patient group.

7.5 DISCUSSION

This chapter has presented some of the most important data acquired during the NCRP research. Our primary interest was in the data generated from the retraining programs themselves. Table 7.1 provides ample testimony to the improvement in functioning of our patients using these retraining routines. On some variables it seemed clear that intra-group variability, leading to high

TABLE 7.17
Significant Changes in Ratings During Training

(A) Patient Sample

Item	Chi^2	Sig. level
1.	9.51	p<.01
3.	6.87	p<.05
5.	9.54	p<.01
7.	6.79	p<.05
11.	6.89	p<.05
16.	8.39	p<.02
17.	16.13	p<.001
19.	19.39	p<.001
23.	23.89	p<.001
31.	15.87	p<.001
33.	8.76	p<.02
36.	7.73	p<.05
37.	10.14	p<.01
47.	39.04	p<.001

(B) Carer Sample

Item	Chi^2	Sig. level
3.	14.07	p<.001
4.	6.53	p<.05
8.	7.52	p<.05
16.	6.06	p<.05
18.	9.90	p<.01

standard deviation values, made the achievement of t-test significance difficult. However, the employment of Chi² analyses, the results of which are detailed in Table 7.2, further emphasise the gains during training. In particular, use of Chi² analysis led to significant findings on some programs (SPEED, VISCAN, ROADRIGHT) where t-test examination alone had failed to detect significant change. A combination of these two approaches to analysis yielded a clear picture of comprehensive gains in performance across the cognitive systems outlined in Table 6.3 (including aspects of memory, visuospatial performance, and information processing). We view the group results provided in 7.2 in this chapter as offering strong evidence of improvement in some areas of cognitive deficit associated with the use of the microcomputer retraining programs.

Given the heterogeneity of the experimental group in terms of underlying neuropathological process, time since brain damage acquired, age, and premorbid IQ, further examination of the data was undertaken to take account of these factors. Fortuitously, there were no significant differences between the two main subgroups (HI, ST) in terms of time since acquisition of brain damage and premorbid IQ, thereby aiding comparison of their performance on the NCRP.

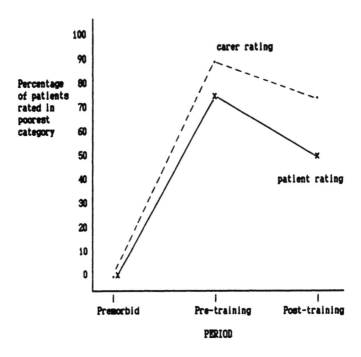

	Premorbid	Pre-training	Post-training
Patient	0	76	47
Carer	0	83	73

FIG. 7.13a.   Percentage of patients rated in the poorest category for the item "How would you rate your memory?"

We feel that an important question for micro-based CRPs is the range of their applicability: For example, are some programs only suitable for younger patients, or higher IQ patients? The results we presented in 7.2.3 in this chapter are generally reassuring in this respect. On many NCRP variables the scores at the start of training were similar for both HI and ST subgroups. Even where the HI group (being younger) did have an initial advantage, the amount of improvement across training of the ST and HI subgroups tended not to differ: For example, although HI subjects scored more highly at the start and end of training in the three-digits condition of the ATTENTION program, the ST subjects showed a similar level of gain in performance during training, as shown in Fig. 7.1. A similar finding was noted for the PROMEM "total correct" variable, 2 (Fig. 7.2). On some variables the ST subgroup performance seemed even more impressive, with these subjects starting training in a significantly poorer position than HI subjects, but managing to close the gap during training by a significant improvement (see Fig. 7.3). It should be pointed out, however, that ceiling effects may have begun to operate on the scores of the HI subgroup, so the comparative data in Fig. 7.3 should be viewed with some caution. Therefore, our findings when comparing the two experimental subgroups lead us to be optimistic regarding the general applicability of the NCRP to patients with various diagnoses. This position is perhaps illustrated by case 15, who was a CVA patient of 66 years of age who suffered his stroke 4 years before starting the NCRP. The subjective judgement of case 15 and his carer was that he had shown

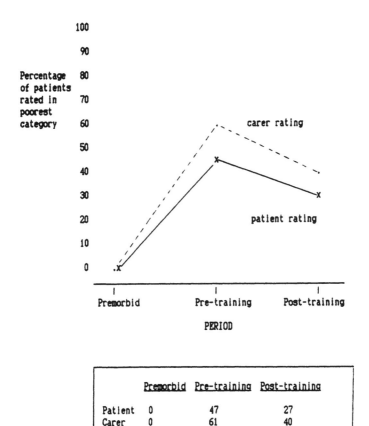

FIG. 7.13b.   Percentage of patients rated in the poorest category for the item "Do you forget to do things?"

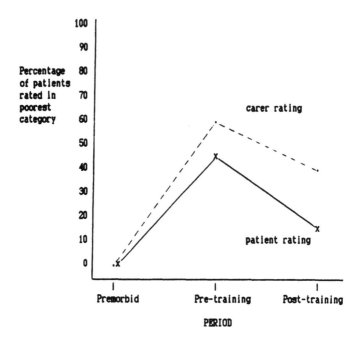

FIG. 7.13c.   Percentage of patients rated in the poorest category for the item "Do you feel listless and lacking in drive?"

a large cognitive improvement as a result of undertaking the NCRP, an opinion supported by a number of his results (e.g. see Fig. 7.4).

Within the ST subgroup generally there were few significant correlations with age, IQ, or time since lesion acquired, thereby reinforcing the general applicability of the NCRP. On a variable with the highest information processing load (three digits, ATTENTION) the older ST subjects scored poorly, as might be predicted. If there was a disappointing finding for the ST subgroup it was the lack of consistency and good outcome in relation to some of the response time variables (see Figures 7.5, 7.6), except where decision time was involved (see Fig. 7.7).

When obtained, the ratings of HI subjects and their carers indicated that they had perceived improvement during the NCRP. As with the ST group, few significant correlations with background variables were noted. On the MEM-CHAT high information load condition a significant correlation was noted with premorbid IQ, but this was an isolated finding. Older HI subjects started training on ROADRIGHT with significantly lower orientation times, though they also tended to make greater gains during training.

As indicated above, the most interesting question for us was the generalisation of any noted NCRP effects across different patients, and the results outlined earlier suggest that neuropathological process, age, time since acquiring brain damage, and premorbid intellectual level are not limiting factors upon the widespread use of our training package. We also wish to have some methods for checking transfer of effects into "real life". It can be argued that the questionnaire data considered in 7.4 in this chapter offers the best mechanism for

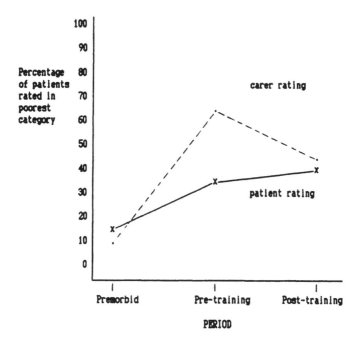

FIG. 7.13d.   Percentage of patients rated in the poorest category for the item "Are you tactful?"

achieving this, although the subjective nature of the data gained and the "demand characteristics" associated with offering a highly desirable treatment for patients, counsels caution in interpretation of results obtained.

A step towards generalisation is the consideration of more objective neuropsychological assessment data obtained before and after training. Perhaps not surprisingly, this data was less impressive than that gained from the NCRP process itself. Evidence of improvement in visuospatial performance across training was provided by the LM results (Table 7.10), though this was not supported by other visual perceptual tasks involving line bisection and cancellation. Significant improvements in information processing ability during training was confirmed using the digit symbol and Coughlan test (Table 7.11), though it was disappointing to find no clearcut evidence of significant improvement in memory functioning using objective neuropsychological tests. Absence of change in pure motor functioning during training, given the nature of the NCRP, was an expected finding.

Although only non-significant improvements in LM performance were noted for the whole of the experimental group across training when examined using t-test, some evidence of significant change was noted for HI subjects using this analysis method. Case comparisons with control subjects were, however, generally disappointing in suggesting that the LM test involves a major task-learning component.

Assessment of information processing ability via digit symbol scores yielded results suggesting that at each assessment point, including pre-training, there was a tendency for ST subjects to perform at a higher level than the HI subgroup. The ST subgroup also showed a significantly better initial assessment performance compared with the C subgroup. Although changes in digit symbol scores across training were unpredictable for individual patients, there was a good correlation between premorbid IQ and changes in these scores during training for patients in the E group. This latter finding was not observed on the corresponding Coughlan information processing measure, though again ST subjects performed better than the HI subgroup at pre-training assessment.

As Fig. 7.10 shows, the HI subgroup improved across training, although these gains were not related to age or time since lesion. Although the opportunity for case matching with C subjects was limited, the available data underlined the gains of HI subjects and the lack of improvement in C subjects (Fig. 7.12).

The degree of rating agreement between patient and carer in terms of questionnaire responses was reassuring, though it is worthy of note that carers tended to view their patient relatives as performing more poorly at pre-training and at post-training follow-up. Both patients and their carers rated "memory and concentration" items as having improved most across the retraining programme, thus supplying some additional validation of the NCRP.

7.6 SUMMARY

This chapter has provided information on the Newcastle Cognitive Retraining Programme study (NCRP). The study involved intensive research on a group of patients with a range of cognitive deficits. The background to the study is provided in Chapter 6, and this chapter has concentrated upon the actual results obtained. Analysis focused upon examination of NCRP data, but also included pre- and post-training neuropsychological assessment data and the ratings of change gained from patients and carers. Some subgroup and C subject investigation is reported within this chapter and relevant variables such as premorbid IQ, time since acquisition of brain damage, and age have also been included. Consideration of the heterogeneity of patients with regard to these, and other potentially relevant, variables led to the adoption of a combined approach to statistical analysis, including t-test, Chi^2, and examinations of individual patient data.

The results obtained from the NCRP confirm the value of the microcomputer-based cognitive retraining approach. Patients showed gains across a wide range of retraining tasks, including those relating to visuospatial, information processing, and memory functions. Our findings also clearly suggest that the general approach and the particular software used will generalise—i.e. will have an applicability to a wide range of neurological patients. We feel optimistic concerning the extension of our NCRP to other groups of patients with cognitive impairment. Interestingly, the validity of our position received support from the ratings of cognitive performance obtained from participating patients and their carers.

Whilst the question of direct transfer of patients' cognitive improvement into real-life situations was beyond the scope of our study, we did include reference data obtained from pre- and post-training neuropsychological assessment. Findings from this aspect of the research were very persuasive in relation to information processing ability, with the results from some areas of visuoperceptual performance and from memory functioning being disappointing.

8 Towards a Model of Rehabilitation

8.1 NEUROLOGICAL REHABILITATION SERVICES IN THE UNITED KINGDOM

In the United Kingdom the need for neurological rehabilitation services has long been recognised (Mair Report, 1972). However, in the early 1990s there is still little evidence of a coordinated rehabilitation service in individual health districts and only a few specialist Regional Rehabilitation Centres are in existence. The need for such services continues unabated. Wade and Langton Hewer (1987b) estimate that an average Health Authority of 250,000 people would include 5,000 individuals with disabling neurological disease, head injury and stroke accounting for a large proportion of these individuals. The annual rate of hospital admission following head injury is thought to be around 650 per health district (report of MRC Coordinating Group, 1982, and Royal College of Physicians, 1986). This means that 45 severe head injuries are admitted to hospital from each health district in each year.

Given a relatively normal life-span and the fact that most head injuries occur during the second and third decades of life, the accumulative total of surviving severely brain damaged individuals in any of the 192 health districts in England and Wales is extremely large—i.e. approximately 2000 for severe head injury alone—and certainly those in need of relatively intensive rehabilitation at any one time could be as many as 200 per health district. The lack of special services is emphasised by the fact that brain-injured individuals are often found in orthopaedic wards of general hospitals or in inappropriate mental illness or mental handicap facilities. More commonly, the post-acute aspects of long-term care are carried out by relatives at home, often with quite inadequate levels of support and advice. The sad fact remains that the problems encountered by relatives do not diminish over the years and, if anything, there is evidence to suggest reduced ability to cope 5 years after the onset of the trauma, compared to 2 years post-injury (Brooks, 1986). Support networks via voluntary agencies such as Headway do help the caregivers to share the burden and to obtain advice. However, such support networks are entirely dependent upon the quality and specific needs of local groups and organising committees and therefore it is not possible for local voluntary agencies to provide a consistent level of advice and support or to be subject to quality assurance measures.

The current situation regarding a rehabilitation service for stroke is also bleak. The trend is towards a policy of diagnosis without hospital admission, which has immediate cost benefits, but assessment of need and rehabilitation services can be quite variable. There are considerable benefits to both the victim of stroke and the carer, in centring treatment upon an individual's home. It is acknowledged that needs relating to continence and mobility can often be met fully in the acute stages but there is an enormous need for better coordination of longer-term problems resulting from stroke and far greater emphasis on matters such as emotional adjustment, long-term occupation, and family and social support (e.g. Smith et al., 1981).

8.1.1 Approaches to Post-acute Rehabilitation

The problems with post-acute rehabilitation of neurological patients have been addressed to some extent in other countries of the world, e.g. USA, Israel, and Sweden. Much can be learned from their experiences (e.g. Ben Yishay, Rattok, & Ross, 1982; Prigatano et al., 1986; Rosenbaum, Lipsitz, Abraham, & Najenson, 1978). A feature of some well-established rehabilitation services is a rehabilitation centre which acts in close concert with acute general hospital services, family support schemes, and employment centres. Prevailing opinion would tend to suggest that such a rehabilitation centre be non-residential (Oddy et al., 1989). It would provide the focus for retraining activities at different stages of the recovery process. An alternative trend in rehabilitation following head injury is towards the development of "rehabilitation systems rather than single stand-alone rehabilitation units" (Brooks, 1991). Within such systems provision is made for a wide range of intervention which may be located in a range of settings including the patient's home although they are coordinated by the professional team by means of care plans for each patient. Evaluations of the effectiveness of two such systems organised by profit-making companies in the USA have recently been carried out by Cope, Cole, Hall, and Barkan, (1991a,b) and Johnston (1991) and Johnston and Lewis (1991). Both groups found evidence for the effectiveness of this type of rehabilitation in terms of outcome measures such as degree of dependence and productivity. The types of intervention provided within such rehabilitation systems are similar to those provided within a service based at a single centre, which should have links with residential living and employment training establishments, sheltered workshops, and so on. Cope et al. argue that the rehabilitation system approach permits rehabilitation to be performed in "as close to a 'real-world' environment as possible" and therefore has advantages relating to improved patient motivation and acceptance of treatment and a potential increase in the patients' ability to generalise treatment gains from treatment to community settings. Such an approach does assume that various premises which can be dedicated to different types of intervention are available; this may not always be the case within UK Health Districts. There are also potential advantages in basing rehabilitation in a single regional rehabilitation centre. For example, the centre provides a focal point for the activities of voluntary agencies and interdisciplinary coordination and exchange of ideas. Writers on stroke care do not place such emphasis upon a rehabilitation centre. However, coordination of services, easy availability, and a designated team to promote continuity of service provision between hospitals and community care (Wade et al., 1985b) are regarded as of greatest importance.

It is clear that currently both head injury and stroke rehabilitation suffers from the lack of a coordinated and integrated approach to treatment. Principal recommendations identify teams of caregivers who would be expected to have a centralised resource centre at their disposal, although in practice some of the caregivers would be widely dispersed in different settings throughout the community. In general terms it appears that, provided hardware and suitably qualified staff are available, development of a comprehensive cognitive retraining treatment programme (with or without microcomputers) will be a realistic proposition for all health regions.

8.1.2 The Role of Neuropsychology in Rehabilitation

Looking at the structure of potential rehabilitation services (involving realistic cost implications), the model for head injury proposed by Oddy et al. (1989) has much to commend it. For stroke, Wade et al's (1985b) model of service is a good starting point. In this section the role of neuropsychology in models of rehabilitation services is highlighted in order that the full potential of neuropsychology in rehabilitation can be illustrated.

It could be argued that Oddy's model is essentially one of hospital-based rehabilitation services, which traditionally have emphasised medical and nursing care. However, Oddy argues for a very much wider based model of rehabilitation and the rehabilitation centre itself is merely the focus for referral and the physical base in which services are coordinated and expertise is developed.

Models of care such as those described by Cope et al. (1991a), which emphasise community-based services, would be fully endorsed both by the current authors and by Oddy himself. The problem is that, unlike the situation in the US, in the UK rehabilitation services are only now being regarded as an entity in their own right. Until recently community services for TBI patients in the UK were often so fragmented as to be extremely ineffective in their service delivery. Neither the structure nor the resources, nor even the motivation appear to exist to allow community-based programmes to be developed. Therefore a rehabilitation service with a recognised base but with full outreach facilities and a philosophy which embraces the value of community resource provision is felt to be a practical first stage development in the UK before services such as those described by Cope et al. could become a reality.

The essential components of Oddy et al's model of neurological rehabilitation is contained in Fig. 8.1.

Most rehabilitation is started some weeks or months after onset but it may be that in some cases active rehabilitation is best commenced during the acute phases of an illness or injury as some recent research (McMillan & Glucksman, 1987) has suggested that subtle changes in neuropsychological functioning do occur in relatively acute stages. There is also some evidence (Mitchell, Bradley, Welch, & Britton, 1990) that early stimulation, even whilst the patient is in coma, can possibly lead to a better outcome. It is therefore extremely important that rehabilitation is seen as a continual process from the most acute stages in a general hospital through to supported community living some years after the event.

Within such a model of rehabilitation at the acute stage the neuropsychologist can be involved in baseline assessment of neuropsychological functioning and it is possible that rates of recovery could be documented briefly over a number of

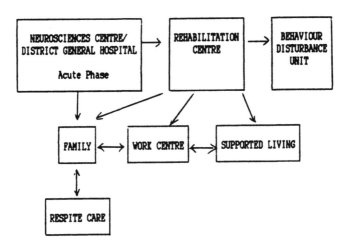

FIG. 8.1. Model of rehabilitation services (from Oddy et al., 1989).

weeks using a few important indices, giving a clear indication of the way in which sensitive abilities such as information processing speed or recall are progressing during the patient's stay in the general hospital. This would have the advantage of commencing the baseline assessment before the patient reaches a rehabilitation centre and making any subsequent improvement due to therapeutic intervention much clearer. The role of the neuropsychologist in an acute setting is of course far wider than that of providing baseline information for neuropsychological rehabilitation staff, but activities such as diagnostic assessment, evaluation of neurosurgical procedures, or investigation of the effects of specific lesions are beyond the scope of this volume.

8.1.3 The Function of the Rehabilitation Centre

In Oddy et al's (1989) model the coordinating centre for rehabilitation services is a non-residential rehabilitation centre serving approximately 200,000–400,000 of the population and this would provide activity and stimulation in the form of retraining at different stages of recovery following acquired brain damage. Such a centre would also provide an opportunity for social and occupational activities, continuing physiotherapy, occupational therapy and assistance with behavioural and emotional problems. In addition such a centre would be considered the focus for cognitive retraining with volunteers and relatives assisting with the monitoring of task performance. The other major function of the centre would be in the provision of an outpatient service which could be provided for patients and their families with daily input from core staff such as specialist speech therapists, clinical neuropsychologists, social workers, physiotherapists, and occupational therapists. Once an individual is making use of a rehabilitation centre, it would not be envisaged that the medical input (apart from those specifically trained in Disability Medicine) would be a particularly prominent feature of treatment, and advice from visiting medical specialists may be the sum total of medical involvement.

A vital aspect of service provision through a rehabilitation centre is to give a focus for involvement by voluntary agencies, such as a head injury support group (e.g. Headway) or interested and involved relatives. As can be seen from our own research the contribution of relatives is extremely important, if only to provide an objective source of information about the patient's progress. However, within a rehabilitation centre the relatives could be become actively involved in all manner of therapies and help to consolidate learning during and outside formal therapy sessions.

As mentioned above the rehabilitation centre would be considered the focus for cognitive retraining and an ideal service would probably have at least four stand-alone computers for daily use. It is felt that any form of linked system is potentially dangerous as, if software does not have sufficient error-protection, only a moment's lapse in concentration by a therapy assistant can lead to random button pressing behaviour by the patient, crashing of the programme and ill-feeling all round. The microcomputer retraining would be considered as one constituent element of a comprehensive programme of neuropsychological rehabilitation which could potentially involve training groups for memory and social skills and individual practical training sessions to include, for example, route-finding and shopping trips, paper and pencil exercises such as the filling in of daily activity schedules or the learning of simple mnemonics to assist recall of information. It is not envisaged that cognitive retraining using microcomputers would form a self-contained package of exercises which could be used as the sole form of neuropsychological rehabilitation.

It is anticipated that other aspects of Oddy's model of rehabilitation such as the work by the family at home, respite care, a behavioural disturbance unit, a work centre, and supported living would all be integrated into the central functions of a rehabilitation centre. For instance, the goals set in the rehabilitation centre must be carried over into other settings such as the work centre. Thus a goal (e.g. to improve recall of information) could, in the first instance, be tackled within the rehabilitation centre on a daily basis but as the recovery process continues the same principles and techniques need to be applied in other settings, e.g. the home and the work centre.

One other advantage of the concept of a rehabilitation centre is that with the involvement of voluntary agencies and families it would be quite possible, with a little relevant training, to use interested caregivers as technicians responsible for the administration of individual micro-computer based cognitive retraining programmes. Such activities would have to be always under the supervision of a trained neuropsychologist whose role it would be to determine level of difficulty and type of task but the use of volunteers and relatives would certainly remove the task of routine administration of training exercises from the remit of trained neuropsychology staff (who are a relatively rare resource within any such service).

8.1.4 Rehabilitation from Stroke

In a similar way to the head injury rehabilitation model, the model for stroke care advanced by Wade et al. (1985b) can evolve in such a way that cognitive retraining through microcomputer becomes an integral part of the therapy service provided. Wade et al., advocate coordination of services such that specialist professional workers will be formed into a single team. Hospital care should be focused on a particular ward or unit with a high proportion of stroke patients (although not solely catering for the needs of this group) and the principles of rehabilitation established within the hospital should be carried through community services. The importance of the role of the stroke team is emphasised by the fact that many patients will not be hospitalised in early stages. Outpatient and day-patient facilities, providing a range of professional help, are a necessary central component of comprehensive stroke care and these facilities should be available, whether the patient be treated initially in hospital or at home. Such a policy would represent a significant step in the direction of improving services for stroke patients as, wherever the patient is located, coordinated or integrated treatment plans are rarely provided, especially during the vitally important early stages of recovery. Currently if patients are in hospital there is a strong possibility that they will be dispersed amongst general medical wards with varying degrees of success in attracting help from professional care workers with the necessary expertise.

Cognitive retraining, with or without microcomputers, represents an important therapeutic intervention commencing at the point where the patient has recovered from the initial acute effects of the stroke. If a rehabilitation centre similar to that described by Oddy et al. is in operation for head injured patients, then it may prove feasible for daily outpatient appointments for therapy to be organised through the centre, and recourse to acute services may only be required when specialist advice on medical problems is required. Although such a shift in emphasis would greatly increase the volume of patients passing through the rehabilitation centre, the overall amount of therapist time used by a stroke patient is likely to be considerably less than that used by a head-injured patient. This being the case, day patient facilities at the rehabilitation centre should be able to cope with the number of stroke patients being admitted for therapeutic intervention during critical phases in the recovery process, i.e. the first 3 months. One further potential advantage would be that specific problems, particularly those associated with higher mental functioning, could be tackled early. If there is no evidence of generalised effects (such as those found in head injury) the response to retraining might be extremely good in such cases.

8.1.5 Example of a Rehabilitation Service from a Case History

To further illustrate the way in which the rehabilitation service would respond to a client's problems a largely hypothetical case (that of CH) is presented here which, whilst including a great number of different problems, is in no sense exaggerated and will be familiar to anyone working with clients who have sustained severe neurological impairment.

Case Report on CH.   Born 1955.
Left school with 3 O levels—English, Geography, and Art. Employed as a clerical worker in the Airforce until his accident in December 1985.
Married—1977, 2 children aged 3 and 6.
Lives in a small market town with both his own parents and his in-laws living within a 2 mile radius.

CH was a keen sportsman and particularly enjoyed distance running. He was a secretary of his local cricket club and both he and his wife enjoyed an active social life.

December 1985.   CH was run over accidentally in the car park of the local cricket club by one of his companions with whom he had been drinking. He sustained a severe head injury and was admitted to his local Regional Neurological Centre some 25 miles from his home, having initially been admitted to his local District General Hospital. He was in coma for 10 days and upon regaining consciousness his injuries and impairments were listed as follows: a fracture to his right leg, gross ataxia of gait, incontinence, poor vision, disorientation, intolerance of ward staff, verbally abusive behaviour, and very poor short-term memory.

Prior to the introduction of an integrated rehabilitation service CH would have been discharged from the acute neurological centre as soon as possible, either to the referring General Hospital or, if his behavioural problems persisted, to the local Mental Health Hospital. However CH was fortunate in living in a progressive health district with well developed services in neurological rehabilitation.

March 1986.   In March 1986, following a slow recovery, particularly with regard to higher mental function, CH was fully ambulant around the ward in the neurological centre but, unfortunately, his inadequate behavioural control was a very troublesome feature. After a number of incidents in which he assaulted nursing staff it was decided that CH should enter the specialised unit for behavioural disturbance on the same hospital site where he would be introduced to a behavioural programme and receive assistance from specialised staff including psychiatric nurses, psychologists, psychiatrists, and occupational therapists. After a month of treatment in the behavioural unit CH no longer struck out at staff and a referral was made to the neurological rehabilitation centre.

Throughout the early part of his recovery CH's wife and family had visited him. Because of his difficulties in tolerating frustration the two young children visited for only short periods of time. His wife remained supportive of her husband and, with advice from the neuropsychologists, she started to try to teach him some simple information pertaining to his home life, occupation, and social life. Visits by people associated with various strands of his life were encouraged by the psychologists in order to help CH make sense of his disordered world. In the behavioural unit his wife was involved in therapy aimed at reducing his anti-social behaviour. The social worker made arrangements with the extended family to meet the needs of the two young children in order that CH's wife could devote as much time to her involvement in the work of the behavioural unit as was practically possible.

May 1986.   CH arrived at the rehabilitation centre some two miles distant from the Regional Neurological Centre. At this time he was still disoriented and had a short attention span. He had impaired verbal expression, limited vocabulary, made frequent semantic errors, and had a tendency to perseverate. Immediate memory span was impaired, preservation of old rote memory preserved, and there was severe impairment of long-term memory and a tendency to confabulate. Severe visuoperceptual problems, and a visual object agnosia were also present. He continued to be verbally abusive to staff although he was no longer physically aggressive. The description of higher mental functions was derived from the initial assessment carried out by the neuropsychologist working in the rehabilitation unit.

A plan of treatment was evolved over the next 2 weeks, which included daily attendance at the social skills group, attendance at an anger control group 3 times weekly, and daily attendance at a memory-retraining group. In addition he had daily sessions of physiotherapy in order to deal with his ataxic gait, and certain behavioural limits were drawn up in order to cope with the aggressive behaviour, the targets of which were made known to all members of staff and to CH's relatives. Finally, daily sessions of cognitive retraining with microcomputers were planned. The cognitive retraining programme concentrated upon the visual-perceptual problem. Route finding exercises, object naming exercises, conversational memory exercises, and exercises designed to compensate for visual neglect were the focus of the 10-week treatment programme. The cognitive retraining using microcomputers, commenced following 2 more assessments at fortnightly intervals in order to extend the baseline and was coordinated by the rehabilitation centre neuropsychologist with day-to-day monitoring and supervision carried out by a clinical psychology assistant and, on occasions, CH's nephew, a 16-year-old school-leaver who was keen to help in his uncle's recovery. In addition to the microcomputing aspects of his treatment programme, orientation exercises, route finding and route planning exercises in hospital and town and exercises for the rehabilitation of visual neglect in the occupational therapy department were introduced. CH's wife was involved in the activities of the social skills group and also the anger control group and on occasions his children were introduced into leisure time in order to allow him a chance to play with them and to learn to adapt to the frustrations that they produced.

August 1986.   A reassessment of cognitive functioning indicated that improvements had occurred in memory and visual-perceptual functioning. Memory remained below the predicted level and CH was instructed in the use of memory aids to help him cope with the residual deficit. There were no problems to be detected with verbal expression or confabulation. His conversations were regarded as being largely appropriate. His physical problems had improved significantly. The ataxic gait was now only evident in the form of a slight limp and he had regained control of his bladder and bowel. CH's aggression had dissipated and he was able to enjoy his children without being frustrated by their noise and behaviour. At this time a number of members of the local Headway group (voluntary agency) had started to visit CH in the rehabilitation centre after his wife had talked to one of the representatives listed in the resource pack issued in the early stages of recovery. The visitor helped CH realise that he was not alone in suffering from such problems and that recovery was possible.

A number of weekends at home had been arranged, coordinated by the unit's social worker, and during the course of the following weeks a member of the local community nursing team who had been to see CH at the rehabilitation centre visited him at home to ensure that the family were coping. The visits home revealed another problem commonly experienced by sufferers of severe closed head injury, namely marital/sexual difficulties due to reduced libido. This problem immediately increased CH's anger and his mood state became less stable. He disclosed the problem to the social worker and in discussion with his wife it was decided to commence marital/sexual counselling with a behavioural psychologist who worked at the rehabilitation centre.

October 1986.   A referral was made to an employment rehabilitation centre and, by the middle of October, CH was attending the centre 3 days a week, being retrained in clerical duties. The employment centre had full access to all of the assessments carried out since the accident occurred and following their own assessment they felt that a return to his previous employment was a possibility.

In the following months a phased discharge from the rehabilitation centre was arranged. Initially, attendance at the day centre associated with the rehabilitation hospital was arranged in order that further training in social skills, and anger management and the marital/sexual counselling could be completed. However, by January 1987 CH was at home full time with continued involvement with the local employment rehabilitation centre and local support from the community nursing team. He attended outpatient follow-up appointments at 3, 6, and 12 months at the rehabilitation centre, being seen by all relevant professionals during the course of a day's visit.

At the 6-month assessment CH reported that he had been discharged from the Air Force with a pension but had managed to get a clerical job through the ERC and was currently enjoying his work. The marital relationship had improved significantly and his sexual difficulties had resolved following treatment. He was also enjoying the responsibilities associated with bringing up his family. Occasional temper outbursts were still in evidence but the family were able to use the strategies advocated by the rehabilitation team to good effect. Finally, CH joined the local Headway support group and was actively supporting others who were going through the long recovery process.

It can be seen from the above illustration that, although CH presented with cognitive and behavioural problems, the cognitive problems were relatively easy to remediate and cognitive retraining formed a very discrete, yet very useful part of a total rehabilitation package. The behavioural problems were ultimately the ones which required most therapist-time, and employment became a major issue in the latter stages. The importance of the rehabilitation model used in this case was that it allowed a continuous process to develop almost from the onset until withdrawal of all services, with each stage merging into the next and specialist services brought in as required. To rely upon only one specialist service in order to provide rehabilitation for an individual (e.g. to prescribe a cognitive retraining programme using microcomputers in isolation from all other aspects of rehabilitation) is felt to be inadequate for the individual's needs and the advantages gained might be insignificant in the context of, for example, gross behavioural problems.

8.1.6 Summary

In summary, current thinking with respect to the rehabilitation of both stroke patients and head injury patients is in favour of a designated team of professional experts and a rehabilitation centre as the core of a coordinated, integrated, and cost effective rehabilitation service. Neuropsychology is regarded as a funda- mental dimension of such a service. If neurological rehabilitation is structured in a way similar to that described above then a cognitive retraining programme will be a feature and microcomputer-based training tasks will be organised and integrated into the overall treatment package.

8.2 COGNITIVE RETRAINING USING MICROCOMPUTERS. AN IMPROVED SERVICE?

If cognitive retraining using microcomputers is acknowledged as an important element within the overall structure of the rehabilitation service, consideration, in the light of our experience, should be given to improvements in service provision of this form of neuropsychological rehabilitation.

Principal recommendations from our research are as follows:

1. The establishment of a good baseline assessment on a small number of repeatable tasks: It seems of paramount importance to repeat assessment as often as possible throughout the early stages of recovery in order that subsequent intervention can be gauged effectively.

2. The use of volunteers, relatives, or clinical psychologists in training. This is essential in order to allow the neuropsychologists to make best use of their own skills. Routine assessments might also be carried out by clinical psychology assistants as long as appropriate training has been given. To make the service cost effective it is recommended that no programme of neuropsychological intervention ought to be considered until relevant helpers and back-up workers have been identified.

3. With regard to computer hardware the keyboard should be made as simple as possible with use of peripherals such as simple YES–NO response buttons. Keeping the patient remote from access to the computer's programs is vital for the preservation of the system.

4. Software should be selected carefully and, whenever possible, preference given to the use of tasks which have been shown to elicit on-task learning, even if evidence of carry-over to psychometric test performance or everyday activities is not available.

5. Cognitive retraining using microcomputers should always be considered as part of an overall neuropsychological retraining programme. Integration with activities within a work centre or a unit which is dealing with emotional and behavioural problems is extremely important if a comprehensive rehabilitation service is to be achieved.

6. Measurement of social, emotional, and functional outcome is as important as measurement of cognitive variables. Improvement in everyday functioning may not always be revealed by standard neuropsychological assessment techniques and there are many reasons why variability can occur in test performance of such patients (e.g. level of anticonvulsants, secondary depression). In the selection of assessment procedures much thought needs to be given in the future to the development of outcome measures. Social, emotional, and functional outcome along the lines of the questionnaire developed for this study (see Appendix III) must be measured in addition to a number of important and highly sensitive cognitive measures, which have shown to reflect changes in ability level or adaptation to disability.

If the model of rehabilitation service provision is an appropriate one it needs to be able to cope with all clients who might be referred to the service regardless of their problems. It is unlikely that problems which could be dealt with by a single discipline (i.e. problems which require only physiotherapy) would find their way into such a service, as the purpose of such a specialised service would be to deal with complex problems which require careful coordination and integration of service provision from a number of disciplines. Thus, leaving aside single discipline referrals, all other referrals should be capable of being channelled through the service following the model outlined above.

Taking the exploration of the model a step further it is possible to demonstrate points at which use of microcomputers can enhance the quality rehabilitation service given. Figures 8.2 and 8.3a,b,c, are modified extracts of Fig. 8.1 (removing the "psychosocial" elements and incorporating the involvement of microcomputers. Programs were selected for inclusion either on the basis of evidence of efficacy provided in published studies (e.g. Ben-Yishay et al., 1987; Ethier et al., 1989a,b) or on the basis of the authors' clinical experience of the programs, which has provided evidence of effectiveness.

We have argued that studies using both group and individual-case design are required to build up a complete picture of the cognitive processes involved in,

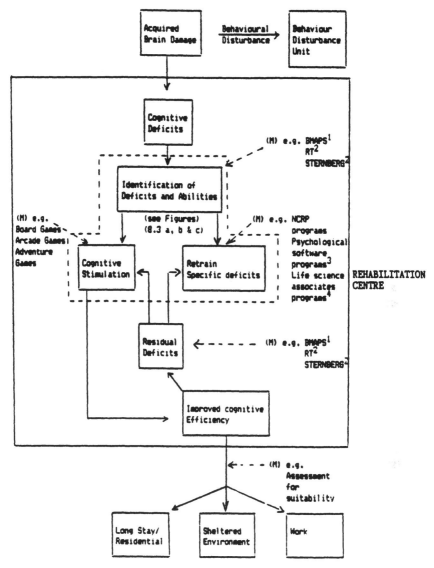

FIG. 8.2.　Assistance of microcomputers in a rehabilitation service.

1.　Acker & Acker (1982).
2.　Skilbeck (1984).
3.　Bracy (1982; 1986). PSYCHOLOGICAL SOFTWARE SERVICES (see Appendix I.1).
4.　Gianutsos & Klitzner (1981); Gianutsos et al. (1983; 1984). LIFE SCIENCE ASSOCIATES (see Appendix I.1).
5.　NCRP programs.
6.　Robertson & Smart (1988). LOCHEESOFT (see Appendix I.1).
7.　Gianutsos & Klitzner (1981). LIFE SCIENCE ASSOCIATES (see Appendix I.1).
8.　Bracy (1982). PSYCHOLOGICAL SOFTWARE SERVICES PACKAGE (1983) (see Appendix I.1).
9.　Braun et al. (1985) (see Appendix I.2).
10.　Johnson (1989) (see Appendix I.2).
11.　Warburg (1988) (see Appendix I.2).
12.　Gianutsos et al. (1984). LIFE SCIENCE ASSOCIATES (see Appendix I.1).
13.　Piasetsky et al. (1983). RUSK INSTITUTE OF REHABILITATION MEDICINE (see Appendix I.1).

185

and the effectiveness of different approaches to retraining. One of the most basic questions relating to microcomputer-based retraining has received very little attention so far. This is the question of the relative merits of different training tasks in eliciting on-test learning. Some are clearly more effective than others in this respect and we need to identify those tasks which are most effective and to try to understand the task differences in the context of theories of learning and recovery of functions. The memory tasks used in the NCRP, and in the majority of other memory-training programmes reported in the literature, have focused on improving "explicit" memory and learning, that is learning in which the individual is able to recall the presentation as well as the content of the to-be-remembered material and in which he or she makes a conscious effort to retain the material. It has been suggested that one of the reasons for the effectiveness

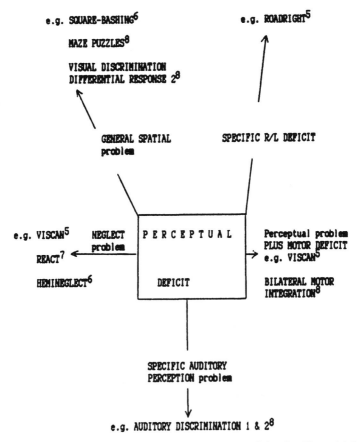

FIG. 8.3a.   Selection of appropriate software for perceptual deficits. (See Figure 8.2 for key to superscript numbers.)

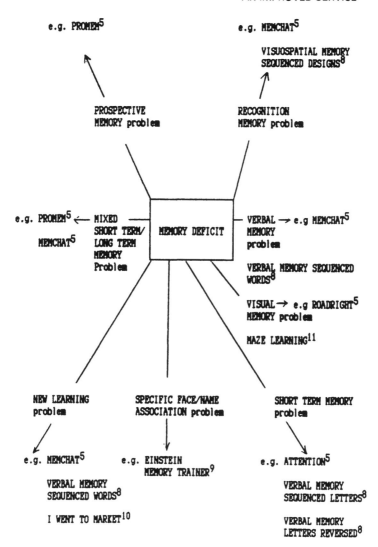

FIG. 8.3b.   Selection of appropriate software for memory deficits. (See Figure 8.2 for key to superscript numbers.)

of the "vanishing cues" technique used by Glisky et al., (1986a,b) is that it taps "implicit" learning processes. In implicit learning the subject does not remember the learning episodes and, although attending to the stimulus, makes no conscious effort to retain the material presented. That learning takes place is demonstrated by the effect which the stimuli presented have upon the subjects' responses in related tasks (Squire, 1987; Squire, Shimamura, & Amaral, 1989).

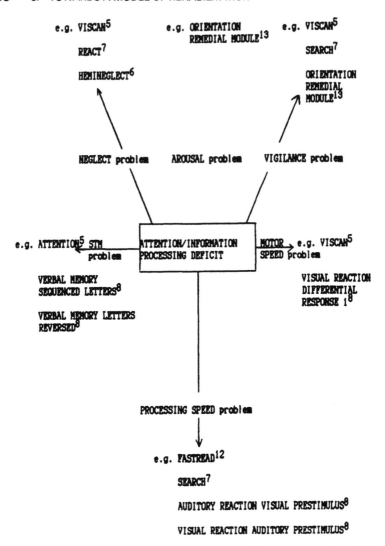

FIG. 8.3c.   Selection of appropriate software for attention/information processing deficits. (See Figure 8.2 for key to superscript numbers.)

It has been demonstrated that implicit learning processes are spared in amnesia (Parkin & Russo, 1990). A recent, and exciting, development in the field of memory remediation is the attempt to utilise these implicit learning processes rather than targeting explicit memory processes (Leng & Copello, 1990; Leng, Copello, & Sayegh, in press).

Comparisons also need to be made between different types of training schedules. Does a massed or spaced-practice schedule lead to greater on-task gains? We do not as yet know the optimum length for a training programme. A first step towards answering questions such as these has been taken by Ethier et al. (1989a,b). Further research is needed to identify any patient characteristics, such as neurological condition, age, and premorbid intellectual condition, that affect outcome.

If a training programme is shown to be effective, then evaluative studies should attempt to replicate any positive findings at different centres since the processes involved in cognitive retraining are highly complex and site-specific variables may have significant effects on outcome. In terms of the outcome measures themselves, researchers in the field may need to look carefully at the outcome measures used. Psychometric tests traditionally in clinical use may not be sensitive enough to pick up subtle changes in cognitive functioning. These tests are in use because they have been shown to be efficient in detecting and localising damage to the brain. They may continue to detect brain damage after cognitive retraining, which does not heal the damage, but might nevertheless do much to improve cognitive functioning. More sensitive tests of cognitive functioning may need to be developed and emphasis should be placed on measures of functional change.

Finally, the interaction of cognitive retraining programmes with other types of service provision has not as yet been investigated. We have argued strongly, on the basis of surveys of the needs of the brain-damaged population and their families, that the cognitive retraining programmes should be delivered as part of a comprehensive rehabilitation programme. Evidence from comprehensive programmes containing a cognitive retraining module run in the United States suggest that these can lead to significant improvements in cognitive and psychosocial functioning. Studies comparing the effectiveness of cognitive retraining programmes carried out in isolation and as part of a comprehensive programme are required if service planners are to have all relevant data at their disposal but may be difficult to justify on ethical grounds since both intuition and experience tend to suggest that the latter option is the most effective.

8.3 SUMMARY AND CONCLUDING REMARKS

The primary focus of this book is the use of microcomputers in cognitive retraining following acquired brain damage. The effects of such damage on the individual are rarely confined to cognitive deficits, although these may be highly significant in determining the degree of disability, and we have aimed, from the outset, to set cognitive retraining in context rather than to confine ourselves to detailed description of retraining techniques in isolation. The reader will, by now, be aware that there are a great many factors which need to be taken into consideration when utilising cognitive retraining techniques, although the techniques may appear straightforward in themselves.

The first area to be discussed is the nature of the cognitive deficits reported in three of the major conditions—head injury, stroke, and herpes simplex encephalitis. The patterns of spontaneous recovery following each of these conditions have been described. This information is relevant in three areas. The first is the evaluation of a cognitive retraining programme when account must be taken of the effects of spontaneous recovery. The second is the timing of the intervention (is it preferable to intervene during the period of spontaneous recovery or to wait until cognitive function has stabilised?) and the third is the area of patient selection.

The two areas last mentioned are discussed in the second chapter of this volume which addresses some of the practical and theoretical issues which require consideration before a decision is made to offer cognitive retraining to a patient or a group of patients. We conclude that early intervention can improve both rate and eventual level of recovery, but that late intervention can also result in significant improvement in level of functioning and that retraining should not, therefore, be withheld simply because brain injury is not recent. We raise an ethical question relating to intervention in relation to prognosis for spontaneous recovery and ask whether, when resources are limited, patients with good or bad prognoses should be given priority.

Another major issue considered in this chapter is the recognised need to demonstrate functional improvement as well as, or in preference to, improved performance on clinical tests. We then move into a discussion of assessment for rehabilitation. This is necessary both to identify individual deficits and strengths and to provide baseline measurements against which to compare eventual outcome. The importance of considering functional improvements has just been mentioned; within Chapter 3 we draw attention to the difficulties inherent in assessing changes in the efficiency with which an individual performs everyday tasks and advocate that assessment should not be limited to performance of psychometric tests. Behaviour rating scales and subjective reports may be extremely valuable in measuring the outcome of a rehabilitative intervention. In Chapter 4 we review the literature on cognitive retraining, selecting for discussion studies carried out at major rehabilitation centres and emphasising those which have used computer-based retraining techniques. A model of disability and rehabilitation is introduced at this point in order to draw attention to the way in which cognitive factors interact with psychosocial and environmental factors to influence eventual outcome following brain damage. Cognitive retraining programmes may target individual systems or may be broad-based, targeting a range of deficits. They may be designed for use with individual patients or may be used with a group of patients. The majority of studies discussed have reported gains on psychometric tests, although some negative findings have been reported. We conclude that insufficient attention has been given to the demonstration of gains in activities of daily living, although a minority of studies have incorporated functional outcome measures.

In Chapter 5 we list the advantages and disadvantages of using computerised as opposed to non-computerised techniques and conclude that computer-based techniques, provided they are used sensibly and by qualified therapists, have much to recommend them. Returning to the practicalities of designing a microcomputer-based rehabilitation programme, we consider some of the issues which relate to program design and outlined the different preparation stages.

In Chapter 6 we discuss the Newcastle Cognitive Retraining Programme and its evaluation. This used a set of programs for the BBC B and Commodore 64 microcomputers and targeted a range of cognitive deficits. Its efficacy when used with a group of brain-damaged individuals was evaluated.

Chapter 7 details the results of this study. Improvements on the training tasks themselves were recorded on the majority of tasks. Few significant improvements in psychometric measures were found for the group as a whole, although certain individuals did show significant improvement on psychometric measures. Significant improvements in everyday functioning in the areas of memory and concentration were found following analysis of the questionnaire data for the group.

In Chapter 8 we return to practical considerations, in this case the importance of providing cognitive retraining within a comprehensive rehabilitation programme. We outline the type of programme which we would regard as representing satisfactory provision and emphasise the need for providing an integrated service. The Newcastle CRP was designed with considerations relating to service delivery and cost-effectiveness in mind; a programme of this type fits well within the comprehensive rehabilitation programme in both theoretical and practical terms.

Although the literature relating to cognitive retraining has burgeoned over the past decade, it is a technique which must, in many respects, be regarded as being in its infancy. Many of the methodological difficulties in evaluating its effectiveness have been discussed in this volume. The Newcastle study, while providing valuable information for service planning, raised as many questions as it answered. We have made a number of suggestions for further research in the area and conclude by emphasising the enormous potential of microcomputers in the rehabilitation, management, and employment of brain-injured individuals.

APPENDIX I: LIST OF SUPPLIERS

I.1 Commercially Available Software

BRAIN-LINK SOFTWARE
317 MONTGOMERY Anne Arbor, MI48103, USA. Tel. (313) 995-0604.

Produces a multi-purpose reading recognition program for the Apple II+, IIe and IIc microcomputer.

BRAIN TRAIN
P.O. Box 1510, Beaverton OR97075-1510, USA. Tel. (503) 228-9117.

Brain Train Vol.I is a set of 55 computer programs designed to assist in the remediation of a wide range of cognitive and behavioural deficits.
   Runs on the Apple IIe and Apple GS and IBM PC (and compatible) microcomputers.

COMMUNICATION SKILL BUILDERS
3830 E Bellevue/P.O. Box 42050, Tucson, Arizona 85733, USA. Tel. (602) 323-7500.

Supply mainly non-computerised materials for use with communication-disordered adults and children. Offer a limited range of computer programs for practising language skills.

Programs run on the Apple series microcomputers.

DLM/TEACHING RESOURCES

Parrot Software, P.O. Box 1139, State College, PA 16804, USA. Tel. (800) 727-7681.

The Parrot Software range has been developed for use in the remediation of cognitive and communication disorders.

Programs run on the Apple II range and IBM (or compatible) computers.

FAR COMMUNICATIONS

5 Harcourt Estate, Kibworth, Leicestershire, LE8 0NE, UK. Tel. (0533) 796166.

Suppliers of The Computerised Boston.

HARTLEY COURSEWARE INC.

P.O. Box 419, Dimondale, MI48821, USA. Tel. 1-800-247-1380.

Suppliers of the "Cognitive Rehabilitation" series. Consists of five programs targeting organisational deficits in the brain-damaged patient.

Programs run on the Apple series and IBM PC computers.

LAUREATE LEARNING SYSTEMS INC.

110 East Spring Street, Winooski, Vermont 05404, USA. Tel. (802) 655-4755.

Suppliers of educational software which includes programs designed for remediation in children with communication disorders.

Programs run on the Apple series of microcomputers.

LIFE SCIENCE ASSOCIATES

One Fennimore Road, Bayport, New York, NY 11705, USA. Tel. (516) 472-2111.

Suppliers of the computer programs for Cognitive Rehabilitation developed by R. Gianutsos and colleagues.

A wide range of programs is available. Programs run on IBM PC (or compatibles) and Apple II series.

See Park Lodge Associates for UK distribution.

LOCHEESOFT

Orders or requests for information to: Software Director LOCHEE Publications Ltd., Oak Villa, New Alyth, Perthshire, PH11 8NN, UK. Tel. (0382) 832154 (orders) or (0382) 532805 (technical queries).

Supply retraining software for the BBC microcomputer developed by Robertson, Gray, Smart, and Richards at the Astley Ainslie Hospital, Edinburgh.

NFER-NELSON

Darville House, 2 Oxford Road East, Windsor, Berkshire, SL4 1DF, UK. Tel. (0753) 858961.

PARK LODGE ASSOCIATES

47 Four Oaks Road, Sutton Coldfield, Birmingham, B74 2XU, UK. Tel. (021) 323-2282.

Distributors for a wide range of psychology software including the Life Science Associates Cognitive Rehabilitation programs. The cost of each package will be more than if obtained direct but the company provide a user support service as well as taking care of the practical problems often associated with making payment in a foreign currency.

PSYCHOLOGICAL CORPORATION LTD

Harcourt Brace Jovanovich Publishers, Foots Cray High Street, Sidcup, Kent, DA14 5HP, UK. Tel. 081 300 1149/1140.

PSYCHOLOGICAL SOFTWARE SERVICES INC.

6555 Carollton Avenue, Indianapolis, IN46220, USA. Tel. (317) 257-9672.

Suppliers of software for Cognitive Rehabilitation therapy developed by Odie L Bracy. A wide range of programs is available.

Programs run on Apple, Atari and IBM computers.

RUSK INSTITUTE OF REHABILITATION MEDICINE
New York University Medical Centre, School of Dentistry Building, 345 East 24th Street, Room 818, New York, NY 10010, USA. Tel. (212) 340-7156.

Suppliers of the Computerised Orientation Remediation Module.
    Runs on the Apple IIc or IIe and IBM XT (or compatibles).

SUNSET SOFTWARE
11750 Sunset Boulevard, Suite 414, Los Angeles, CA 90049, USA. Tel. (213) 476-0245.

Speech, language and cognitive remediation software for the Apple II series of microcomputers.

GROUPE ZORGLUB
Contact: Francois Coyette, Centre de Revalidation Neuropsychologique, Cliniques Universitaires, Saint Luc, Avenue Hippocrate 10, B-1200, Bruxelles, Belgium. Tel. (02) 764-13-05.

Programs for diagnosis and retraining of visual inattention.
    Runs on the Apple IIe computer, with versions for the Apple II+ and Apple GS in the course of development.

I.2 Software and Information Available from Authors/Users

Mr R. Beresford, Department of Speech, Old Medical School, University of Newcastle upon Tyne, NE1 7RU, UK.

Enquiries about the Newcastle Speech Assessment.

Dr C.M.J. Braun, Department de Psychologie, Universitée du Quebec à Montreal, CP 8888, succ. "A", Montreal PQ, Canada H3C 3P8.

Enquiries about software for cognitive rehabilitation.
    Programs run on the Apple IIe microcomputer.

Burden Neurological Institute, Stoke Lane, Stapleton, Bristol, Avon, BS16 1QT, UK. Tel. (0272) 567444/565656.

The Cognitive Rehabilitation Suite is a suite of 56 programs designed to stimulate and challenge recovering head injury patients.
     Runs on the BBC microcomputer, minimum RAM requirement 1Mb. Supplied free to non-profit-making organisations.

Professor D.L. Chute, Neuropsychology Program and Software Development Group, Drexel University, Philadelphia, Pennsylvania 19104, USA.

Further information about "Prosthesis Ware" software: Speak Easy, Speak Easier, and Speak Easiest.

Dr Alan J. Finlayson, Chedoke–McMaster Hospitals, Box 2000, Station "A", Hamilton, L8N 3Z5, Canada. Tel. (416) 521-2100.

Copies of the programs "Sink the ship," "Simon says," "Intercept" and "Driver" can be supplied free of charge.
     The programs run on the Apple series of microcomputers. Driver works best with a game paddle or joystick.

Dr Roger Johnson, Department of Clinical Psychology, The Rehabilitation Unit, Addenbrooke's Hospital, Cambridge, CB2 2QQ, UK.

Author and supplier of the Memory Training Disc.
     Programs run on the BBC B or BBC Master. Send blank formatted disc.

Dr Phillip Lowe, Department of Medical Physics, Newcastle General Hospital, Westgate Road, Newcastle upon Tyne, NE4 6BE, UK.

The VISCAN keyboard and software were developed in this department.

Dr Richard J. Warburg, Department of Psychology, North Manchester General Hospital, Crumpsall, Manchester, M8 6RB, UK.

Author of programs for the assessment of memory impairment.

Programs run on the BBC microcomputer. They are still under development. The author would be interested in comments from those wishing to use the disc on an experimental basis.

Dr R.T. Woods, Department of Clinical Psychology, Institute of Psychiatry, De Crespigny Park, London, SE5 8AF, UK.

Further details and copies of automated cognitive tests developed for elderly patients.

Run on the commodore 64 microcomputers.

I.3 Suppliers of Non-computerised Assessment/ Rehabilitation Materials Described in this Book

Dr A.K. Coughlan, Psychology Department, St. James' University Hospital, Beckett St., Leeds, L79 7TF, UK.

Author and supplier of The Adult Memory and Information Processing Battery.

Thames Valley Publishing Company, 22 Bulmershe Road, Reading, RG1 5RJ, UK.

Suppliers of the Rivermead Behavioural Memory Test and the Behavioural Inattention Test.

Winslow Press, Telford Road, Oxon, OX6 0TS, UK. Tel. (0869) 244644,.

Supply Communication Stickers/Colour Communication Stickers, Colour Cards and other cognitive and communication aids and training materials.

I.4 Suppliers of Electronic and Peripheral Devices Described in this book

British Telecom, British Telecom Materials Department, Queens Drive House, 5 Dudmore Road, Swindon, SN3 1AH, UK. Tel. (0793) 484201.

Supply the Claudius Converse Electronic Voice.

Datamed, 39 Thorburn Road, Edinburgh, EH13 0BH, UK. Tel. (031) 441-3185.

Suppliers of communication aids.

MARDIS, Microprocessor Assistance for the Disabled, Room B22, Engineering Building, University of Lancaster, Bailrigg, Lancaster, CA1 4YW, UK.

Supply the MARDIS "Orac" portable speech communication system.

Micro Express, A.B. European Marketing Ltd., Wharfdale Road, Pentwyn, Cardiff, CF2 7HB, UK. Tel. (0222) 733485.

Suppliers of the Concept Keyboard. The keyboard can be used with most makes of computer. Interface leads/cards are available for IBM PCs (and clones), Apple IIe, Apple GS, Apple MacIntosh, Commodore 64, Commodore Amiga, Acorn Archimedes, Acorn BBC and RM Nimbus.

Microvitec plc., Futures Way, Bolling Road, Bradford, West Yorkshire, BD4 7TU, UK.

Suppliers of the Microvitec Touchtec 501 Touch Sensitive Screen.

APPENDIX II: SOURCES OF INFORMATION

Compaid Trust, Unit CH.1, Pembury Hospital, Tunbridge Wells, Kent, TN2 4OJ, UK. Tel. (0892) 82-4060.

Postal and telephone advice on issues relating to the use of computers by disabled people.

Disabled clients in the Tunbridge Wells area spend time working on computers at the Centre. The trust has been asked to set up a similar Advice Centre in the north of England.

Computers in Aphasia Working Party (CAW), Coordinator: Claire Kinsey, Research Speech Therapist, Frenchay Hospital, Frenchay, Bristol, Avon, BS16 1LE, UK.

CAW Holds regular meetings to discuss research projects in the area and acts as a core information source.

Director of Research into Automated (Psychological and Psychiatric) Testing (DRAT). Available from: Ms Linda Marshall, Ergonomics Research Group, Department of Psychology, University of Hull, Cottingham Road, HU6 7RX, UK. Tel. (0482) 465932.

Entries in the directory relate to research projects in computer-based psychological or psychiatric assessment. Information on software and hardware used is provided in addition to the authors' names and addresses.

HEADWAY—National Head Injuries Association, 200 Mansfield Road, Nottingham, NG1 3HX, UK. Tel. (0602) 622382.

National Speech Therapy Equipment Guide. Available from: S. Kirkby, 4 Albert Street, Western Hill, Durham, DH1 4RL, UK.

Open Software Library. Contact: Graham Wright, Education Centre, Warrington District School of Nursing, Lovely Lane, Warrington, UK.

A voluntary resource for health workers using microcomputers. It aims to collect computer programs which might not be generally available and disseminate them on either cassette tape or floppy disc.

SEND, Michael Thomas, SEND Project Officer, Micro-electronics Education Support Unit, Unit 6, Sir William Lyons Road, Science Park, University of Warwick, Coventry, CV4 7EZ, UK. Tel. (0203) 416994.

A special educational needs database available as part of the PRESTEL Education Service. Information on peripheral devices and software for use with children with special needs.

The CTI Directory of Psychology Software, supported by the Computer Board for Universities and Research Councils and the IBM UK Trust. Available from: CTI Centre for Psychology, Department of Psychology, University of York, York, YO1 5DD, UK.

APPENDIX III: AN INVESTIGATION INTO THE ECOLOGICAL VALIDITY OF TWO TRAINING TASKS

Background

The relationship between performance on memory tests administered in the clinical or laboratory setting and memory functioning in everyday life has been a matter of some concern over the past 2 to 3 decades (Erickson & Scott, 1977). The relationship between laboratory or clinically-based cognitive training tasks and performance of tasks in everyday life is similarly of concern, in relation to the issue of generalisation of improvements in training tasks to activities of daily living.

Boorman (1989) carried out a study which compared performance on the retraining tasks MEMCHAT and ROADRIGHT with performance on analogous behavioural tasks. The aim was to establish whether or not there was evidence of involvement of the same cognitive processes in the training and behavioural tasks.

Subjects

Fourteen of the subjects in the experimental group of the evaluation study took part in this experiment. These were subject 1 and subjects 3 to 15. Subject details are provided in Table 6.1.

Procedure

Two "real-life" tasks, one involving verbal memory (for conversational material) and the other right–left orientation and visual memory were devised. The aim was for these tasks to be analogous to the training tasks MEMCHAT and ROADRIGHT.

The following account of the procedure and the tasks used is quoted from Boorman's thesis:

ANALOGOUS VERBAL MEMORY TASK
I was familiar with many of the subjects, having supervised most of their cognitive retraining programmes, consequently trying to produce a "real-to-life" situation was made that much easier. Subjects were used to hearing about my ecological grievances which often came out during "between test" chats, and so were not the slightest bit suspicious when they entered the office to find me writing a letter to Margaret Thatcher about a Save the Whale campaign—all part of the experiment!
Dialogue for the Verbal Memory Task:
"Hello [name]. Come in, sit down. I'll be with you in a minute. I'm just writing a letter to (1) MARGARET THATCHER about a (2) SAVE THE WHALE CAMPAIGN that I'm involved with. Are you going anywhere nice for your holidays? I'm going to (3) PORTUGAL with my (4) PARENTS. The only problem is we've got to go from (5) GATWICK AIRPORT which is quite a drive. I'm holding the fort today as (6) DR BRADLEY and (7) MR WELCH have gone to a meeting at (8) WASHINGTON."

* The numbered points denote information that the subject will later be asked to recall. Two of the points being part of the instructions for the left/right orientation task (see below).

ANALOGOUS LEFT/RIGHT ORIENTATION TASK
Instructions:
"I want you to do a short test involving you reading a map. I'll show you what to do, and then you continue. You begin here at the (9) NEUROLOGICAL CENTRE marked START on the map."
Proceed to Demonstrate
The supervisor unfolds the map and orientates herself. Using the map she guides herself and the subject to the short path leading to the main corridor. The map is then folded up again and handed to the subject.

Then:
"From now on it is up to you to follow the arrows around the hospital to the point marked STOP. That is the (10) PSYCHOLOGICAL MEDICINE BUILDING. Go as quickly as you can, making sure that you follow the arrows carefully."
There is a total of 6 corners for the subject to make a right/left discrimination on. The subject is timed using a stopwatch over the 338 metre route. If the subject takes a wrong turning, the supervisor stops the clock, calls back the subject to the decision corner and corrects the error. The clock is started again. The total time

taken for the subject to complete the 338m route is noted. (Total of 6 corners, 1 point per corner). The subject is then taken back to the main building.

To determine the subject's average decision time per corner, the subject is timed over a 10 metre stretch of corridor at normal walking speed.

Calculation is:
S takes x seconds to walk 10 metres (corridor)
S takes x/10 seconds to walk 1 metre
S takes x/110 * 338 seconds to walk 338m
Predicted time for subject to walk 338m = 338x/10.

Average left/right decision time:
Decision time = R (time for 338m route) = 338x/10
Average decision time per corner = R–(338x/10)/6

NB. A negative score means that actual time was quicker than predicted time due to a lack of consistency in walking speed.

Then (back in the office):
"I'm just going to ask you a few questions about what we were talking about earlier."
Questions:
1) When you first came into the office, who did I say I was writing to? (MARGARET THATCHER)
2) About what? (SAVE THE WHALE)
3) Where am I going on holiday? (PORTUGAL)
4) Who am I going with? (PARENTS)
5) Which airport are we going from? (GATWICK)
6) What are the names of the people who I said I was holding the fort for? (DR BRADLEY AND MR WELCH—2 points)
7) Where have they gone? (WASHINGTON)
8) What was the name of the building marked START on the map? (NEURO-LOGICAL CENTRE)
9) What was the name of the building marked STOP on the map? (PSYCHO-LOGICAL MEDICINE BUILDING)

The subjects' total score for verbal memory (delayed recall of information) is determined. One point per correct answer, maximum score possible = 10. Where the answer approximated the correct answer but was not absolutely accurate, it was scored 0.5.

Results and Analysis of Results

Table III.1 shows the scores for each subject on the real-life verbal memory task and the MEMCHAT training task at each of the 3 levels of difficulty. The MEMCHAT scores were those obtained in the pos.-training administration of the tasks. Total score for each task is 10.

TABLE III.1
Raw Scores on the Real-life Verbal Memory Task and the MEMCHAT
Training Task

Subject	Verbal Memory Task	MEMCHAT		
		Level 1	Level 2	Level 3
1	9	7	10	8
3	8	10	10	10
4	3	8	7	7
5	8.5	10	10	9
6	2	6	5	9
7	9	9	10	9
8	9	10	9	10
9	5	8	8	8
10	4	9	8	7
11	2	5	9	7
12	10	10	10	10
13	7.5	9	10	10
14	9	8	8	8
15	8.5	10	9	10

Pearson's correlation coefficient was calculated. Statistically significant correlations on a 2-tail test were obtained between scores on the real-life task and scores on each level of the training task (Level 1: $r = 0.7$, $p < .01$; Level 2: $r = 0.72$, $p < .001$; Level 3: $r = 0.71$, $p < .01$).

Table III.2 shows the scores for each subject on the real-life orientation and visual memory task and the ROADRIGHT training task. Subject 13 obtained a negative decision time score as a result of inconsistency in walking speed, as well as rapid decision time. Because rapid decision time contributed to the score it was not omitted from the analysis. Number of errors and mean decision time per corner were calculated for the real-life and training task, scores for the latter being taken from the post-training administration of the orientation task only. The administration included items at all 4 difficulty levels.

Pearson's correlation coefficient was calculated. No statistically significant correlations were found between performance on the real-life and training tasks. Correlation coefficients were as follows: Orientation task errors (OTE) and training task errors (TTE): $r = 0.082$, $p > .05$. Orientation task decision time (OTD) and training task decision time (TTD): $r = 0.013$, $p > .05$; OTE and TTD: $r = 0.118$, $p > .05$. OTD and TTE: $r = 0.325$, $p > .05$.

TABLE III.2
Raw Scores on the Real-life Orientation Task and the ROADRIGHT Training Task

Subject	Orientation Task		ROADRIGHT	
	No. of of Errors	Mean Decision Time per Corner	No. of of Errors	Mean Decision Time per Corner
1	1	7.57	1	5.83
3	0	14.4	0	8.52
4	2	0.23	0	4.01
5	0	9.53	1	5.32
6	1	7.23	8	16.3
7	0	1.9	0	3.06
8	0	10.57	0	6.38
9	4	42.9	0	9.11
10	3	19.77	0	7.52
11	0	7.43	1	7.12
12	1	25.13	0	3.19
13	0	-5.56	0	6.78
14	0	11.86	0	39.85
15	0	1.8	3	6.42

Discussion

Highly significant correlations were obtained between the scores on the real-life verbal memory task and the scores on the MEMCHAT training task. This result suggests that the tasks are subserved by the same underlying cognitive processes and that the computerised training task has ecological validity.

The same cannot be said of the real-life orientation task and the training task ROADRIGHT, where no significant correlations were obtained. The differences between the 2 tasks were described by Boorman (1989) as follows:

> The computer program was presented to the subjects on a V.D.U. requiring the subjects to make an initial mental rotation through a horizontal axis, so as to enable them to imagine themselves "setting off" from one of the houses. Whereas when presented with the map, the subjects generally held the map flat and viewed it from above, eliminating the mental rotation involved in the computerised task. The subjects could then orientate themselves at different stages along the route by turning the map. Of course, the computer screen has no such flexibility. Another difference between the 2 tasks is their presentation. The map gives the subjects a number of clues which aid orientation, such as names of corridors and buildings

etc. (although this was kept to an absolute minimum) whereas the houses in the computerised exercise were merely coloured squares with little resemblance to real houses.

Observation of subject number 6 illustrates the functional differences between the 2 tasks beautifully. Over the 9 weeks of retraining, despite the measures taken to help him, he showed no improvement on the training task. Having been a keen cyclist prior to his head injury (and so presumably competent at making left/right discriminations) it was assumed that his poor performance score on ROAD-RIGHT indicated an orientation deficit occurring as a result of the cerebral insult he has received. This was confirmed by the subject's father who reported that since his accident, he often lost his way. The only way that he could achieve an acceptable result on the training task was to transfer the task from the screen to the floor, marking out a path running between two houses and getting him physically to start at one marked house and to verbalise his route as he walked to the other. This avoided a mental rotation through a horizontal plane. Not so surprisingly then, this subject performed extremely well on the "real-life" left/right orientation task, tackling 5 out of the 6 corners successfully!

APPENDIX IV

TABLE IV.1
Percentage Reduction in Patients Rated in Poorest Category After NCRP

Memory and Concentration	Respondent	
	Patient	Carer
1. Rate Memory	29%	10%
2.	19%	15%
3. Forget to do things	20%	21%
4. Forget lists	20%	3%
5. Family/Friends	40%	17%
6. Conversation track	22%	12%
7. Concentrate	13%	26%
8. Think quickly	-6%	-33%
9.	9%	4%
10.	9%	15%
11.	-15%	-10%
Feeling		
12. Worry	20%	11%
13.	11%	16%
14.	-3%	10%
15. Mood change	26%	29%

(Continued)

TABLE IV.1
(Continued)

	Respondent	
Memory and Concentration	Patient	Carer
16. Drive	31%	21%
17. Cheerful	29%	9%
18.	-3%	19%
19. Speak up for self	46%	13%
Spend Time		
20.	16%	9%
21.	6%	-16%
22.	12%	5%
23. Repair jobs	31%	-5%
24.	3%	1%
25.	-4%	-11%
26.	-1%	2%
27.	16%	-16%
28.	-6%	3%
29.	-12%	2%
30. Travel public	16%	-22%
31.	13%	19%
32. Visit friends	30%	-9%
33.	13%	-11%
34. Pub/club	21%	8%
35.	15%	1%
36.	11%	-1%
37.	11%	-9%
38. Hobbies	8%	23%
39.	-4%	-9%
40.	10%	-8%
41.	13%	14%
42.	3%	9%
43. Help outside house	5%	29%
44.	-7%	-7%
45.	1%	-9%
46.	6%	6%
47. Make understand	40%	23%
48.	-25%	-16%
49.	-17%	-10%
50.	-5%	14%

PRE-TRAINING QUESTIONNAIRE (PATIENT'S VERSION)

Name ....

Today's date ....

Employment
(most recent full-time job if unemployed now) ....

Mode of completion ....

Please put a tick in the box ☑ next to the word that best describes how things are *now* (meaning the last 2 or 3 weeks). Also put a tick in the box ☑ next to the word that best describes how things were before your illness or accident. Please answer all the questions.

	Now	*Before Illness/Accident*

Your memory and concentration

1. How would you rate your memory?
   - [ ] very good
   - [ ] good
   - [ ] average
   - [ ] poor
   - [ ] very poor

   Before Illness/Accident
   - [ ] very good
   - [ ] good
   - [ ] average
   - [ ] poor
   - [ ] very poor

2. Do/did you lose your way?
   - [ ] never
   - [ ] occasionally
   - [ ] sometimes
   - [ ] often
   - [ ] very often

   Before Illness/Accident
   - [ ] never
   - [ ] occasionally
   - [ ] sometimes
   - [ ] often
   - [ ] very often

3. Do/did you forget to do things?
   - [ ] never
   - [ ] occasionally
   - [ ] sometimes
   - [ ] often
   - [ ] very often

   Before Illness/Accident
   - [ ] never
   - [ ] occasionally
   - [ ] sometimes
   - [ ] often
   - [ ] very often

4. Do/did you forget messages and lists?
   - [ ] never
   - [ ] occasionally
   - [ ] sometimes
   - [ ] often
   - [ ] very often

   Before Illness/Accident
   - [ ] never
   - [ ] occasionally
   - [ ] sometimes
   - [ ] often
   - [ ] very often

	Now	*Before Illness/Accident*

5. Do/did you forget important details about family and close friends?

Now	Before Illness/Accident
☐ never	☐ never
☐ occasionally	☐ occasionally
☐ sometimes	☐ sometimes
☐ often	☐ often
☐ very often	☐ very often

6. Do/did you lose track of the conversation?

Now	Before Illness/Accident
☐ never	☐ never
☐ occasionally	☐ occasionally
☐ sometimes	☐ sometimes
☐ often	☐ often
☐ very often	☐ very often

7. Is/was it difficult to concentrate?

Now	Before Illness/Accident
☐ no	☐ no
☐ a bit difficult	☐ a bit difficult
☐ moderately difficult	☐ moderately difficult
☐ very difficult	☐ very difficult

8. Is/was it difficult to think quickly?

Now	Before Illness/Accident
☐ no	☐ no
☐ a bit difficult	☐ a bit difficult
☐ moderately difficult	☐ moderately difficult
☐ very difficult	☐ very difficult

9. Do/did you confuse right and left?

Now	Before Illness/Accident
☐ never	☐ never
☐ occasionally	☐ occasionally
☐ sometimes	☐ sometimes
☐ often	☐ often
☐ very often	☐ very often

10. Do/did you bump into things because you don't see them?

Now	Before Illness/Accident
☐ never	☐ never
☐ occasionally	☐ occasionally
☐ sometimes	☐ sometimes
☐ often	☐ often
☐ very often	☐ very often

	Now	*Before Illness/Accident*
11. Is/was it difficult to recognise people?	☐ no ☐ a bit difficult ☐ moderately difficult ☐ very difficult	☐ no ☐ a bit difficult ☐ moderately difficult ☐ very difficult

How you feel

12. Do/did you worry about things?	☐ never ☐ occasionally ☐ sometimes ☐ often ☐ very often	☐ never ☐ occasionally ☐ sometimes ☐ often ☐ very often
13. Are/were you irritable?	☐ never ☐ occasionally ☐ sometimes ☐ often ☐ very often	☐ never ☐ occasionally ☐ sometimes ☐ often ☐ very often
14. Do/did you get very angry?	☐ never ☐ occasionally ☐ sometimes ☐ often ☐ very often	☐ never ☐ occasionally ☐ sometimes ☐ often ☐ very often
15. Does/did your mood change suddenly?	☐ never ☐ occasionally ☐ sometimes ☐ often ☐ very often	☐ never ☐ occasionally ☐ sometimes ☐ often ☐ very often
16. Do/did you feel listless and lacking in drive?	☐ never ☐ occasionally ☐ sometimes ☐ often ☐ very often	☐ never ☐ occasionally ☐ sometimes ☐ often ☐ very often

	Now	*Before Illness/Accident*
17. Do/did you feel cheerful?	☐ never ☐ occasionally ☐ sometimes ☐ often ☐ very often	☐ never ☐ occasionally ☐ sometimes ☐ often ☐ very often
18. Are/were you tactful?	☐ no ☐ not very ☐ moderately ☐ very	☐ no ☐ not very ☐ moderately ☐ very
19. Do/did you speak up for yourself?	☐ never ☐ occasionally ☐ sometimes ☐ often ☐ very often	☐ never ☐ occasionally ☐ sometimes ☐ often ☐ very often

How you spend your time

	Now	*Before Illness/Accident*
20. Do/did you prepare snacks or meals?	☐ never ☐ occasionally ☐ sometimes ☐ often ☐ very often	☐ never ☐ occasionally ☐ sometimes ☐ often ☐ very often
21. Do/did you wash up?	☐ never ☐ occasionally ☐ sometimes ☐ often ☐ very often	☐ never ☐ occasionally ☐ sometimes ☐ often ☐ very often
22. Do/did you do housework?	☐ never ☐ occasionally ☐ sometimes ☐ often ☐ very often	☐ never ☐ occasionally ☐ sometimes ☐ often ☐ very often

	Now	*Before Illness/Accident*

23. Do/did you do repair jobs about the house?

Now	Before Illness/Accident
☐ never	☐ never
☐ occasionally	☐ occasionally
☐ sometimes	☐ sometimes
☐ often	☐ often
☐ very often	☐ very often

24. Do/did you do your own home improvements? (eg, upholstery, replacing kitchen units)

Now	Before Illness/Accident
☐ never	☐ never
☐ occasionally	☐ occasionally
☐ sometimes	☐ sometimes
☐ often	☐ often
☐ very often	☐ very often

25. Do/did you do repair jobs on a car or bike?

Now	Before Illness/Accident
☐ never	☐ never
☐ occasionally	☐ occasionally
☐ sometimes	☐ sometimes
☐ often	☐ often
☐ very often	☐ very often

26. Do/did you do any painting and decorating?

Now	Before Illness/Accident
☐ never	☐ never
☐ occasionally	☐ occasionally
☐ sometimes	☐ sometimes
☐ often	☐ often
☐ very often	☐ very often

27. Do/did you shop in local shops?

Now	Before Illness/Accident
☐ never	☐ never
☐ occasionally	☐ occasionally
☐ sometimes	☐ sometimes
☐ often	☐ often
☐ very often	☐ very often

28. Do/did you go shopping in a large shopping centre?

Now	Before Illness/Accident
☐ never	☐ never
☐ occasionally	☐ occasionally
☐ sometimes	☐ sometimes
☐ often	☐ often
☐ very often	☐ very often

	Now	*Before Illness/Accident*
29. Do/did you drive a car?	☐ never ☐ occasionally ☐ sometimes ☐ often ☐ very often	☐ never ☐ occasionally ☐ sometimes ☐ often ☐ very often
30. Do/did you travel by public transport?	☐ never ☐ occasionally ☐ sometimes ☐ often ☐ very often	☐ never ☐ occasionally ☐ sometimes ☐ often ☐ very often
31. Do/did you go for walks?	☐ never ☐ occasionally ☐ sometimes ☐ often ☐ very often	☐ never ☐ occasionally ☐ sometimes ☐ often ☐ very often
32. Do/did you visit friends and relatives at home?	☐ never ☐ occasionally ☐ sometimes ☐ often ☐ very often	☐ never ☐ occasionally ☐ sometimes ☐ often ☐ very often
33. Do/did friends and relatives visit you at home?	☐ never ☐ occasionally ☐ sometimes ☐ often ☐ very often	☐ never ☐ occasionally ☐ sometimes ☐ often ☐ very often
34. Do/did you go out to a pub or a club?	☐ never ☐ occasionally ☐ sometimes ☐ often ☐ very often	☐ never ☐ occasionally ☐ sometimes ☐ often ☐ very often

	Now	*Before Illness/Accident*

35. Do/did you spend time gardening?

Now	*Before Illness/Accident*
☐ never	☐ never
☐ occasionally	☐ occasionally
☐ sometimes	☐ sometimes
☐ often	☐ often
☐ very often	☐ very often

36. Do/did you read books or newspapers?

Now	*Before Illness/Accident*
☐ never	☐ never
☐ occasionally	☐ occasionally
☐ sometimes	☐ sometimes
☐ often	☐ often
☐ very often	☐ very often

37. Do/did you join in any games or sports?

Now	*Before Illness/Accident*
☐ never	☐ never
☐ occasionally	☐ occasionally
☐ sometimes	☐ sometimes
☐ often	☐ often
☐ very often	☐ very often

38. Do/did you have any other hobby, interest or voluntary work which you are/were engaged in?

If yes, please specify:

☐_____

Now	*Before Illness/Accident*
☐ never	☐ never
☐ occasionally	☐ occasionally
☐ sometimes	☐ sometimes
☐ often	☐ often
☐ very often	☐ very often

39. Do/did you have a paid job?

Now	*Before Illness/Accident*
☐ full-time	☐ full-time
☐ part-time	☐ part-time
☐ occasional casual work	☐ occasional casual work
☐ no	☐ no

You and your family

40. Do/did you spend time alone in the house?

Now	*Before Illness/Accident*
☐ never	☐ never
☐ occasionally	☐ occasionally
☐ sometimes	☐ sometimes
☐ often	☐ often
☐ very often	☐ very often

	Now	Before Illness/Accident

41. Do/did you go out of the house alone?
Now	Before Illness/Accident
☐ never	☐ never
☐ occasionally	☐ occasionally
☐ sometimes	☐ sometimes
☐ often	☐ often
☐ very often	☐ very often

42. Do/did you need help getting about in the house?
Now	Before Illness/Accident
☐ no	☐ no
☐ a little help	☐ a little help
☐ a lot of help	☐ a lot of help

43. Do/did you need help getting about outside the house?
Now	Before Illness/Accident
☐ no	☐ no
☐ a little help	☐ a little help
☐ a lot of help	☐ a lot of help

44. Can/could you manage your own cooking and washing if necessary?
Now	Before Illness/Accident
☐ no	☐ no
☐ yes, with difficulty	☐ yes, with difficulty
☐ yes, easily	☐ yes, easily

45. Can/could you take responsibility for looking after children or sick or elderly relatives if necessary?
Now	Before Illness/Accident
☐ no	☐ no
☐ yes, with difficulty	☐ yes, with difficulty
☐ yes, easily	☐ yes, easily

46. Do/did you find it difficult to work out change when paying for something?
Now	Before Illness/Accident
☐ no	☐ no
☐ a bit difficult	☐ a bit difficult
☐ moderately difficult	☐ moderately difficult
☐ very difficult	☐ very difficult
☐ don't handle money	☐ don't handle money

47. Do/did you find it difficult to make yourself understood when out alone?
Now	Before Illness/Accident
☐ no	☐ no
☐ a bit difficult	☐ a bit difficult
☐ moderately difficult	☐ moderately difficult
☐ very difficult	☐ very difficult
☐ don't go out alone	☐ don't go out alone

	Now	*Before Illness/Accident*
48. Do/did you take responsibility for paying bills?	☐ never ☐ occasionally ☐ sometimes ☐ often ☐ very often	☐ never ☐ occasionally ☐ sometimes ☐ often ☐ very often
49. Are/were you involved in decisions about how money is spent in your family?	☐ never ☐ occasionally ☐ sometimes ☐ often ☐ very often	☐ never ☐ occasionally ☐ sometimes ☐ often ☐ very often
50. Are/were you involved in decisions about family matters (e.g. holidays, children's schooling)?	☐ never ☐ occasionally ☐ sometimes ☐ often ☐ very often	☐ never ☐ occasionally ☐ sometimes ☐ often ☐ very often

POST-TRAINING QUESTIONNAIRE (PATIENT'S VERSION)

Name ....

Today's date ....

Employment
(most recent full-time job if unemployed now) ....

Mode of completion ....

Please put a tick in the box ☑ next to the word that best describes how things are *now* (meaning the last 2 or 3 weeks).

Your memory and concentration

1. How would you rate your memory?

☐ very good
☐ good
☐ average
☐ poor
☐ very poor

2. Do you lose your way?

☐ never
☐ occasionally
☐ sometimes
☐ often
☐ very often

3. Do you forget to do things?

☐ never
☐ occasionally
☐ sometimes
☐ often
☐ very often

4. Do you forget messages and lists?

☐ never
☐ occasionally
☐ sometimes
☐ often
☐ very often

5. Do you forget important details about family and close friends?

☐ never
☐ occasionally
☐ sometimes
☐ often
☐ very often

6. Do you lose track of the conversation?

☐ never
☐ occasionally
☐ sometimes
☐ often
☐ very often

7. Is it difficult to concentrate?

☐ no
☐ a bit difficult
☐ moderately difficult
☐ very difficult

8. Is it difficult to think quickly?

☐ no
☐ a bit difficult
☐ moderately difficult
☐ very difficult

9. Do you confuse right and left?

☐ never
☐ occasionally
☐ sometimes
☐ often
☐ very often

10. Do you bump into things because you don't see them?

☐ never
☐ occasionally
☐ sometimes
☐ often
☐ very often

11. Is it difficult to recognise people?

☐ no
☐ a bit difficult
☐ moderately difficult
☐ very difficult

How you feel

12. Do you worry about things?

☐ never
☐ occasionally
☐ sometimes
☐ often
☐ very often

13. Are you irritable?

☐ never
☐ occasionally
☐ sometimes
☐ often
☐ very often

14. Do you get very angry?

☐ never
☐ occasionally
☐ sometimes
☐ often
☐ very often

15. Does your mood change suddenly?

☐ never
☐ occasionally
☐ sometimes
☐ often
☐ very often

16. Do you feel listless and lacking in drive?

☐ never
☐ occasionally
☐ sometimes
☐ often
☐ very often

17. Do you feel cheerful?

☐ never
☐ occasionally
☐ sometimes
☐ often
☐ very often

18. Are you tactful?

☐ no
☐ not very
☐ moderately
☐ very

19. Do you speak up for yourself?

☐ never
☐ occasionally
☐ sometimes
☐ often
☐ very often

How you spend your time

20. Do you prepare snacks or meals?

☐ never
☐ occasionally
☐ sometimes
☐ often
☐ very often

21. Do you wash up?

☐ never
☐ occasionally
☐ sometimes
☐ often
☐ very often

22. Do you do housework

☐ never
☐ occasionally
☐ sometimes
☐ often
☐ very often

23. Do you do repair jobs about the house?

☐ never
☐ occasionally
☐ sometimes
☐ often
☐ very often

24. Do you do your own home improvements? (e.g., upholstery, replacing kitchen units)

- [ ] never
- [ ] occasionally
- [ ] sometimes
- [ ] often
- [ ] very often

25. Do you do repair jobs on a car or bike?

- [ ] never
- [ ] occasionally
- [ ] sometimes
- [ ] often
- [ ] very often

26. Do you do any painting and decorating?

- [ ] never
- [ ] occasionally
- [ ] sometimes
- [ ] often
- [ ] very often

27. Do you shop in local shops?

- [ ] never
- [ ] occasionally
- [ ] sometimes
- [ ] often
- [ ] very often

28. Do you go shopping in a large shopping centre?

- [ ] never
- [ ] occasionally
- [ ] sometimes
- [ ] often
- [ ] very often

29. Do you drive a car?

- [ ] never
- [ ] occasionally
- [ ] sometimes
- [ ] often
- [ ] very often

30. Do you travel by public transport?

☐ never
☐ occasionally
☐ sometimes
☐ often
☐ very often

31. Do you go for walks?

☐ never
☐ occasionally
☐ sometimes
☐ often
☐ very often

32. Do you visit friends and relatives at home?

☐ never
☐ occasionally
☐ sometimes
☐ often
☐ very often

33. Do friends and relatives visit you at home?

☐ never
☐ occasionally
☐ sometimes
☐ often
☐ very often

34. Do you go out to a pub or a club?

☐ never
☐ occasionally
☐ sometimes
☐ often
☐ very often

35. Do you spend time gardening?

☐ never
☐ occasionally
☐ sometimes
☐ often
☐ very often

36. Do you read books or newspapers?

☐ never
☐ occasionally
☐ sometimes
☐ often
☐ very often

37. Do you join in any games or sports?

☐ never
☐ occasionally
☐ sometimes
☐ often
☐ very often

38. Do you have any other hobby, interest or voluntary work which you are engaged in?

    If yes, please specify:

    [   ]

☐ never
☐ occasionally
☐ sometimes
☐ often
☐ very often

39. Do you have a paid job?

☐ full-time
☐ part-time
☐ occasional casual work
☐ no

You and your family

40. Do you spend time alone in the house?

☐ never
☐ occasionally
☐ sometimes
☐ often
☐ very often

41. Do you go out of the house alone?

☐ never
☐ occasionally
☐ sometimes
☐ often
☐ very often

42. Do you need help getting about in the house?

☐ no
☐ a little help
☐ a lot of help

43. Do you need help getting about outside the house?

☐ no
☐ a little help
☐ a lot of help

44. Can you manage your own cooking and washing if necessary?

☐ no
☐ yes, with difficulty
☐ yes, easily

45. Can you take responsibility for looking after children or sick or elderly relatives if necessary?

☐ no
☐ yes, with difficulty
☐ yes, easily

46. Do you find it difficult to work out change when paying for something?

☐ no
☐ a bit difficult
☐ moderately difficult
☐ very difficult
☐ don't handle money

47. Do you find it difficult to make yourself understood when out alone?

☐ no
☐ a bit difficult
☐ moderately difficult
☐ very difficult
☐ don't go out alone

48. Do you take responsibility for paying bills?

☐ never
☐ occasionally
☐ sometimes
☐ often
☐ very often

49. Are you involved in decisions about how money is spent in your family?

☐ never
☐ occasionally
☐ sometimes
☐ often
☐ very often

50. Are you involved in decisions about family matters (e.g. holidays, children's schooling)?

☐ never

☐ occasionally

☐ sometimes

☐ often

☐ very often

References

Acker, W. & Acker, C. (1982). *Bexley–Maudsley automated psychological screening and category sorting tests.* Windsor: NFER–Nelson.

Adamovich, B.R., Henderson, J.A., & Auerbach, S. (1985). *Cognitive rehabilitation of closed head injured patients: A dynamic approach.* San Diego, California: College Hill Press. London: Taylor and Francis.

Albert, M.L. & Obler, L. (1978). *The bilingual brain.* New York: Academic Press.

Allport, A. (1980). Attention and performance. In G. Claxton (Ed.), *Cognitive psychology: New directions.* London: Routledge & Kegan Paul.

Andrews, K., Brocklehurst, J.C., Richards, B, & Laycock, P.J. (1980). The prognostic value of picture drawings by stroke patients. *Rheumatology Rehabilitation, 19,* 180–188.

Angle, H.B., Hay, L.R., Hay, W.M., & Ellinwood, E.H. (1977). Computer-aided interviewing in comprehensive behavioural assessment. *Behaviour Therapy, 8,* 747–754.

Baddeley, A.D. (1982). Implications of neuropsychological evidence for theories of normal memory. *Philosophical Transactions of the Royal Society of London B., 298,* 59–72.

Baddeley, A.D. & Wilkinson, A. (1983). Taking memory out of the laboratory. In J. Harris & P.E. Morris (Eds), *Everyday memory, actions & absent mindedness.* London: Academic Press.

Baringer, J.R. (1978). Simplex virus infections of the nervous system. In P.J. Vinken & G.W. Bruys (Eds), *Handbook of clinical neurology 34: Infections of the nervous system, Part II.* Amsterdam: North Holland Publishing Company.

Barlow, D.H. & Hersen, M. (1984). *Single case experimental designs* (Second Edition). New York: Pergamon Press.

Bartram, D., Beaumont, J.G., Cornford, T., Dann, P.L., and Wilson, S.L. (1987). Recommendations for the design of software for computer based assessment—Summary statement. *Bulletin of the British Psychological Society, 40,* 86–87.

Basso, A. (1987). Approaches to neuropsychological rehabilitation: language disorders. In M.J. Meier, A.L. Benton & L. Diller (Eds), *Neuropsychological Rehabilitation.* New York and London: Churchill Livingstone.

229

Basso, A., Capitani, E., & Moraschini, S. (1982a). Sex differences in recovery from aphasia. *Cortex, 18*, 469–475.

Basso, A., Capitani, E., & Zanobio, M.C. (1982b). Pattern of recovery of oral and written expression and comprehension in aphasic patients. *Behavioural Brain Research, 6*, 115–128.

Battersby, W.S., Bender, M.B., Pollack, M., & Kahn, R.L. (1956). Unilateral "spatial agnosia" ("inattention") in patients with cortical lesions. *Brain, 79*, 68–93.

Bayless, J.D., Varney, N.R., & Roberts, R.T. (1989). Tinkertoy test performance and vocational outcome in patients with closed head injuries. *Journal of Clinical & Experimental Neuropsychology, 11*, 913–917.

Beaumont, J.G. (1975). The validity of the category test administered by on-line computer. *Journal of Clinical Psychology, 31*, 458–462.

Beaumont, J.G. (1981). Microcomputer aided assessment using standard psychometric procedures. *Behaviour Research Methods and Instrumentation, 13*, 430–433.

Beaumont, J.G. & French, C.C. (1987). A clinical field study of eight automated psychometric procedures: The Leicester/DHSS project. *International Journal of Man–Machine Studies, 26*, 661–682.

Bender, L. (1938). A visual motor gestalt test and its clinical use. *American Orthopsychiatric Association Research Monographs, No. 3.*

Bender, M.B. (1979). Defects in reversal of serial order of symbols. *Neuropsychologia, 17*, 125–138.

Benjamin, R.M. & Thompson, R.F. (1959). Differential effects of cortical lesions in infant and adult cats on roughness discrimination. *Experimental Neurology, 1*, 305–321.

Bennett-Levy, J. & Powell, G.E. (1980). The subjective memory questionnaire: An investigation into the self-reporting of "real life" memory skills. *British Journal of Social and Clinical Psychology, 19*, 177–188.

Benton, A.L. (1950). A multiple choice type of the visual retention test. *Archives of Neurology & Psychiatry, 64*, 699–707.

Benton, A.L. (1968). Differential behavioural effects in frontal lobe disease. *Neuropsychologia, 6*, 53–60.

Benton, A.L. (1974). *The revised visual retention test* (Fourth Edition). New York: Psychological Corporation.

Benton, A.L. (1979). Visuoperceptive, visuospatial and visuoconstructive disorders. In K.M. Heilman & E. Valenstein (Eds), *Clinical neuropsychology*. New York: Oxford University Press.

Benton, A.L., Elithorn, A., Fogel, M.L., & Kerr, M.A. (1963). A perceptual maze test sensitive to brain damage. *Journal of Neurology, Neurosurgery & Psychiatry, 26*, 540–544.

Benton, A.L. & Hamsher, K. de S. (1976). *Multilingual aphasia examination: Manual.* Iowa City: University of Iowa.

Benton, A.L., Hamsher, K. de S., Varney, N.R., & Spreen, O. (1983). *Contributions to neuropsychological assessment.* New York: Oxford University Press.

Benton, A.L. & van Allen, M.W. (1968). Impairment in facial recognition in patients with cerebral disease. *Cortex, 4*, 344–358.

Ben-Yishay, Y., Gerstman, L.J., Diller, L., & Haas, A. (1970). Prediction of the rehabilitation outcomes from psychometric parameters in left hemiplegics. *Journal of Consulting and Clinical Psychology, 34*, 436–441.

Ben-Yishay, Y., Piasetsky, E.B., & Diller, L. (1978). A modular approach to training (verbal) abstract thinking in brain injured people. In Y. Ben-Yishay (Ed.), Working approaches to remediation of cognitive deficits in brain damaged persons. *Rehabilitation Monographs, 59*. New York: New York University Medical Center.

Ben-Yishay, Y., Piasetsky, E.B., & Rattok, J. (1987). A systematic method for ameliorating disorders in basic attention. In M.J. Meier, A.C. Benton, & L. Diller (Eds), *Neuropsychological rehabilitation*. Edinburgh and New York: Churchill Livingstone.

Ben-Yishay, Y., Rattok, J., & Diller, L. (1979). A clinical strategy for the systematic amelioration of attentional disturbances in severe head trauma patients. In Y. Ben-Yishay (Ed.), Working approaches to remediation of cognitive deficits in brain-damaged persons. *Rehabilitation Monograph, No. 60,* 1–27. New York: New York University Medical Center.

Ben-Yishay, Y., Rattok, J., & Ross, B. (1982). *Working approaches to remediation of cognitive deficits in brain damage. Supplement to the 7th annual workshop for rehabilitation professionals.* New York: University Institute of Rehabilitation Medicine.

Ben-Yishay, Y., Rattok, J., Ross, B., Lakin, P., Cohen, J., & Diller, L. (1980). A remedial module for the systematic amelioration of basic attentional disturbances in head trauma patients. In Y. Ben-Yishay (Ed.), Working approaches to remediation of cognitive deficits in brain-damaged persons. *Rehabilitation Monograph, No. 61,* 70–127. New York: New York University Medical Center.

Beresford, R. (1988). *The Newcastle Speech Assessment.* Newcastle upon Tyne: Department of Speech, University of Newcastle upon Tyne.

Berg, E.A. (1948). A simple objective test for measuring flexibility in thinking. *Journal of General Psychology, 39,* 15–22.

Bergman, M., Hirsch, S., & Nagenson, T. (1977). Tests of auditory perception in the assessment and management of patients with cerebral cranial injury. *Scandinavian Journal of Rehabilitation Medicine, 9,* 173–177.

Black, P., Markowitz, R.S., & Cianci, S. (1975). Recovery of motor function after lesions in the motor cortex of the monkey. In R. Porter & D.W. Fitzsimmons (Eds) *Outcome of severe damage to the central nervous system.* CIBA Foundation Symposium No 34. Amsterdam: Elsevier.

Boller, R. & Vignolo, L.A. (1966). Latent sensory aphasia in hemisphere-damaged patients: An experimental study with the Token Test. *Brain, 89,* 815–830.

Bond, M.R. (1975). Assessment of psychosocial outcome after severe head injury. In R. Porter & D.W. Fitzsimmons (Eds), *Outcome of severe damage to the central nervous system* (CIBA Foundation Symposium No. 34). Amsterdam: Elsevier.

Bond, M.R. (1976). Assessment of psychosocial outcome of severe head injury. *Acta Neurochirrurgica, 34,* 57–70.

Bond, M.R. (1979). The stages of recovery from severe head injury with special reference to late outcome. *International Rehabilitation Medicine, 1,* 155–159.

Bond, M.R. (1984). The psychiatry of closed head injury. In N. Brooks, *Closed head injury: Psychological social and family consequences.* Oxford: Oxford University Press.

Bond, M.R. (1986). Neurobehavioural sequelae of closed head injury. In I. Grant & K.M. Adams (Eds), *Neuropsychological assessment of neuropsychiatric disorders.* New York: Oxford University Press.

Bond, M.R. & Brooks, D.N. (1976). Understanding the process of recovery as a basis for the investigation of rehabilitation for the brain injured. *Scandinavian Journal of Rehabilitation Medicine, 8,* 127.

Boorman, T. (1989). *An investigation into whether laboratory based cognitive tests and analogous behavioural tasks utilise the same mental processes.* Unpublished dissertation submitted in part-fulfilment of the requirements for BA (Social Sciences), Middlesex Polytechnic, July 1989.

Botvin, V.G., Keith, R.A., & Johnston, M.V. (1978). Relationship between primitive reflexes in stroke patients and rehabilitation outcome. *Stroke, 9,* 256–258.

Bracy, O. (1982). *Cognitive rehabilitation programs for brain injured and stroke patients.* Indianapolis: Psychological Software Services.

Bracy, O. (1983). Computer based cognitive rehabilitation. *Cognitive Rehabilitation, 1,* 7–8 & 18.

Bracy, O. (1986). *Programs for cognitive rehabilitation.* Indianapolis: Psychological Software Services.

Bracy, O. (1987). *Programs for cognitive rehabilitation.* Indianapolis: Psychological Software Services.

Bracy, O., Lynch, W., Sbordone, R., & Berrol, S. (1985). Cognitive retraining through computers: fact or fad? *Cognitive Rehabilitation, 3,* 10–24.

Bradley, V.A. & Welch, J.L. (1987). *Pre- and post-training questionnaires for patients and carers.* Unpublished questionnaires developed at the Department of Psychology, Regional Neurological Centre, Newcastle upon Tyne.

Braun, C.M.J., Bartolini, G., & Bouchard, A. (1985). *Cognitive rehabilitation software.* Montreal: University of Quebec at Montreal.

Brierley, H. (1971).A fully automated intellectual test. *British Journal of Social & Clinical Psychology, 10,* 286–288.

Brierley, J.B. (1977). Neuropathology of amnesic states. In C.W.M. Whitty & O.L. Zangwill (Eds.), *Amnesia (2nd ed.).* London: Butterworths.

Brooks, D.N. (1972). Memory and head injury. *Journal of Nervous and Mental Disease, 155,* 350–355.

Brooks, D.N. (1979). Psychological deficits after severe blunt head injury: their significance and rehabilitation. In D.J. Oborne, M.M. Gruneberg, & J.R. Eiser (Eds), *Research in psychology and medicine, 2.* London: Academic Press.

Brooks, D.N. (1984). *Closed head injury: Psychological, social and family consequences.* Oxford: Oxford University Press.

Brooks, D.N. (1987). Measuring neuropsychological and functional recovery in neurobehavioural recovery. In H.S. Levin, J. Grafman, & H.M. Eisenbergh (Eds), *Neurobehavioural recovery from head injury.* Oxford: Oxford University Press.

Brooks, D.N. (1991). The effectiveness of post-acute rehabilitation. *Brain Injury 5,* 103–109.

Brooks, D.N. & Aughton, M.E. (1979). Psychological consequences of blunt head injury. *International Rehabilitation Medicine, 1,* 160–165.

Brooks, D.N., Campsie, L., & Simonton, C. (1986). The five year outcome of severe blunt head injury: A relative's view. *Journal of Neurology, Neurosurgery & Psychiatry, 49,* 764–770.

Brooks, D.N., Deelman, B.G., van Zomeren, A.H., van Dongen, H., van Harskamp, F., & Aughton, M.E. (1984). Problems in measuring cognitive recovery after acute brain injury. *Journal of Clinical Neuropsychology, 6,* 71–85.

Brooks, D.N., McKinlay, W., Symington, C., Beattie, A., & Campsie, L. (1987). Return to work within the first seven years of severe head injury. *Brain Injury, 1,* 5–19.

Brookshire, R., Nicholas, L., Redmond, K., & Krueger, K. (1979). Effect of clinician behaviours on acceptability of patient responses in aphasia treatment sessions. *Journal of Communication Disorders, 12,* 369–384.

Bruce, C. (1987). *Improving aphasic naming with computer generated phonemic cues.* Paper presented to the British Aphasiology Society National Conference, Newcastle upon Tyne, September, 1987.

Bruce, C. & Howard, D. (1987). Computer generated phonemic cues: an effective aid for naming in aphasia. *British Journal of Disorders of Communication, 22,* 191–201.

Bruckner, F.E. & Randle, P.H. (1972). Return to work after severe head injuries. *Rheumatology and Physical Medicine, 11,* 344–348.

Burke, W.H., Wesolowski, M.D., & Guth, M.L. (1988). Comprehensive head injury rehabilitation: an outcome evaluation. *Brain Injury, 2,* 313-322.

Burton, E., Burton, A., & Lucas, D. (1988). The use of microcomputers with aphasic patients. *Aphasiology, 2,* 479–491.

Butters, N., Lewis, R., Cermak, L.S., & Goodglass, H. (1973). Material-specific memory deficits in alcoholic Korsakoff patients. *Neuropsychologia, 11,* 291–299.

Butters, N. & Miliotis, P. (1985). Amnesic disorders. In K.M. Heilman & E. Valenstein (Eds), *Clinical neuropsychology* (Second Edition), 403–452. New York: Oxford University Press.

Byng, S. & Coltheart, M. (1986). Aphasia therapy research: Methodological requirements and illustrative results. In E. Hjelmquist & L.B. Nilsson (Eds), *Communication and handicap*. Amsterdam: North Holland Publishing Company.

Caramazza, A. & McCloskey, M. (1988). The case for single patient studies. *Cognitive Neuropsychology, 5*, 517–528.

Carlsson, C.A., van Essen, C., & Lofgren, J. (1968). Factors affecting the clinical course of patients with severe head injury. *Journal of Neurosurgery, 29*, 242–251.

Carr, A.C., Ghosh, A., & Ancill, R.J. (1983). Can a computer take a psychiatric history? *Psychological Medicine, 13*, 151–158.

Carr, A.C., Woods, R.T., & Moore, B.J. (1986). Developing a microcomputer based automated testing system for use with psychogeriatric patients. *Bulletin of the Royal College of Psychiatrists, 10*, 309–311.

Cermak, L.S. (1976). The encoding capacity of a patient with amnesia due to encephalitis. *Neuropsychologia, 19*, 311–326.

Cermak, L.S. & O'Connor, M. (1983). The anterograde and retrograde retrieval ability of a patient with amnesia due to encephalitis. *Neuropsychologia, 21*, 213–234.

Chelune, G.J. & Moehle, K.A. (1986). Neuropsychological assessment and everyday functioning. In D. Wedding, A. Horton, & J. Webster (Eds), *The Neuropsychology Handbook*. New York: Springer Publishing Company.

Christensen, A-L. (1975). *Luria's neuropsychological investigation*. New York: Spectrum.

Christie, D. (1982). Aftermath of stroke: an epidemiological study in Melbourne, Australia. *Journal of Epidemiological Community Health, 14*, 311–326.

Chute, D.L., Conn, G., Dipasquale, M.C., & Hoag, M. (1988). Prosthesis Ware: A new class of software supporting the activities of daily living. *Neuropsychology, 2*, 41–57.

Chute, D.L. & Hoag, M. (1988). *Speak Easy, Speak Easier & Speak Easiest, HyperCard ProsthesisWare*. Santa Barbara: Kinkos Academic Courseware Exchange.

Cliffe, M.J. (1985). Microcomputer implementation of an idiographic psychological instrument. *International Journal of Man–Machine Studies, 23*, 89–96.

Cockburn, J.M. & Smith, P.T. (1989). *The Rivermead Behavioural Memory Test, supplement 3: Elderly people*. Reading: Thames Valley Test Company.

Code, C., Heer, M., & Schofield, M. (1989). *The computerized Boston*. Kibworth, Leics: Far Communications.

Colby, K.M., Christinaz, D., Parkison, R.C., Graham, S., & Karpf, C. (1981). A word-finding computer program with a dynamic lexical-semantic memory for patients with anomia using an intelligent speech prosthesis. *Brain & Language, 14*, 272–281.

Coltheart, M. (1987). Functional architecture of the language-processing system. In M. Coltheart, G. Sartori & R. Job (Eds), *The cognitive neuropsychology of language*. Hillsdale, NJ: Lawrence Erlbaum Associates Inc.

Coltheart, M., Sartori, G., & Job, R. (1987). *The cognitive neuropsychology of language*. Hillsdale, NJ: Lawrence Erlbaum Associates Inc.

Conder, R., Evans, D., Faulkner, P., Henley, K., Kreutzner, J., Lent, B., Maxwell, J., McNeny, R., Morrison, C., Pinter, B., Richerson, G., & Stith, F. (1988). Programme description: an interdisciplinary programme for cognitive rehabilitation. *Brain Injury, 2*, 365–385.

Conkey, R.C. (1938). Psychological changes associated with head injuries. *Archives of Psychology (Frankfurt), 232*, 1–62.

Cope, D.N., Cole, J.R., Hall, K.M., & Barkan, H. (1991a). Brain injury: analysis of outcome in a post-acute rehabilitation system Part 1: General analysis. *Brain Injury, 5*, 111–125.

Cope, D.N., Cole, J.R., Hall, K.M., & Barkan, H. (1991b). Brain injury: analysis of outcome in a post-acute rehabilitation system Part 2: Subanalyses. *Brain Injury, 5*, 127–139.

Cope, D.N. & Hall, K.M. (1982). Head injury rehabilitation: Benefit of early intervention. *Archives of Physical Medicine and Rehabilitation, 63*, 433–437.

Coughlan, A.K. & Hollows, S.E. (1985). *Adult memory and information processing battery (AMIPB)*. Psychology Department, St James' University Hospital, Beckett St., Leeds, LS9 7TF: First Author.

Craik, F.I.M. & Lockhart, R.S. (1972). Levels of processing: a framework for memory research. *Journal of Verbal Learning and Verbal Behaviour, 11,* 671–684.

Craine, J.F. (1982). The retraining of frontal lobe dysfunction. In L.E. Trexler (Ed.), *Cognitive rehabilitation: Conceptualization and intervention.* New York: Plenum Press.

Cramond, H.J., Clark, M.S., & Smith, D.S. (1989). The effect of using the dominant or non-dominant hand on performance of the Rivermead Perceptual Assessment Battery. *Clinical Rehabilitation, 3,* 215–221.

Crook, T.H. & Larrabee, G.J. (1988). Inter-relationships among everyday memory tests: Stability of factor structure with age. *Neuropsychology, 2,* 1–12.

Crosson, B. & Buenning, W. (1984). An individualised memory retraining program after closed head injury: A single case study. *Journal of Clinical Neuropsychology, 6,* 287–301.

Culton, G.L. (1969). Spontaneous recovery from aphasia. *Journal of Speech & Hearing Research, 12,* 825–832.

Damasio, A.R. (1979). The frontal lobes. In K.M. Heilman & E. Valenstein (Eds), *Clinical neuropsychology.* New York: Oxford University Press.

Damasio, A.R., Graff-Radford, N.R., Eslinger, P.J., Damasio, H., & Kassell, N. (1985). Amnesia following basal forebrain lesions. *Archives of Neurology, 42,* 263–271.

Darley, F.L. (1975). Treatment of acquired aphasia. In W.J. Friedlander (Ed.), *Advances in neurology, 7.* New York: Raven Press.

David, R.M. & Skilbeck, C.E. (1984). Raven's IQ and language recovery following stroke. *Journal of Clinical Neuropsychology, 6,* 302–308.

Dean, A.C. (1987). Microcomputers and aphasia. *Aphasiology, 1,* 267–270.

De Haan, E.H.F., Young, A.W., & Newcombe, F. (1987). Face recognition without awareness. *Cognitive Neuropsychology, 4,* 385–415.

De Kosky, S.T., Heilman, K.M., Bowers, D., & Valenstein, E. (1980). Recognition and discrimination of emotional faces and pictures. *Brain and Language,* 9, 206–214.

Deloche, G., Seron, X., Coyette, F., Wendling, I., Hirnsbrunner, T., & van Eeckhout, P. (1983). *Microcomputer-assisted rehabilitation programs for patients with aphasia or visual neglect.* Paper presented at the 6th Annual Meeting, International Neuropsychological Society European Conference, Lisbon, 14–17 June.

Denes, G., Semenza, C., Stoppa, E., & Lis, A. (1982). Unilateral spatial neglect and recovery from hemiplegia: A follow-up study. *Brain, 105,* 543–552.

Denker, S.J. & Lofving, B. (1958). A psychometric study of identical twins discordant for closed head injury. In *Acta Psychiatrica et Neurologica Scandinavica, 33, Supplement 122.*

De Renzi, E. & Faglioni, P. (1978). Normative data and screening power of a shortened version of the Token Test. *Cortex, 14,* 41–49.

De Renzi, E. & Vignolo, L.A. (1962). The Token Test: A sensitive test to detect receptive disturbances in aphasics. *Brain, 85,* 665–678.

Diller, L. (1987). Neuropsychological rehabilitation. In M.J. Meier, A.L. Benton, & L. Diller (Eds), *Neuropsychological rehabilitation.* Edinburgh and London: Churchill Livingstone.

Diller, L., Ben-Yishay, Y., Gerstman, L.J., Goodkin, R., Gordon, W.A. & Weinberg, J. (1974). Studies in cognition and rehabilitation in hemiplegia. *Rehabilitation Monograph, No. 50.* New York: New York University Medical Centre.

Diller, L. & Gordon, W.A. (1981). Rehabilitation and clinical neuropsychology. In S.B. Filskov & T.J. Boll (Eds), *Handbook of clinical neuropsychology.* New York and Chichester: Wiley.

Diller, L. & Weinberg, J. (1972). Differential aspects of attention in brain damaged persons. *Perceptual and Motor Skills, 35,* 71–81.

Diller, L. & Weinberg, J. (1977). Hemi-inattention in rehabilitation: The evolution of a rational remediation program. In E. Weinstein & R. Friedland (Eds), *Advances in neurology, 18*. New York: Raven Press.

Diller, L., Weinberg, J., Piasetsky, E.B., Ruckdeschel-Hibbard, M., Egelko, S., Scotzin, M., Couniotakis, J., & Gordon, W.A. (1980). Methods for the evaluation and treatment of the visual perceptual difficulties of right brain-damaged individuals. *Manual Supplement to the 8th Annual Workshop for Rehabilitation Professionals*, Institute of Rehabilitation Medicine, New York University Medical Centre.

Dresser, A.C., Meirowsky, A.M., Weiss, G.H., McNeal, M.L., Simon, G.A., & Caveness, W.F. (1973). Gainful employment following head injury. *Archives of Neurology, 29*, 111–116.

Dunn, L.M. (1965). *Expanded manual for the Peabody Picture Vocabulary Test*. Minneapolis: American Guidance Service.

Dye, O.A., Milby, J.B., & Saxon, S.A. (1979). Effects of early neurological problems following head trauma on subsequent neuropsychological performance. *Acta Neurologica Scandinavica, 59, 10–14.*

Eames, P. (1987). Head injury rehabilitation: time for a new look. *Clinical Rehabilitation, 1*, 53–57.

Edmans, J.A. & Lincoln, N.B. (1989). Treatment of visual perceptual deficits after stroke: four single case studies. *International Disability Studies, 11*, 25–33.

Ellis, A.W. (1982). Spelling and writing (and reading and speaking). In A.W. Ellis (Ed.), *Normality and pathology in cognitive function*. London: Academic Press.

Ellis, A.W. (1987). Intimations of modularity, or the modelarity of mind: doing cognitive neuropsychology without syndromes. In M. Coltheart, G. Sartori, & R. Job (Eds), *The cognitive neuropsychology of language*. London: Lawrence Erlbaum Associates Ltd.

Elwood, D.L. (1969). Automation of psychological testing. *American Psychologist, 24*, 287–289.

Elwood, D.L. (1972a). Test-retest reliability and cost analyses of automated face-to-face intelligence testing. *International Journal of Man–Machine Studies, 4*, 1–22.

Elwood, D.L. (1972b). Automated WAIS testing correlated with face-to-face WAIS testing: a validity study. *International Journal of Man–Machine Studies, 4*, 129–137.

Elwood, D.L. & Clark, C.L. (1978). Computer administration of Peabody Picture Vocabulary Test to young children. *Behaviour Research Methods and Instrumentation, 10*, 43–46.

Enderby, P. (1983). *Frenchay dysarthria assessment and computer differential analysis*. Windsor: NFER–Nelson.

Enderby, P. (1987). Microcomputers in assessment, rehabilitation and recreation. *Aphasiology, 1*, 151–156.

Erickson, R.C. & Scott, M.L. (1977). Clinical memory testing: A review. *Psychological Bulletin, 84*, 1130–1149.

Ethier, M., Braun, C.M.J., & Baribeau, J.M.C. (1989a). Computer dispensed cognitive-perceptual training of closed head injury patients after spontaneous recovery. Study 1: Speeded tasks. *Canadian Journal of Rehabilitation, 2*, 223–233.

Ethier, M., Baribeau, J.M.C., & Braun, C.M.J. (1989b). Computer dispensed cognitive-perceptual training of closed head injury patients after spontaneous recovery. Study 2: Non-speeded tasks. *Canadian Journal of Rehabilitation, 3*, 7–16.

Farmer, J.E. & Frank, R.G. (1988). The BIRS (Brain Injury Rehabilitation Scale): A measure of change during post-acute rehabilitation. *Brain Injury, 2*, 323–333.

Farnsworth, D. (1943). Farnsworth–Munsel 100-hue and dichotomous test for colour vision. *Journal of the Optical Society of America, 33*, 568–578.

Feibel, J.H. & Springer, C.J. (1982). Depression and failure to resume social activities after stroke. *Archives of Physical Medicine and Rehabilitation, 63*, 276–278.

Feigenson, V.S., McCarthy, M.L., Greenberg, S.D., & Feigenson, W.D. (1977). Factors influencing outcome and length of stay in a stroke rehabilitation unit. *Stroke, 8*, 657–662.

Finlayson, M.A.J., Alfano, D.P., & Sullivan, J.F. (1987). A neuropsychological approach to cognitive remediation: Microcomputer applications. *Canadian Psychology, 28*, 180–190.

Finlayson, M.A.J. & Rourke, B.P. (1978). Locus of control as a predictor variable in rehabilitation medicine. *Journal of Clinical Psychology, 34*, 367–368.

Fitz-Gibbon, C.T. (1984). Meta-analysis: An explication. *British Educational Research Journal, 10*, 135–144.

Fitz-Gibbon, C.T. (1986). In defence of randomised controlled trials, with suggestions about the possible use of meta-analysis. *British Journal of Disorders of Communication, 21*, 117–124.

Fodor, J.A. (1983). *The modularity of mind.* Cambridge, Mass.: The MIT Press/Bradford.

Frederiks, J.A.M. (1969). Disorders of the body schema. In P.J. Vinken & G.W. Bruyn (Eds), *Handbook of clinical neurology, 4*, Amsterdam: North Holland Publishing Company.

French, C.C. (1990). Computer assisted assessment. In J.R. Beech & L. Harding (Eds), *Testing people: A practical guide to psychometrics.* Windsor: NFER–Nelson.

French, C.C. & Beaumont, J.G. (1987). The reaction of psychiatric patients to computerised assessment. *British Journal of Clinical Psychology, 26*, 267–278.

French, C.C. & Beaumont, J.G. (1990). A clinical study of the automated assessment of intelligence by the Mill Hill Vocabulary Test and the Standard Progressive Matrices Test. *Journal of Clinical Psychology, 46*, 129–140.

Fridlund, A.J. & Delis, D.C. (1983). *The California Neuropsychological System.* Bayport, New York: Life Science Associates.

Gasparrini, B. & Satz, P. (1979). A treatment for memory problems in left hemisphere CVA patients. *Journal of Clinical Neuropsychology, 1*, 137–150.

Gianutsos, R. (1980). What is cognitive rehabilitation? *Journal of Rehabilitation July–Sep.*, 37–40.

Gianutsos, R. (1981). Training the short and long term recall of a post-encephalitis amnesic. *Journal of Clinical Neuropsychology, 3*, 143–153.

Gianutsos, R., Cochran, E.E., & Blouin, M. (1984). *Computer programs for cognitive rehabilitation, III: therapeutic memory exercises for independent use.* Bayport, New York: Life Science Associates.

Gianutsos, R. & Gianutsos, J. (1979). Rehabilitating the verbal recall of brain injured patients by mnemonic training: An experimental demonstration using single case methodology. *Journal of Clinical Neuropsychology, 1*, 117–135.

Gianutsos, R. & Grynbaum, B.B. (1983). Helping brain-injured people contend with hidden cognitive deficits. *International Journal of Rehabilitation Medicine, 5*, 37–40.

Gianutsos, R. & Klitzner, C. (1981). *Computer programs for cognitive rehabilitation.* Bayport, New York: Life Science Associates.

Gianutsos, R. & Matheson, P. (1987). The rehabilitation of visual perceptual disorders attributable to brain injury. In M.J. Meier, A.L. Benton, & L. Diller (Eds) *Neuropsychological rehabilitation.* Edinburgh and New York: Churchill Livingstone.

Gianutsos, R., Vroman, G.M., & Matheson, P. (1983). *Computer programs for cognitive rehabilitation, II: further procedures for visual imperception.* Bayport, New York: Life Science Associates.

Giles, G.M. & Fussey, I. (1988). Models of brain injury rehabilitation: from theory to practice. In I. Fussey & G.M. Giles (Eds), *Rehabilitation of the severely brain injured adult.* Sydney: Croom Helm.

Glasgow, R., Zeiss, R., Barrera, M., & Lewinsohn, P. (1977). Case studies on remediating memory deficits in brain damaged individuals. *Journal of Clinical Psychology, 33*, 1049–1054.

Glass, G.V., McGaw, B., & Smith, M.L. (1981). *Meta-analysis in social research.* Beverley Hills and London: Sage Publications.

Glisky, E.L., Schacter, D.L., & Tulving, E. (1986a). Learning and retention of computer related vocabulary in memory impaired patients: Method of vanishing cues. *Journal of Clinical and Experimental Neuropsychology, 8*, 292–312.

Glisky, E.L., Schacter, D.L., & Tulving, E. (1986b). Computer learning by memory impaired patients: acquisition and retention of complex knowledge. *Neuropsychologia, 24*, 313–328.

Golden, C., Hammeke, T., & Purisch, A. (1981). *The Luria-Nebraska neuropsychological battery: Manual.* Los Angeles: Western Psychological Services.

Goldman, P.S. (1974). An alternative to developmental plasticity: Heterology of CNS structures in infants and adults. In D.G. Stern, J.J. Rosen & N. Butters (Eds), *Plasticity and recovery of function in the central nervous system.* New York: Academic Press.

Goldman, P.S. (1976). The role of experience in recovery of function following orbital prefrontal lesions in infant monkeys. *Neuropsychologia, 14,* 401–412.

Goldstein, H. (1952). The effect of brain damage on the personality. *Psychiatry, 15,* 245–260.

Gollin, E.S. (1960). Developmental studies of visual recognition of incomplete objects. *Perceptual and Motor Skills, 11,* 289–298.

Goodglass, H. & Kaplan, E. (1983). *The assessment of aphasia and related disorders* (Second Edition). Philadelphia: Lea & Febiger.

Gordon, W.A. (1987). Methodological considerations in cognitive remediation. In M.J. Meier, A.L. Benton, & L. Diller (Eds), *Neuropsychological rehabilitation.* Edinburgh and London: Churchill Livingstone.

Gordon, W.A. & Diller, L. (1983). Stroke: coping with a cognitive deficit. In T.E. Burish & L.A. Bradley (Eds), *Coping with chronic disease: research and applications.* New York: Academic Press.

Gordon, W.A., Hibbard, M., Diller, L., Egelko, S., Scotzin, M., Lieberman, A., & Ragnarsson, K.T. (1985). The impact of a comprehensive program of perceptual retraining on right brain damaged stroke patients. *Archives of Physical Medicine and Rehabilitation, 66,* 350–359.

Gouvier, W.D. (1982). Using the digital alarm chronograph in memory retraining. *Behavioural Engineering, 7,* 134.

Gouvier, W.D. & Warner, M.S. (1987). Treatment of visual imperception and related disorders. In J.M. Williams and C.J. Long (Eds), *The rehabilitation of cognitive disorders.* New York: Plenum Press.

Gouvier, W.D., Webster, J.S., & Blanton, P.D. (1986). Cognitive retraining with brain damaged patients. In D. Wedding, A.M. Horton, & D. Webster (Eds), *The neuropsychology handbook.* New York: Springer.

Grant, D.A. & Berg, E.A. (1981). *Wisconsin Card Sorting Test.* Windsor: NFER–Nelson.

Gray, J.M. & Robertson, I. (1988). Microcomputer based attentional retraining after brain injury: a randomised group-controlled trial. Paper presented at the International Neuropsychological Society, Finland, 1988. *Journal of Clinical and Experimental Neuropsychology, 10,* 332 (abstract).

Gray, J.M. & Robertson, I.H. (1989). Remediation of attentional difficulties following brain injury: three experimental single case studies. *Brain Injury, 3,* 163–170.

Gresham, G.E., Phillips, T.F., & Labi, M.L.C. (1980). ADL status in stroke: Relative merits of three standard indexes. *Archives of Physical Medicine and Rehabilitation, 61,* 355–358.

Gresham, G.E., Phillips, T.F., Wolfe, P.A., McNamara, P.M., Kinnel, W.B., & Dawber, T.R. (1979). Epidemiologic profile of long term stroke disability: The Framingham Study. *Archives of Physical Medicine and Rehabilitation, 60,* 487–491.

Groher, M. (1977). Language and memory disorders following closed head trauma. *Journal of Speech and Hearing Research, 20,* 212.

Groher, M. (1983). Communication disorders. In Rosenthal, M. Griffith, E.R., Bond, M.R., & Miller, J.D. (Eds), *Rehabilitation of the head injured adult.* Philadelphia: F.A. Davis Company.

Gronwall, D.M. & Sampson, H. (1974). *The psychological effects of concussion.* Auckland: Auckland University Press.

Gross, Y., Ben-Nahum, Z., & Munk, G. (1982). Techniques and application of simultaneous information processing. In L.E. Trexler (Ed.), *Cognitive rehabilitation: Conceptualization and intervention.* New York: Plenum Press.

Hagen, C. (1973). Communicative abilities in hemiplegia: Effect of speech therapy. *Archives of Physical Medicine and Rehabilitation, 54,* 454–463.

Hall, J. (1980). Word-rating scales for long-stay patients: A review. *Psychological Medicine, 10,* 277–288.

Halligan, P.W. & Marshall, J.C. (1989). Perceptual cuing and perceptuo-motor compatibility in visuospatial neglect: A single case study. *Cognitive Neuropsychology, 6,* 423–435.

Halstead, W.C. (1947). *Brain and intelligence.* Chicago: University of Chicago Press.

Halstead, W.C. & Wepman, J.M. (1959). The Halstead–Wepman aphasia screening test. *Journal of Speech and Hearing Disorders, 14,* 9–15.

Hanley, J.R., Young, A.W., & Pearson, N.A. (1989). Defective recognition of familiar people. *Cognitive Neuropsychology, 6,* 179–210.

Harrington, D.E. & Levandowski, D.H. (1987). Efficacy of an educationally based cognitive retraining programme for traumatically head injured as measured by LNNB pre- and post-test scores. *Brain Injury, 1,* 65–72.

Harris, J.E. (1978). External memory aids. In M.M. Gruneberg, P.E. Morris & R.N. Sykes (Eds), *Practical aspects of memory.* London: Academic Press.

Harris, J.E. (1984). Methods of improving memory. In B.A. Wilson & N. Moffatt (Eds), *Clinical management of memory problems.* London and Sydney: Croom Helm.

Heaton, R.K., Chelune, G.J., & Lehman, R.A.W. (1978). Using neuropsychological and personality tests to assess the likelihood of patient employment. *The Journal of Nervous and Mental Disease, 166,* 408–416.

Heaton, R.K. & Pendleton, M.G. (1981). Use of neuropsychological tests to predict adult patients' everyday functioning. *Journal of Consulting and Clinical Psychology, 49,* 807–821.

Hebb, D.O. (1945). Man's frontal lobes. *Archives of Neurology and Psychiatry, 54,* 10–24.

Hecaen, H. (1962). Clinical symptomatology in right and left hemispheric lesions. In V.B. Mountcastle (Ed.), *Interhemispheric relations and cerebral dominance.* Baltimore: Johns Hopkins Press.

Heilman, K.M., Safran, A., & Geschwind, N. (1971). Closed head trauma and aphasia. *Journal of Neurology, Neurosurgery, and Psychiatry, 34,* 265–269.

Herbert, C.M. & Powell, G.E. (1989). Insight and progress in rehabilitation. *Clinical Rehabilitation, 3,* 125–130.

Hersen, M. & Barlow, D.H. (1976). *Single case experimental designs: Strategies for studying behaviour change.* New York: Pergamon Press.

Hier, D.B., Mondlock, J., & Caplan, L.R. (1983). Recovery of behavioural abnormalities after right hemisphere stroke. *Neurology, 33,* 345–350.

Holbrook, M. (1982). Stroke: Social & emotional outcomes. *Journal of the Royal College of Physicians, 16,* 100–104.

Holbrook, M. & Skilbeck, C.E. (1983). An activities index for use with stroke patients. *Age and Ageing, 12,* 166–170.

Holden, U.P. & Woods, R.T. (1982). *Reality orientation: Psychological approaches to the confused elderly.* Edinburgh: Churchill Livingstone.

Holland, A.L. (1980). *Communicative abilities in daily living: Manual.* Baltimore: University Park Press.

Howard, D. & Hatfield, F.M. (1987). *Aphasia therapy: Historical and contemporary issues.* Hove: Lawrence Erlbaum Associates Ltd.

Huppert, F. (1989). *Dementia of the Alzheimer type: A longitudinal study.* Paper presented to the Neurological Research Group, General Hospital, Newcastle upon Tyne, Spring 1989.

Hyman, M.D. (1972). Social psychological determinants of patients' performance in stroke rehabilitation. *Archives of Physical Medicine and Rehabilitation, 53,* 217.

Incagnoli, T. (1986). Current directions and future trends in clinical neuropsychology. In T. Incagnoli, G. Goldstein, & C.J. Golden (Eds), *Clinical application of neuropsychological test batteries.* New York and London: Plenum Press.

Ishihara, S. (1954). *Ishihara tests of colour blindness.* Windsor: NFER–Nelson.

Ishihara, S. (1985). *Ishihara tests of colour blindness.* Windsor: NFER–Nelson.

Jackson, H. (1989). Transitional Rehabilitation. *Headway Newsletter, March*, 4–7.

James, W. (1890). *The Principles of Psychology*, I. New York: Holt & Co.

Jenkins, J.J., Jimenez-Pabon, E., Shaw, R.E., & Sefer, J.W. (1975). *Schuell's Aphasia in adults.* New York and London: Harper & Row.

Jennett, B., Snoek, J., Bond, M.R., & Brooks, B. (1981). Disability after severe head injury: Observations on the use of the Glasgow Outcome Scale. *Journal of Neurology, Neurosurgery & Psychiatry, 44*, 285–293.

Johnson, R. (1989). *Memory training software.* Prepared at Addenbrooke's Hospital, Cambridge, UK. Available from the author.

Johnson, R. & Garvie, C. (1985). The BBC microcomputer for therapy of intellectual impairment following acquired brain damage. *Occupational Therapy, Feb.*, 46–48.

Johnston, M.V. (1991). Outcome of community re-entry programmes for brain injury survivors Part 2: Further investigations. *Brain Injury, 5*, 155–169.

Johnston, M.V. & Lewis, F.D. (1991). Outcomes of community re-entry programmes for brain injury survivors Part 1: Independent living and productive activities. *Brain Injury, 5*, 141–154.

Kagan, J., Rosman, B.L., Day, D., Albert, J., & Phillips, W. (1964). Information processing in the child: Significance of analytic and reflective attitudes. *Psychological Monographs, 78* (1), (Whole No. 578), 1–37.

Katz, M.M. & Lyerly, S.B. (1963). Methods of measuring adjustment and social behaviour in the community: 1. Rationale, description, discriminative validity and scale development. *Psychological Reports, 13*, 503–535.

Katz, R.C. (1986). *Aphasia treatment and microcomputers.* London: Taylor & Francis.

Katz, R.C. (1987a). Efficacy of aphasia treatment using microcomputers. *Aphasiology, 1*, 141–149.

Katz, R.C. (1987b). Reply: Common Ground. *Aphasiology, 1*, 171–175.

Katz, R.C. (1989). Treatment software for aphasic adults. In E. Perecman (Ed.), *Integrating theory and practice in clinical neuropsychology.* Hillsdale, NJ: Lawrence Erlbaum Associates Inc.

Katz, R.C. & Nagy, V. (1982). A computerised treatment system for chronic aphasic patients. In R.H. Brookshire (Ed.), *Clinical aphasiology: Conference proceedings*, 153–160. Minneapolis: BRK Publishers.

Katz, R.C. & Nagy, V. (1983). A computerised approach for improving word recognition in chronic aphasic patients. In R.H. Brookshire (Ed.), *Clinical aphasiology: Conference proceedings*, 65–72. Minneapolis: BRK Publishers.

Katz, R.C. & Nagy, V. (1984). An intelligent computer based spelling task for chronic aphasia patients. In R.H. Brookshire (Ed.), *Clinical aphasiology: Conference proceedings*, 65–72. Minneapolis: BRK Publishers.

Katz, R.C. & Nagy, V. (1985). A self-modifying computerised reading program for severely impaired aphasic adults. In R.H. Brookshire (Ed.), *Clinical aphasiology: Conference proceedings*, 184–188. Minneapolis: BRK Publishers.

Kaufman, A. (1968). The substitution test: A survey of studies on organic mental impairment and the role of learning and motor factors in test performance. *Cortex, 4*, 47–63.

Kazdin, A.E. (1982). *Single case research designs: Methods for clinical and applied settings.* New York: Open University Press.

Kemp, R. & Earp, P. (1990). The development of microcomputer based applications. In R. West, M. Christie, & J. Weinman (Eds), *Microcomputers, psychology & medicine.* Chichester: John Wiley.

Kennard, M.A. (1936). Age and other factors in motor recovery from precentral lesions in monkeys. *American Journal of Physiology, 115*, 138.

Kennard, M.A. (1940). Relation of age to motor impairment in man and subhuman primates. *Archives of Neurology and Psychiatry, 44*, 377–397.

Kennard, M.A. (1942). Cortical reorganisation of motor function: Studies on series of monkeys of various ages from infancy to maturity. *Archives of Neurology and Psychiatry, 48,* 227–240.

Kertesz, A. (1982). *The Western Aphasia Battery.* New York: Grune & Stratton.

Kertesz, A. (1989). Assessing aphasic disorders. In E. Perecman (Ed.), *Integrating theory and practice in clinical neuropsychology.* Hillsdale, NJ: Lawrence Erlbaum Associates Inc.

Kertesz, A. & McCabe, T. (1977). Recovery patterns and prognosis in aphasia. *Brain, 100,* 1.

Kewman, D.G., Yanus, B., & Kirsch, N. (1988). Assessment of distractability in auditory comprehension after traumatic brain injury. *Brain Injury, 2,* 131–137.

Kinsey, C. (1986). Microcomputer speech therapy for dysphasic adults: a comparison with two conventionally administered tasks. *British Journal of Disorders of Communication, 21,* 125–133.

Kinsey, C. (1987). *Analysis of dysphasics' behaviour.* Unpublished paper presented to British Aphasiology Society National Conference, Newcastle, Sept. 1987.

Kinsey, C. (in press). Analysis of dysphasics' behaviour in computer and conventional therapy environments. *Aphasiology.*

Kirk, S.A., McCarthy, J.J., & Kirk, W.D. (1968). *Illinois Test of Psycholinguistic Abilities examiners manual* (Revised Edition). Urbana, Ill.: University of Illinois Press.

Klonoff, P.S., Costa, L.D., & Snow, W.G. (1986). Predictors and indicators of quality of life in patients with closed head injury. *Journal of Clinical & Experimental Neuropsychology, 8,* 469–485.

Kotila, M., Waltimo, O., Niemi, M-L., Laaksonen, R., & Lempinen, M. (1984). The profile of recovery from stroke and factors influencing outcome. *Stroke, 15,* 1039–1044.

Kreutzer, J.S. & Zasler, N.D. (1989). Psychosexual consequences of traumatic brain injury: Methodology and preliminary findings. *Brain Injury, 3,* 177–186.

Kurlychek, R.T. & Levin, W. (1987). Computers in the cognitive rehabilitation of brain injured persons. *CRC Critical Reviews in Medical Informatics, 1,* 241–257.

Laatsch, L. (1983). *Computer programs for cognitive rehabilitation, 4.* Bayport, New York: Life Science Associates.

Larrabee, G.J. & Levin, H.S. (1986). Memory self-ratings and objective test performance in a normal elderly sample. *Journal of Clinical and Experimental Neuropsychology, 8,* 275–284.

Lashley, K.S. (1938). Factors limiting recovery after central nervous lesions. *Journal of Nervous and Mental Disorders, 88,* 733–755.

Lehmann, J.F., Delateur, B.J., Fowler, R.S., Warren, C.G., & Arnhold, R. (1975). Stroke rehabilitation: Outcome and prediction. *Archives of Physical Medicine and Rehabilitation, 56,* 383–389.

Lendrem, W., McGuirk, E., & Lincoln, N.B. (1988). Factors affecting language recovery in aphasic stroke patients receiving speech therapy. *Journal of Neurology, Neurosurgery & Psychiatry, 51,* 1103.

Leng, N.R.C. & Copello, A.G. (1990). Rehabilitation of memory after brain injury: Is there an effective technique? *Clinical Rehabilitation, 4,* 63–69.

Leng, N.R.C., Copello, A.G., & Sayegh, A. (in press). Learning after brain injury by the method of vanishing cues: A case study. *Behavioural Psychotherapy.*

Levin, H.S., Grossman, R.G., Rose, J.E., & Teasdale, G. (1979). Long term neuropsychological outcome of closed head injury. *Journal of Neurosurgery 50,* 412–422.

Lezak, M.D. (1978). Subtle sequelae of brain damage: Perplexity, distractability and fatigue. *American Journal of Physical Medicine, 57,* 9–15.

Lezak, M.D. (1982). *The test–retest stability and reliability of some tests commonly used in neuropsychological assessment.* Unpublished paper presented at the 5th European Conference of the International Neuropsychological Society, Deauville, France, June, 1982.

Lezak, M.D. (1983). *Neuropsychological assessment.* New York: Oxford University Press.

Lezak, M.D. (1987). Assessment for rehabilitation planning. In M.J. Meier, A.L. Benton, & L. Diller (Eds), *Neuropsychological rehabilitation.* Edinburgh and London: Churchill Livingstone.

Likert, R. & Quasha, W.H. (1970). *The revised Minnesota paper formboard test. Manual.* New York: Psychological Corporation.

Lincoln, N.B. & Edmans, J.A. (1989). A shortened version of the Rivermead Perceptual Assessment Battery? *Clinical Rehabilitation, 3,* 199–204.

Loftus, G.R. & Loftus, E.T. (1976). *Human memory. The processing of information.* Hillsdale, NJ.: Lawrence Erlbaum Associates Inc.

Logie, R. (1986). *Visual span task adapted for the Apple Microcomputer.* Software prepared at the MRC Applied Psychology Unit, Cambridge.

Long, C.J. & Wagner, M. (1986). Computer applications in neuropsychology. In D. Wedding, A. Horton, & J. Webster (Eds), *The neuropsychology handbook.* New York: Springer Publishing Company.

Loverso, F.L. (1987). Unfounded expectations: Computers in rehabilitation. *Aphasiology, 1,* 157–159.

Lucas, R.W. (1977). A study of patients' attitudes to computer interrogation. *International Journal of Man-Machine Studies, 9,* 69–86.

Luria, A.R. (1963). *Restoration of function after brain injury.* New York: MacMillan.

Luria, A.R. (1966). *Higher cortical functions in man* (B. Haigh, transl.) New York: Basic Books.

Luria, A.R. (1973). *The working brain.* New York: Basic Books.

Lynch, W. (1982). The use of electronic games in cognitive rehabilitation. In L.E. Trexler (Ed.), *Cognitive rehabilitation: Conceptualization and intervention.* New York: Plenum Press.

McGlone, J. (1980). Sex differences in human brain asymmetry: A critical view. *Behavioural and Brain Sciences, 3,* 215–263.

McKenna, P. & Warrington, E.K. (1983). *Graded Naming Test.* Windsor: NFER–Nelson.

McKinlay, W., Brooks, D.N., Bond, M.R., Martinage, D.P., & Marshall, M.M. (1981). The short term outcome of severe blunt head injury as reported by relatives of the injured persons. *Journal of Neurology, Neurosurgery & Psychiatry, 44,* 527–533.

McKinlay, W., Brooks, N. & Hickox, A. (1986). *Questionnaire for relatives.* Unpublished questionnaire developed at the Department of Psychology, the Western General Hospital, Edinburgh.

McKinlay, W. & Pentland, B. (1987). Developing rehabilitation services for the head injured: A UK perspective. *Brain Injury,1,* 3–4.

McLeary, R. & Hay, R.A. (1980). *Applied time series analysis for the social sciences.* Beverley Hills and London: Sage Publications.

McMillan, T.M., Brooks, D.N., McKinlay, W., Oddy, M., Tyerman, A., & Wilson, B.A. (1989). *Services for young adult patients with acquired brain damage.* British Psychological Society Working Party Report.

McMillan, T.M. & Glucksman, E.E. (1989). Neuropsychology of moderate head injury. *Journal of Neurology, Neurosurgery & Psychiatry, 50,* 393–397.

Mahoney, F.I. & Barthel, D.W. (1965). Functional evaluation: The Barthel Index. *Maryland State Medical Journal, 14,* 61–65.

Mair Report. (1972). *Medical rehabilitation. The pattern for the future.* Edinburgh: Scottish Home and Health Department.

Malec, J. & Questad, K. (1983). Rehabilitation of memory after craniocerebral trauma: Case report. *Archives of Physical Medicine and Rehabilitation, 64,* 436–438.

Malone, T.W. (1981). Toward a theory of intrinsically motivating instruction. *Cognitive Science, 4,* 333–369.

Mandelberg, I.A. & Brooks, D.N. (1975). Cognitive recovery after severe head injury: 1, Serial Testing on WAIS. *Journal of Neurology, Neurosurgery and Psychiatry, 38,* 1121–1126.

Marshall, J.C. (1982). Models of the mind in health and disease. In A.W. Ellis (Ed.), *Normality and pathology in cognitive functioning.* London: Academic Press.

Marshall, J.C. & Newcombe, F. (1984). Putative problems and pure progress in neuropsychological single case studies. *Journal of Clinical Neuropsychology, 6*, 65–70.

Marshall, R.C. (1987). Reapportioning time for aphasia rehabilitation: A point of view. *Aphasiology, 1*, 59–73.

Marslen-Wilson, W.D. & Teuber, H-L. (1975). Memory for remote events in anterograde amnesia: Recognition of public figures from newsphotographs. *Neuropsychologia, 13*, 353–364.

Matthews, W.B. & Oxbury, J.M. (1975). Prognostic factors in stroke. In R. Porter & D.W. Fitzsimmons (Eds) *Outcome of severe damage to the central nervous system.* (Ciba Foundation Symposium. No. 34.) Amsterdam. Elsevier, 279–289.

Meerwaldt, J.D. (1983). Spatial disorientation in right-hemisphere infarction: A study of the speed of recovery. *Journal of Neurology, Neurosurgery and Psychiatry, 46*, 426–429.

Meier, M.J., Strauman, S., & Thompson, W.G. (1987). Individual differences in neuropsychological recovery: An overview. In M.J. Meier, A.L. Benton & L. Diller (Eds), *Neuropsychological rehabilitation.* Edinburgh and New York: Churchill Livingstone.

Meudell, P.R., Northern, B., Snowden, J., & Neary, D. (1980). Long term memory for famous voices in amnesic and normal subjects. *Neuropsychologia, 18*, 133–139.

Miller, E. (1984). *Recovery and management of neuropsychological impairments.* Chichester and New York: Wiley.

Mills, R.H. (1982). Microcomputerised auditory comprehension training. In R.H. Brookshire (Ed.), *Clinical aphasiology: Conference proceedings.* Minneapolis: BRK Publishers.

Milner, B. (1966). Amnesia following operation on the temporal lobes. In C.W.M. Whitty & O. Zangwill (Eds), *Amnesia.* London: Butterworths.

Milner, B., Corkin, S., & Teuber, H-L. (1968). Further analysis of the hippocampal amnesic syndrome: 14 year follow-up of H.M. *Neuropsychologia, 6*, 215.

Mirsky, A.F. (1989). The neuropsychology of attention: Elements of a complex behaviour. In E. Perecman (Ed.), *Integrating theory and practice in clinical neuropsychology.* Hillsdale, NJ: Lawrence Erlbaum Associates Inc.

Mitchell, S., Bradley, V.A., Welch, J.L., & Britton, P.G. (1990). Coma arousal procedure: A therapeutic intervention in the treatment of head injury. *Brain Injury, 4*, 273–279.

Moerland, M.C., Alderkamp, A.P., & de Alpherts, W.C.J. (1986). A neuropsychological test battery for the Apple IIe. *International Journal of Man–Machine Studies, 25*, 453–467.

Money, J.A. (1976). *A standardised road map test of direction sense. Manual.* San Rafael, California: Academic Therapy Publications.

Mooney, C.M. (1957). Age in the development of closure ability in children. *Canadian Journal of Psychology, 2*, 219–226.

Moore, A.D., Stambrook, M., & Peters, L.C. (1989). Coping strategies and adjustment after closed head injury: A cluster analytical approach. *Brain Injury, 3*, 171–175.

MRC Coordinating Group. (1982). Research aspects of rehabilitation after acute brain damage in adults. *Lancet, 2*, 1034–1036.

Mutchnick, M.G. (1988). The role of motivation in rehabilitation. In J.M. Williams & C.J. Long (Eds), *Cognitive approaches to neuropsychology.* New York: Plenum Press.

Najenson, T. (1978). Recovery of communication function after prolonged coma. *Scandinavian Journal of Rehabilitation Medicine, 10*, 15.

Nelson, H.E. (1982). *National Adult Reading Test: Test manual.* Windsor: NFER–Nelson.

Newcombe, F. (1982). The psychological consequences of closed head injury: Assessment and rehabilitation. *Injury: the British Journal of Accident Surgery, 14*, 111–136.

Newcombe, F. (1985). Rehabilitation in clinical neurology: Neuropsychological aspects. In J.A.M. Fredericks (Ed.), *Handbook of clinical neurology, 2, (46). Neurobehavioural disorders.* Amsterdam and New York; Elsevier Science.

Newcombe, F. & Fortuny, L.A.I. (1979). Problems and perspectives in the evaluation of psychological deficits after cerebral lesions. *International Rehabilitation Medicine, 1*, 182-192.

Newcombe, F., Marshall, J.C., Caravick, P.J., & Hiorns, R.W. (1975). Recovery curves in acquired dyslexia. *Journal of Neurological Science, 24*, 127-133.

Newcombe, F. & Russell, W.K. (1969). Dissociated visual perceptual and spatial deficits in focal lesions of the right hemisphere. *Journal of Neurology, Neurosurgery and Psychiatry, 32*, 73-81.

Nordstrom, C-H., Messeter, K., Sundbarg, G., & Wahlander, S. (1989). Severe traumatic brain lesions in Sweden. Part I: Aspects of management in non-neurosurgical clinics. *Brain Injury, 3*, 247-265.

Norris, D.E., Skilbeck, C.E., Hayward, A.E., & Torpy, D.M. (1985). *Microcomputers in clinical practice*. Chichester and New York: John Wiley & Sons.

O'Connor, M. & Cermak, L.S. (1987). Rehabilitation of organic memory disorders. In M.J. Meier, A.L. Benton & L. Diller (Eds), *Neuropsychological rehabilitation*. Edinburgh and New York: Churchill Livingstone.

Oddy, M. (1984). Head injury and social adjustments. In N. Brooks (Ed.), *Closed head injury: Psychological, social and family consequences*. Oxford: Oxford University Press.

Oddy, M., Bonham, E., McMillan, T.M., Stroud, A., & Rickard, S. (1989). A comprehensive service for rehabilitation and long term care of head injury survivors. *Clinical Rehabilitation, 3*, 253-259.

Oddy, M. & Humphrey, M. (1980). Social recovery during the year following severe head injury. *Scandinavian Journal of Rehabilitation Medicine, 6*, 5-14.

Oddy, M., Humphrey, M., & Uttley, D. (1978). Stresses upon the relatives of head injured patients. *British Journal of Psychiatry, 133*, 507-513.

Osterrieth, P.A. (1944). Le test de copie d'une figure complexe. *Archives de Psychologie, 30*, 206-356.

Palin, M.W. & Mordecai, D.R. (1984). *Lingquest, 2 Phonological Analysis*. Sidcup, Kent: Psychological Corporation.

Palin, M.W., Mordecai, D.R., & Palmer, C.B. (1985). *Lingquest, 1, Language Sample Analysis*. Sidcup, Kent: Psychological Corporation.

Panting, A. & Merry, P. (1972). The long term rehabilitation of severe head injuries with particular reference to the need for social and medical support for the patient's family. *Rehabilitation, 38*, 33-37.

Parente, R. & Anderson, J. (1983). Techniques for improving cognitive rehabilitation: Teaching organisation and encoding skills. *Cognitive Rehabilitation, 1*, 20-22.

Parkin, A.J. & Russo, R. (1990). Implicit and explicit memory and the automatic/effortful distinction. *European Journal of Cognitive Psychology, 2*, 71-80.

Parmar, V. & Lawlor, M. (1990). Use of a microcomputer network for people with a mental handicap. In R. West, M. Christie, & J. Weinman (Eds), *Microcomputers, psychology and medicine*. Chichester: Wiley.

Patten, B.M. (1972). The ancient art of memory. *Archives of Neurology, 26*, 25-31.

Patterson, K.E. & Shewell, C. (1987). Speak and spell: Dissociations and word class effects. In M. Coltheart, G. Sartori, & O.R. Job (Eds), *The cognitive neuropsychology of language*. Hove: Lawrence Erlbaum Associates Ltd.

Pattie, A.H. & Gilleard, C.J. (1979). *Manual for the Clifton Assessment Procedures for the Elderly*. Sevenoaks: Hodder & Stoughton Educational.

Peck, D.F. (1970). The conversion of progressive matrices and Mill Hill vocabulary raw scores into deviation IQs. *Journal of Clinical Psychology, 26*, 67-70.

Piasetsky, E.B., Ben-Yishay, Y., Weinberg, J., & Diller, L. (1982). The systematic remediation of specific disorders: Selected application of methods derived in a clinical research setting. In L.E. Trexler (Ed.), *Cognitive rehabilitation*. New York and London: Plenum Press.

Piasetsky, E.B., Rattok, J., Ben-Yishay, Y., Ross, B., & Diller, L. (1983). Computerised ORM: A manual for clinical and research uses. In Y. Ben-Yishay (Ed.), Working approaches to remediation of cognitive deficits in brain damaged patients. *Rehabilitation Monograph, No. 64.* New York: New York University Medical Centre.

Pizzamiglio, L., Mammucari, A., & Razzano, C. (1985). Evidence for sex differences in brain organisation from recovery in aphasia. *Brain and Language, 25,* 213–232.

Ponsford, J. (1990). The use of computers in the rehabilitation of attention disorders. In R.H. Wood & I. Fussey (Eds), *Cognitive rehabilitation in perspective.* London: Taylor & Francis.

Poppelreuter, W. (1917). *Die psychischen Schadigungen durch Kopfschuss im Kriege, 1914/16.* Leipzig: Verlag von Leopold Voss.

Porch, B.E. (1967). *The Porch Index of Communicative Ability.* Palo Alto: Consulting Psychologists Press.

Powell, G.E. (1981). *Brain function therapy.* London: Gower.

Powell, G.E. (1986). The self after brain injury: Theory, research and rehabilitation. *Journal of Clinical and Experimental Neuropsychology, 8,* 115.

Powell, T. (1990). A district service for people with acquired brain injury. *Clinical Psychology Forum, No. 25.*

Prescott, R.J., Garraway, W.M., & Akhtar, A.N. (1982). Predicting functional outcome following acute stroke using a standard clinical examination. *Stroke, 13,* 641–647.

Prigatano, G.P. (1986). *Neuropsychological rehabilitation after brain injury.* Baltimore: John Hopkins University Press.

Prigatano, G.P. (1987). Personality and psychosocial consequences after brain injury. In M.J. Meier, A.C. Benton, & L. Diller (Eds), *Neuropsychological rehabilitation.* Edinburgh and New York: Churchill Livingstone.

Prigatano, G.P., Fordyce, V.J., & Zinen, H.K. (1986). *Neuropsychological rehabilitation after brain injury.* Baltimore: John Hopkins University Press.

Prins, R.S., Snow, C.E., & Wagenaar, E. (1978). Recovery from aphasia: Spontaneous speech versus language comprehension. *Brain and Language, 6,* 191–211.

Ratcliff, G. (1979). Spatial thought, mental rotation and the right cerebral hemisphere. *Neuropsychologia, 17,* 49–54.

Ratcliff, G. & Newcombe, F. (1973). Spatial orientation in man: Effects of left, right and bilateral posterior lesions. *Journal of Neurology, Neurosurgery & Psychiatry, 36,* 448–454.

Raven, J.C. (1960). *Guide to the standard progressive matrices.* London: H.K. Lewis.

Raven, J.C. (1965). *Guide to using the coloured progressive matrices.* London: H.K. Lewis.

Reitan, R.M. (1958). Validity of the trail making test as an indication of organic brain damage. *Perceptual and Motor Skills, 8,* 271–276.

Reitan, R.M. (1979). *Neuropsychology and rehabilitation.* Tucson: Author.

Reitan, R.M. & Davison, L.A. (1974). *Clinical neuropsychology: Current status and applications.* Washington DC: Winston.

Rey, A. (1941). L'examen psychologique dans les cas d'encephalopathie traumatique. *Archives de Psychologie, 28,* N. 112, 286–340.

Rey, A. (1964). *L'examen clinique en psychologie.* Paris: Presses Universitaires de France.

Richards, D. (1986). *Therapy Games. Software for the BBC microcomputer.* New Alyth, Perthshire: Lochee Publications Ltd.

Riddoch, M.J. & Humphreys, G.W. (1986). Neurological impairments of object constancy: The effects of orientation and size disparities. *Cognitive Neuropsychology, 3,* 207–224.

Roberts, A.H. (1979). *Severe accidental head injury.* London: McMillan.

Robertson, I.H., Gray, J.M., & McKenzie, S. (1988). Microcomputer based cognitive rehabilitation of visual neglect: Three multiple baseline single case studies. *Brain Injury, 2,* 151–163.

Robertson, I.H., Gray, J.M., Pentland, D., & Waite, L.J. (1990). Randomised controlled trial of microcomputer based rehabilitation for unilateral left visual neglect. *Archives of Physical Medicine and Rehabilitation, 71,* 663–668.

Robertson, I.H. & Smart, S. (1987). *Simple and choice reaction time tasks.* Unpublished software prepared at the Astley Ainslie Hospital, Edinburgh.

Robertson, I.H. & Smart, S. (1988). *Attention training programs.* New Alyth, Perthshire: Lochee Publications.

Robinson, R.G. & Price, T.R. (1982). Post-stroke depressive disorders: A follow-up study of 103 stroke patients. *Stroke, 13,* 635–641.

Romanczyk, R.G. (1986). *Clinical utilisation of microcomputer technology.* New York and Oxford: Pergamon Press.

Rose, F.C. & Symonds, C.P. (1960). Persistent memory defect following encephalitis. *Brain, 83,* 195–212.

Rosenbaum, M., Lipsitz, N., Abraham, J., & Najenson, P. (1978). A description of an intensive treatment project for the rehabilitation of severely brain injured soldiers. *Scandinavian Journal of Rehabilitation Medicine, 10,* 1–6.

Rosenthal, M. & Bond, M.R. (1990). Behavioural and psychiatric sequelae. In M. Rosenthal, E.R. Griffith, M.R. Bond, & J.D. Miller (Eds), *Rehabilitation of the adult and child with traumatic brain injury.* Philadelphia: Davis Company.

Royal College of Physicians. (1986). *Physical disability in 1986 and beyond.* National report prepared by the Royal College of Physicians.

Ruff, R.M., Baser, C.A., Johnston, J.W., Marshall, L.F., Klauber, S.K., Klauber, M.R., & Minteer, M. (1989). Neuropsychological rehabilitation: An experimental study with head injured patients. *Journal of Head Trauma Rehabilitation, 4,* 20–36.

Sarno, M.T. (1969). *The functional communication profile: Manual of directions.* New York: Institute of Rehabilitation Medicine, New York University Medical Centre.

Sarno, M.T. (1980). Language rehabilitation outcome in the elderly aphasic. In L.K. Obler & M.L. Albert (Eds), *Language and communication in the elderly.* Lexington, Mass.: Lexington Press.

Sarno, M.T. & Levita, E. (1971). Natural course of recovery in severe aphasia. *Archives of Physical Medicine and Rehabilitation, 52,* 175–179.

Schenkenberg, T., Bradford, D.C., & Ajax, E.T. (1980). Line bisection and unilateral visual neglect in patients with neurological impairment. *Neurology, 30,* 509–517.

Schuell, H. (1965). *The Minnesota test for differential diagnosis of aphasia.* Minneapolis: University of Minnesota Press.

Schwartz, M.F. & Schwartz, B. (1984). In defence of Organology. *Cognitive Neuropsychology, 1,* 25–42.

Scott, C. (1987). *Cognitive neuropsychological remediation.* Paper presented to British Aphasiology Society National Conference, Newcastle, Sept. 1987.

Scott, C. & Byng, S. (1989). Computer assisted remediation of a homophone comprehension disorder in surface dyslexia. *Aphasiology, 3,* 301–320.

Semmes, J., Weinstein, S., Ghent, L., & Teuber, H-L. (1955). Spatial orientation in man after cerebral injury, I: Analysis by locus of lesion. *Journal of Psychology, 39, 227–244.*

Seron, X. (1987a). Neuropsychological rehabilitation in European French-language countries. In M.J. Meier, A.L. Benton, & L. Diller (Eds), *Neuropsychological rehabilitation.* Edinburgh and New York: Churchill Livingstone.

Seron, X. (1987b). Cognition first, microcomputer second. *Aphasiology, 1,* 161–163.

Seron, X., Deloche, G., Moulard, G., & Rousselle, M. (1980). A computer based therapy for the treatment of aphasic subjects with writing disorders. *Journal of Speech & Hearing Disorders, 45,* 45–48.

Shallice, T. (1979). Case study approach in neuropsychological research. *Journal of Clinical Neuropsychology, 1,* 183–211.

Shewan, C.M. & Bandur, D.L. (1986). *Treatment of aphasia. A language-oriented approach.* London: Taylor and Francis.

Siegel, S. (1956). *Non-parametric statistics for the behavioural sciences.* New York: McGraw-Hill.

Skilbeck, C.E. (1983). Perceptual deficit and memory disturbance. In G. Lubbock (Ed.), *Stroke care—An interdisciplinary approach*. London: Faber & Faber.

Skilbeck, C.E. (1984). Computer assistance in the management of memory and cognitive impairment. In B. Wilson & N. Moffat (Eds), *Clinical management of memory problems*. London: Croom Helm.

Skilbeck, C.E. (1990). Computer assistance in the management of memory and cognitive impairment. In B. Wilson & N. Moffat (Eds), *The clinical management of memory problems*. London: Croom Helm.

Skilbeck, C.E. (1991). Microcomputer-based cognitive rehabilitation. In A. Ager (Ed.), *Micro-computers and clinical psychology: Issues, applications and future developments*. Chichester: John Wiley & Sons.

Skilbeck, C.E., Wade, D.T., Langton-Hewer, R., & Wood, V.A. (1983). Recovery after stroke. *Journal of Neurology, Neurosurgery and Psychiatry, 46,* 5–8.

Skilbeck, C.E. & Woods, R.T. (1980). The factorial structure of the Wechsler Memory Scale: Samples of neurological and psychogeriatric patients. *Journal of Clinical Neuropsychology, 2,* 293–300.

Skinner, C., Wirz, S., Thompson, I., & Davidson, J. (1984). *Edinburgh Functional Communication Profile*. Bicester, Oxon: Winslow Press.

Slack, W.V. & Slack, C.W. (1977). Talking to a computer about emotional problems: A comparative study. *Psychotherapy, 14,* 156–164.

Smart, S. (1987). *Hemi-neglect software*. New Alyth, Perthshire: Lochee Publications.

Smith, A. (1967). The serial sevens subtraction test. *Archives of Neurology, 17,* 78–80.

Smith, A. (1975). Neuropsychological testing in neurological disorders. In W.J. Friedlander (Ed.), *Advances in neurology, 7*. New York: Raven Press.

Smith, D.S., Goldenberg, E., & Ashburn, A. (1981). Remedial therapy after stroke: A randomised control trial. *British Medical Journal, 282,* 517–520.

Smith, E. (1974). Influence of site of impact on cognitive impairment persisting long after closed head injury. *Journal of Neurology, Neurosurgery & Psychiatry, 37,* 719–726.

Sohlberg, M.M. & Mateer, C.A. (1986). *Attention process training (APT)*. Puyallup, Washington: Association for Neuropsychological Research and Development.

Sohlberg, M.M. & Mateer, C.A. (1987). Effectiveness of an attention training program. *Journal of Clinical and Experimental Neuropsychology, 9,* 117–130.

Sohlberg, M.M. & Mateer, C.A. (1989). *Introduction to cognitive rehabilitation: Theory and Practice*. New York and London: Guildford Press.

South East Thames Neuropsychology Working Party. (1987). *Rehabilitation services for adults with acquired brain damage in South East Thames region*. Unpublished report prepared for South East Thames Regional Health Authority.

South East Thames Working Party on Severe Brain Injury. (1990). *Severe brain injury*. Unpublished reported prepared for South East Thames Regional Health Authority.

Southampton General Hospital Rehabilitation Unit. (1988). *Survey of severely head injured people in Southampton and South West Hampshire Health Authority*. Unpublished report prepared for South West Hampshire Health Authority.

Space, L.G. (1981). The computer as psychometrician. *Behaviour Research Methods and Instrumentation, 13,* 595–606.

Squire, L.R. (1975). Short term memory as a biological entity. In D. Deutsch & J.A. Deutsch (Eds), *Short term memory*. New York: Academic Press.

Squire, L.R. (1987). *Memory and brain*. New York and Oxford: Oxford University Press.

Squire, L.R., Shimamura, A.P., & Amaral, D.G. (1989). Memory and the hippocampus. In J. Byrne & W. Berry (Eds), *Neural models of plasticity*. New York: Academic Press.

Sternberg, S. (1969). Memory scanning: Mental processes revealed by RT experiments. *American Scientist, 57,* 421–457.

Street, R.F. (1931). *A Gestalt completion test. Contributions to education, No. 481.* New York: Bureau of Publications, Teachers College, Columbia University.

Sunderland, A., Harris, J.E. & Baddeley, A.D. (1983). Do laboratory tests predict everyday memory? A neuropsychological study. *Journal of Verbal Learning and Verbal Behaviour, 22,* 341–357.

Sunderland, A., Harris, J.E. & Baddeley, A.D. (1984). Assessing everyday memory after severe head injury. In J.E. Harris & P.E. Morris (Eds), *Everyday memory, actions and absentmindedness.* London: Academic Press.

Sundet, K., Finset, A., & Reinvang, I. (1988). Neuropsychological predictors in stroke rehabilitation. *Journal of Clinical & Experimental Neuropsychology, 10,* 363–379.

Susset, V., Vorbecky, J., & Black, R. (1979). Disability outcome and self assessment outcome of disabled persons: An analysis of 506 cases. *Archives of Physical Medicine and Rehabilitation, 60,* 50–60.

Swiercinsky, D.P. (1978). *Computerised SAINT: System for analysis and interpretation of neuropsychological tests.* Unpublished paper presented at the meeting of the American Psychological Association, Toronto, Sept. 1978.

Swiercinsky, D.P. (1984). *Computerised neuropsychological assessment.* Unpublished paper presented to the symposium of ethical issues in the use of computers in neuropsychological assessment (Chair: A.J. McSweeney) at the meeting of the International Neuropsychological Society, Houston, Feb. 1984.

Talland, G.A. (1965). *Deranged memory.* New York: Academic Press.

Talland, G.A. & Schwab, R.S. (1964). Performance with multiple sets in Parkinson's disease. *Neuropsychologia, 2,* 45–53.

Tallis, R. (1987). Measurement in rehabilitation: An introduction. *Clinical Rehabilitation, 1,* 1–3.

Taylor, E.M. (1959). *The appraisal of children with cerebral deficits.* Cambridge, Massachusetts: Harvard University Press.

Taylor, L.B. (1979). Psychological assessment of neurosurgical patients. In T. Rasmussen & R. Marino (Eds), *Functional neurosurgery.* New York: Raven Press.

Taylor, M.M., Schaeffer, J.N., Blumenthal, F.S., & Grisell, J.L. (1971). Perceptual training in patients with left hemiplegia. *Archives of Physical Medicine and Rehabilitation, 52,* 163–169.

Teasdale, G. & Jennett, B. (1974). Assessment of coma and impaired consciousness. *Lancet, 2,* 81.

Terman, L.M. & Merrill, M.A. (1960). *Stanford-Binet intelligence scale* (Revised version). Boston: Houghton Mifflin.

Teuber, H-L. (1975). Recovery of function after brain injury. In R. Porter & D.W. Fitzsimmons (Eds), *Outcome of severe damage to the central nervous system.* (Ciba Foundation Symposium, No 34). Amsterdam: Elsevier.

Thomsen, I.V. (1960). Persistent memory deficits following encephalitis. *Brain, 83,* 195–212.

Thomsen, I.V. (1975). Evaluation and outcome of aphasia in patients with severe closed head injury. *Journal of Neurology, Neurosurgery and Psychiatry, 38,* 713–718.

Thomsen, I.V. (1977). Verbal learning and aphasic and non-aphasic patients with severe head injuries. *Scandinavian Journal of Rehabilitation Medicine, 9,* 73–77.

Thomsen, I.V. (1981). Neuropsychological treatment and long time follow-up in an aphasic patient with very severe head trauma. *Journal of Clinical Neuropsychology, 3,* 43–51.

Timming, R., Orrison, W.W., & Mikula, J.A. (1982). Computerised tomography and rehabilitation outcome after severe head trauma. *Archives of Physical Medicine and Rehabilitation, 63,* 154–159.

van Merrienboer, J.J. & Jelsma, O. (1988). The matching familiar figure test. Computer or experimenter controlled administration. *Educational and Psychological Measurement, 48,* 161–164.

van Zomeren, A.H. (1981). *Reaction time and attention after closed head injury.* Lisse, Netherlands: Swets & Zeitlinger.

van Zomeren, A.H., Brouwer, E.H., & Deelman, B.G. (1984). Attention deficits: The riddles of selectivity, speed and alertness. In N. Brooks (Ed.), *Closed head injury: Psychological, social and family consequences.* Oxford: Oxford University Press.

Vernon, P.E. & Parry, J.B. (1949). *Personnel selection in the British Forces.* London: University of London Press.

von Monakow, C. (1914). *Die Lokalisation im Grosshirn und der Abbau der Funktion durch und Kortikale.* Herde, Wiesbaden: J.F. Bergmann.

von Monakow, C. (1969). Diaschisis. In K.H. Pribam (Ed.), *Brain and behaviour, 1, mood states and mind.* Baltimore: Penguin.

Vroman, G.M., Kellar, L., & Cohen, I. (1989). Cognitive rehabilitation in the elderly: a computer based memory training program. In E. Perecman (Ed.), *Integrating theory and practice in clinical neuropsychology.* Hillsdale, NJ: Lawrence Erlbaum Associates Inc.

Wade, D.T., Langton-Hewer, R., Skilbeck, C.E., & David, R.M. (1985a). *Stroke: A critical approach to diagnosis, treatment & management.* London: Chapman & Hall Medical.

Wade, D.T., Langton-Hewer, R., Skilbeck, C.E., Bainton, D., & Burns-Cox, C. (1985b). Controlled trial of a home-care service for acute stroke patients. *Lancet, Feb.,* 323–326.

Wade, D.T. & Langton-Hewer, R. (1987a). Functional abilities after stroke: measurement, natural history and prognosis. *Journal of Neurology, Neurosurgery and Psychiatry, 50,* 177–182.

Wade, D.T. & Langton-Hewer, R. (1987b). Epidemiology of some neurological diseases with special reference to workload on the NHS. *International Rehabilitation Medicine, 8,* 129–137.

Wade, D.T., Parker, V., & Langton-Hewer, R. (1986). Memory disturbance after stroke: Frequency and associated losses. *International Rehabilitation Medicine, 8,* 60–64.

Wade, D.T., Skilbeck, C.E., & Langton-Hewer, R. (1989). Selected cognitive losses after stroke: Frequency, recovery & prognostic importance. *International Disability Studies, 11,* 34–39.

Walsh, K.W. (1978). *Neuropsychology: a clinical approach.* Edinburgh: Churchill Livingstone.

Warburg, R.J. (1988). *Assessment of memory impairments. Programs for the BBC microcomputer.* Unpublished software, developed in the Department of Psychology, North Manchester General Hospital. Available from the author.

Warrington, E.K. (1984). *Recognition memory test.* Windsor: NFER–Nelson.

Warrington, E.K. & Taylor, A.M. (1973). The contribution of the right parietal lobe to object recognition. *Cortex, 9,* 152–164.

Weber, A.M. (1988). *Attentional capacity test.* Unpublished paper presented at the International Neuropsychology Meeting, New Orleans, LA.

Wechsler, D. (1955). *Wechsler Adult Intelligence Scale. Manual.* New York: Psychological Corporation.

Wechsler, D. (1976). *Wechsler Intelligence Scale for Children* (Anglicized Revised Edition). Sidcup, Kent: Psychological Corporation.

Wechsler, D. (1981). *Wechsler Adult Intelligence Scale—Revised.* Cleveland: Psychological Corporation.

Wechsler, D. (1988). *Wechsler Memory Scale—Revised edition (WMS-R).* New York: Psychological Corporation.

Wechsler, D. & Stone, C.P. (1945). *Wechsler Memory Scale. Manual.* New York: Psychological Corporation.

Weddell, R., Oddy, M., & Jenkins, D. (1980). Social adjustment after rehabilitation: a two year follow-up of patients with severe head injury. *Psychological Medicine, 10,* 257–263.

Weinberg, J., Diller, L., Gerstman, L.J., & Schulman, P. (1972). Digit span in right and left hemiplegics. *Journal of Clinical Psychology, 28,* 361.

Weinberg, J., Diller, L., Gordon, W.A., Gerstman, L.J., Lieberman, A., Lakin, P., Hodges, G., & Ezrachi, O. (1977). Visual scanning training effect on reading-related tasks in acquired right brain damage. *Archives of Physical Medicine and Rehabilitation, 58,* 479–486.

Weinberg, J., Diller, L., Gordon, W.A., Gerstman, L.J., Lieberman, A., Lakin, P., Hodges, G., & Ezrachi, O. (1979). Training sensory awareness and spatial organisation in people with right brain damage. *Archives of Physical Medicine and Rehabilitation, 60,* 491–496.

Weinberg, J., Piasketsky, E.B., Diller, L., & Gordon, W.A. (1982). Treating perceptual organisation deficits in non-neglecting right brain damage stroke patients. *Journal of Clinical Neuropsychology, 4,* 59–75.

Weiss, D.N. & Vale, C.D. (1987). Adaptive testing. *Applied Psychology, 36,* 249–262.

West, R. (1990). Data analysis using statistical packages on microcomputers. In R. West, M. Christie, & J. Weinman (Eds), *Microcomputers, psychology and medicine.* Chichester: Wiley.

Whiting, S.E., Lincoln, N.B., Bhavnani, G., & Cockburn, J. (1985). *The Rivermead perceptual assessment battery.* Windsor: NFER–Nelson.

Whurr, R. (1974). *The aphasia screening test.* London: Westminster Hospital.

Willanger, R., Danielsen, U.T., & Ankerhus, J. (1981). Denial and neglect of hemiparesis in right side apoplectic lesions. *Acta Neurologica Scandinavica, 64,* 310–326.

Williams, J.M. (1988). Everyday cognition and the ecological validity of intellectual and neuropsychological tests. In J.M. Williams & C.J. Long (Eds), *Cognitive approaches to neuropsychology.* New York: Plenum Press.

Wilmott, M. (1989). The sick role and related concepts. In A.K. Broome (Ed.), *Health psychology.* London: Chapman Hall.

Wilson, B.A. (1981). A survey of behavioural treatments carried out at a rehabilitation centre for stroke and head injuries. In G. Powell (Ed.), *Brain function therapy.* London: Gower.

Wilson, B.A. (1984). Memory therapy in practice. In B.A. Wilson & N. Moffatt (Eds), *Clinical management of memory problems.* London and Sydney: Croom Helm.

Wilson, B.A. (1987). *Rehabilitation of memory.* New York and London: The Guildford Press.

Wilson, B.A., Baddeley, A.D., & Cockburn, J.M. (1989). How do old dogs learn new tricks: teaching a technological skill to brain injured people. *Cortex, 25,* 115–119.

Wilson, B.A., Cockburn, J.M., & Baddeley, A.D. (1985). *The Rivermead behavioural memory test.* Reading: Thames Valley Publishing Company.

Wilson, B.A., Cockburn, J.M., Baddeley, A.D., & Hiorns, R. (1989). *The Rivermead behavioural memory test: Second supplement.* Reading: Thames Valley Publishing Company.

Wilson, B.A., Cockburn, J.M., & Halligan, P.W. (1987). *Behavioural inattention test.* Reading: Thames Valley Publishing Company.

Wilson, B.A. & Moffat, N. (Eds). (1984a). *Clinical management of memory problems.* London: Croom Helm.

Wilson, B.A. & Moffat, N. (1984b). Rehabilitation of memory for everyday life. In J. Harris & P. Morris (Eds), *Everyday memory: Actions and absent mindedness.* London: Academic Press.

Wilson, J.T.L., Wiedmann, K.D., Hadley, D.M., & Brooks, D.N. (1990). The relationship between visual memory function and lesions detected by magnetic resonance imaging after closed head injury. *Neuropsychology, 3,* 255–265.

Wood, F.B., Ebert, V., & Kinsbourne, M. (1982). The episodic-semantic distinction in memory and amnesia: Clinical and experimental observation. In L. Cermak (Ed.), *Human memory and amnesia.* Hillsdale, New Jersey: Lawrence Erlbaum Associates Inc.

Wood, R.L. (1984). Behaviour disorders following severe brain injury: their presentation and psychological management. In D.N. Brooks (Ed.), *Closed head injury: Psychological, social and family consequences.* New York: Oxford University Press.

Wood, R.L. (1986). Rehabilitation of patients with disorders of attention. *Head Trauma Rehabilitation, 1,* 43–53.

Wood, R.L. (1987). *Brain injury rehabilitation: a neurobehavioural approach.* London and Sydney: Croom Helm.

Wood, R.L. & Fussey, I. (1987). Computer based cognitive retraining: a controlled study. *International Disability Studies, 9,* 149–153.

Woods, R.T. & Britton, P.G. (1985). *Clinical psychology with the elderly.* Beckenham, Kent: Croom Helm.

Woods, B.T. & Teuber, H-L. (1978). Mirror movements after childhood hemiparesis. *Neurology, 28*, 1152–1158.

Young, G.C., Collins, D., & Hren, M. (1983). Effect of pairing scanning training with block design training in the remediation of perceptual problems in left hemiplegia. *Journal of Clinical Neuropsychology, 5*, 201–212.

Zangwill, O.L. (1966). Psychological deficits associated with frontal lobe lesions. *International Journal of Neurology, 5*, 395–402.

Author Index

Subject Index

Printed and bound by CPI Group (UK) Ltd, Croydon, CR0 4YY

22/10/2024

01777627-0011